STAR Parenting
TALES AND TOOLS

T0290331

Wow! This book is filled with old wisdom and fresh ideas! STAR Parenting is outstanding because it is such a complete guide to managing oneself as a parent, and yet it is simply written. Crary balances the needs of the child with the needs of the parent and recognizes temperament and developmental changes in children. I highly recommend this book to parents, grandparents, aunties, uncles, and teachers of young children. What a gift!

— JEAN ILLSLEY CLARKE, PH.D.
author of *How Much Is Enough?* and *Self-Esteem: A Family Affair*

Ms. Crary combines several tried and true parenting theories and resources into one book. Using real examples, a multitude of options is provided that helps both child and parent grow. If I had only one book to buy for parenting strategies, this would be it!

— KAREN L. ZIMMERMAN, M.ED., CFLE
early childhood coach and parent educator, St. Paul Public Schools, Minn.

STAR Parenting provides a framework for problem-solving just about any parenting or discipline issue. . . . The STAR process provides a structure for adjusting to the changing role of discipline, from the early years through the teen years.

— BARBARA LEBLANC, M.S.W., L.C.S.W.
director of The Parenting Center at Children's Hospital, New Orleans

This book is filled with the wisdom of practical parenting concepts and tools that are integrated into a simple and coherent model. We are reminded that there is no one right way to parent, and parents should start with identifying their values so they are clear about what is really important in the long run. The description of the dark side points out that even good ideas can be not only ineffective but also misused, leading to negative results.

— GLEN PALM, PH.D
professor of Child and Family Studies, St. Cloud State University, St. Cloud, Minn.

STAR Parenting is the single most useful tool in helping parents understand and acquire the skills of gaining cooperation with children. It compels the adult to constantly be in motion to use positive caregiving and to instruct children in healthy patterns so they can be productive in society. This model has far-reaching implications in society—beyond parenting to marriages, businesses, and community work.

— LAURIE A. D. KANYER, M.A., CFLE
director of Synapse Consulting and Growing Capable Parents, Yakima, Wash.

STAR Parenting is a solid approach by a dedicated parenting educator to teaching parenting skills that work. Each chapter contains critical concepts and ideas based on sound theory and experiences. A parent educator using this book can easily guide parents through the concepts, activities, and recommended practices. I particularly like the chapter about using the whole star to demonstrate how to actively use the process.

— KAREN DEBORD, PH.D.
professor emerita, North Carolina State University, Raleigh

STAR Parenting is packed with the accumulated wisdom of Crary's years as a parent educator. It sets out a comprehensive foundation for problem solving, then invites the parent's own creative input. We parents often get stuck in a couple of ruts, and Crary's broad, systematic approach leads to new answers, bringing out the best in us.

— HELEN F. NEVILLE, B.S., R.N.
parent educator, author, researcher at Kaiser Permanente Oakland Medical Center, California

STAR Parenting

TALES AND TOOLS

Respectful Guidance Strategies to Increase
Parenting Effectiveness & Enjoyment

ELIZABETH CRARY, M.S.

PARENTING PRESS
Seattle, Washington

Ackowledgments

I wish to acknowledge—

The first STAR parents who helped develop the program and those since, whose questions have helped clarify the process, points, and tools.

All the students, over the years, who have shared their stories with me, which adds a richness to this book.

My colleagues, Jean, Helen, Val, and Rae, for their valuable suggestions.

The STAR helpers, particularly Debi, Jenny, Jennifer, Jill, and Kari, who read the manuscript, offered suggestions, and provided needed examples, which has made this book more enjoyable and useful.

My editor, Carolyn, who has worked valiantly to keep me on the path of clarity and consistency.

And my family, Fred, Karl, Karen, and Sue, who have supported me on this journey and helped when needed, whether it is fixing food, rehabilitating the computer, proofreading, or any number of other things.

Thank you, all!

Printed in the United States of America
Edited by Carolyn J. Threadgill
Designed by Judy Petry

ISBN 978-1-884734-95-3 paperback

Library of Congress Cataloging-in-Publication Data
Available from Parenting Press, 1-800-992-6657

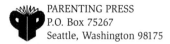 PARENTING PRESS
P.O. Box 75267
Seattle, Washington 98175

To see all our helpful publications and services for parents, caregivers, and children, go to
www.ParentingPress.com.

Contents

Introduction

Two-year-old Michael didn't want to stay in bed. His parents, Richard and Lisa, took turns putting him back in bed. By the time the "active" parent had gotten settled they could hear Michael's door open and footsteps in the hall again.

This continued much of the evening. By the time Michael stayed in bed, Richard and Lisa had put him back forty-five times! The next night it took seventeen trips; and the third night, four trips. After that he accepted the need to stay in bed gracefully.

With a 4-, 3-, and 1-year-old, Teresa wanted to teach the older two how to buckle themselves into their own car seats. She explained that the top buckles "kiss" and then the bottom two buckles "kiss." She cautioned the kids to listen for the three clicking (locking) sounds. Then they practiced and practiced and practiced.

When Teresa decided the kids could do it, she told them when they each buckled themselves in she would reward them each with a penny. "Best two dollars I ever spent!" she reported.

At eight o'clock Elena went to her mother, Carmen, and announced, "I want to stay up late tonight."

Mom, wishing to avoid a major bedtime battle, said in a thoughtful voice, "Hmm, it's your bedtime now. You want to stay up late. I want you to go to bed now. I wonder, what can we do so we can both be happy?"

Elena thought a bit and replied, "I can go to bed in fifteen minutes."
Carmen decided that was fine but didn't wish to accept too easily. She considered her response. "I am willing to go with fifteen minutes, but how will we know when the time is up?"

"I'll set a timer and show you. When it rings, I'll go to bed."
"It's a deal," Mom said as they clapped hands in a "high five."

Christy tells her story: We have a small house and often four people come in and drop their stuff on the living room floor three times a day. Up to four coats, twelve pairs of shoes, and four backpacks create quite a mess. I feel crabby and tense when the house is cluttered.

At first, I just picked everything up and felt resentful. Next, I asked the kids to pick things up (over and over and OVER). Then, I looked at whose stuff comprised the mess. I love shoes and have lots and lots. Beth, 4, has already discovered the joy of shoes, and now has more than I do. Nicholas, 7, and Dad together have nine pairs.

One day I counted only pairs of shoes. The score? Beth:5, Nicholas:3, Dad:2, Mom:6! Oops! I looked at the coats, and noticed that although mine were hung up, I had taken ALL the hooks on the short coat rack that was for the kids! I was part

of the problem, and needed to change my behavior or they never would.

Now, when I come in, I say "Wow, I have three pair of shoes out and I'm putting them ALL away. Now I have two . . . only one more . . . I am hanging my jacket on a hanger! The living room is looking neater!"

Nicholas comes running to be first to put his two pairs away and hang his coat and pack on the rack before I can finish. Although Beth doesn't always find all her shoes, most of them make it into the closet, and she can now at least see hooks to hang her jacket and pack on. Dad takes his cue, "I like putting my shoes where I can find them!" The living room is much tidier these days, and I can breathe.

What do these parents have in common? They are all STAR parents. Each of these parents was trying a new approach to a recurring problem. They knew what they had been doing was not working, so they considered their options before they responded.

So, what is STAR Parenting?

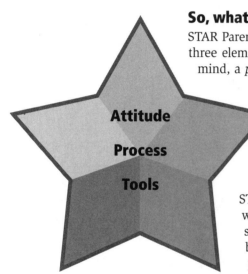

STAR Parenting is an integrated approach to child guidance based on a star. It has three elements: An *attitude* of respect and reflection that keeps the long view in mind, a *process* for dealing with behavior, and *fifteen tools* which are organized into five groups or points. The STAR provides both an acronym for the problem-solving process and offers parents a visual prompt for the STAR points and tools. STAR Parenting allows parents to be flexible, creative, and effective. You can see the STAR Parenting process, points, and tools on page 8.

STAR Parenting's story

STAR Parenting is based on more than twenty years of study and active work with parents and children. It grew out of a conversation with a former student who said she needed a class for people who knew what to do, but couldn't get themselves to do it. We put together a group of frustrated parents and dove into figuring out how to prevent or overcome parent confusion and inertia. Over the years, I have found that parents, like my former student, can have a great deal of theoretical knowledge but not be able to put it to use. They might also have unrealistic expectations regarding their children's attention spans, how long it takes a child to do something, and what kids can do at different ages. We looked at these issues and many others.

STAR Parenting organizes over two decades of experience into an effective parenting approach: it is based in parental experience, puts research to work in practical ways, distills my work guiding parents and children, and is *realistic*. Part of being realistic is providing parents with a flexible structure rather than a set of rigid rules. Each family's situation and experiences are different, so creativity as well as practicality are necessary. STAR Parenting meets the need by providing both a process and a number of flexible tools with an easy way to manage them. The star image helps as a visual reminder of the process and the tools.

What is STAR Parenting's philosophy?

During the first class of parents, a mother complained repeatedly about how slow her young son was at getting into his car seat. Her frustration was obvious. I asked her and all the other parents to record over the next week how long it took their kids to do something they thought took "too long" and report at the next class. Of course, everyone was eager to know the result of data collection on the car seat boy. His mother shared rather sheepishly, "The first time I timed him, it took him thirty seconds to get into the car seat; the second time, one minute; and the third time, twenty seconds. I guess I can give him two minutes."

STAR Parenting would help this parent's problem solving in the future by asking her to:

- *Honor* her values by identifying them and creating a long-term vision for her son.
- *Focus* on her growth and her child's. In my parenting classes we say, "A STAR parent is a growing parent, not a perfect parent." Research suggests that being a good parent eighty percent of the time is good enough. Thank goodness, because about the time you figure out what works, your child enters a new phase and you feel like you're starting all over!
- *Consider* who owns the problem. The child owns the problem if his needs are not met. The parent owns the problem if her needs are not met. They both own it if both have unmet needs. Who owns the problem influences the types of solutions that will work.
- *Acknowledge* that it may take several attempts to solve a problem. The first thing a parent tries does not always work. Nothing is wrong with the child. Nothing is wrong with the parent. The approach just didn't work this time. The STAR Parenting process and tools help parents chose among alternatives.
- *Recognize* that her child's age, temperament, and life experience influence her parenting. What needs to be done at 2 may well be inappropriate at 5. Also, many parents have discovered that what works with one child doesn't always work with a sibling.
- *Understand* that any tool can be used for good or for ill. In STAR Parenting we talk about how parents can unknowingly misuse a tool.

Myths that make effective parenting challenging

While working with STAR Parenting, I noticed that some parents had beliefs that make parenting more difficult. A few of them are:

- *If you read enough books, you will find a way to make parenting easy.* There is no "quick fix." In general, change is made by consistent, gentle persistence over time. This is especially true if the problem is based in temperament or developmental stage.
- *If my kids are unhappy or angry, I must be a bad parent.* Our job as parents is to care for our children and give them experiences and skills needed to become caring, competent adults. Their job is to learn how to make themselves happy, a useful lifelong skill.
- *If my child feels loved, he will grow up just fine.* Children need both love (nurture) and limits (structure). Without structure, children will not know how to follow rules (obey the law), be self-disciplined, or have empathy for others. Some parents hold on to this mistaken belief that love is enough until about the time teachers and peers start to require more maturity in the child.
- *Parenting won't change my life much, I can continue doing things as I used to.*

Parenting is a lifestyle and it is different from the married without children lifestyle. Before kids, many couples were able to arrange things pretty much as they liked. Once the baby is born, time, money, and energy need to be redistributed.

- *Things would be fine if my child did not slow me down.* That might be true . . . but you do have a child, and children are slow. Most children's natural pace is an amble. To expect more speed is to create stress for yourself and your child.
- *Parents must be (or appear to be) perfect so their children have a good role model.* Exhibiting the values and behavior we want from our children is helpful, but expecting perfection from either of us is harmful. Children need to know that it is all right to make mistakes and to learn to fix them. Research shows that children who believe they must be perfect often resist new experiences because they fear they won't measure up. (This belief can be self-induced or imposed from the outside.) Parents can help by trying new things and by sharing mistakes they've made and how they dealt with them.

How does Star Parenting work in daily parenting life?

As mentioned earlier, STAR Parenting is a step-by-step approach to child guidance based on a star. Its main elements are: first, an *attitude of respect and reflection* that keeps your long-term goals for your child in mind; second, a four-step *process* for responding to unwanted behavior; and third, fifteen *specific tools* organized into five groups or points. These tools can be seen on the STAR diagram.

The word STAR provides an acronym for the problem-solving process:

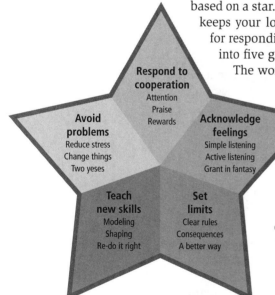

S = *Stop and focus,*
T = *Think of ideas,*
A = *Act effectively,* and
R = *Review, revise, and reward yourself.*

The process can be used casually in the moment for everyday annoyances, or deliberately and thoughtfully for problems that are more frustrating or serious.

The STAR points provide a visual reminder of the five different areas of healthy parenting. On each point are three parent-tested tools, making a total of fifteen tools (see diagram). This STAR approach allows parents a great deal of flexibility, creativity, effectiveness, and relevance to their particular situation.

Let's look back at the stories in the beginning (pages 5 and 6) and see what tools those parents tried. Richard and Lisa chose a simple *consequence* and traded off duty since they knew Michael's persistent temperament would wear either one of them down. Teresa taught the new skill of buckling the seat belt by *modeling* and practicing with her kids. Then she used a *reward* to make the new skill a habit. Carmen chose *a better way* and clarified expectations to get Elena to bed. Christy discovered that she was a significant part of the problem and that when she *modeled* the behavior she wanted things went much better. These are four of the fifteen tools that await you in the coming chapters.

How can you use this book?

STAR Parenting Tales and Tools is divided into three parts. Part One introduces the four-step STAR Parenting process and talks about how unconscious expectations may influence your parenting experience. Part Two teaches the five points of the star and the fifteen STAR Parenting tools. Part Three shows you how to get started solving problems, the dark side of the star (misuse of the process or tools), and what to do if you are still having trouble. In the following chapters, whenever a STAR tool is mentioned it will be in italic and preceded with a star (☆).

Because STAR Parenting is based on parents' experience, there are many stories from parents. Within each chapter there are examples of parents using specific elements of STAR Parenting. At the end of each chapter, there is a "STAR in Action Story" that shows how one parent applied the *whole* STAR Parenting process to her or his problem.

These stories allow you to see how different parents think about their situation and how they decide what to do first. You can see that different parents make different decisions based on their particular values and the nature of their children. There is no one right way.

There are several ways to use *STAR Parenting Tales and Tools.* First, you can read the book, starting at the beginning, and do the activities as you go. When you get to the end, you will probably have a pretty good grasp of STAR Parenting and probably already be successful at using it.

Or, if you are not a sequential person, you can read chapter one to get an overview of STAR Parenting, then jump to whatever part intrigues you and try that. Be aware that we are often drawn to the types of tools that we are already using. If those tools were going to work, they already would have. It has been my observation, and that of successful parents, that when you are having trouble with a situation you usually need to use a different point of the star. Often what your child needs is a response that is new or one that you are less comfortable with.

If you are a social person, you may prefer to learn with someone—your parenting partner or a friend. Choose a regular time to meet (once or twice a month), read a chapter, and use the book club questions from ParentingPress.com to get you going and guide your study.

In chapter one, "STAR Parenting in Action," we will start with an overview of the STAR Parenting process by following Debra as she deals with daughter Tami's tantrum in the toy store.

Part One

STAR Parenting Process

Stop and focus

Think of ideas

Act effectively

Review, revise,
and reward

Chapter 1

STAR Parenting in Action

~~~~~~

STAR Parenting offers help

~~~~~~

*Whenever Tami, 3, can't have what she wants she has a fit. For example, yesterday afternoon we were at a toy store to buy a birthday present. After we chose a present, she wanted to buy a large, fancy birthday card. I told her that it was too expensive and she started yelling. When I said it was time to go home, she tried to hit me, saying, "I won't go home. Sally **needs** the card."*

Parenting is such a mixed bag of fun and frustration. When your child spontaneously hugs you, parenting is delightful. When she screams, pulls away, and refuses to cooperate, it is maddening. At those maddening times a parent often wishes for help. STAR Parenting offers that help and makes living and working with kids easier and more fun.

The STAR Parenting process—an overview

The STAR Parenting process, as we saw in the introduction, is based on the word Star. Each letter stands for a different step of the problem-solving process:

S — *Stop and focus*
T — *Think of ideas*
A — *Act effectively*
R — *Review, revise, and reward yourself*

As we consider an overview of this process, we'll look at how Tami's mother, Debra, can use the steps to solve her problem.

S—*Stop and focus* on yourself, the child, and the problem. When you find yourself getting angry or frustrated, stop and take several deep breaths to calm yourself. Focus on what is bothering you and where you want to go before you do something that may make life more difficult for you and your child. Think about what you want for your child in the long run (your goals) and what the child is like (temperament and experience).

If the problem is ongoing, you may find it helpful to collect data on it. For example, how often does it happen? Is your child tired or frustrated when it happens? Are you stressed? Sometimes the problem is different than you think. Let's see how this process might work for Debra.

Tami's mom, Debra, might have taken a deep breath to calm herself and said, "I can handle this with the STAR. Let me see: stop, calm myself, and focus on the situation. Okay, Tami and I are both tired and hungry. Tami is upset because I won't buy a card. Since Tami often reacts intensely that's no surprise. I want Tami to become a capable, caring, assertive adult. Right now she is being caring and assertive, but she needs more skill in asserting constructively. In the short run, I want her to learn to calm herself so she can think. I need to start collecting data on how often she is upset."

T—*Think of ideas.* Lots of ideas. Different ideas. Include some silly ideas. When your mind is free enough to think of silly ideas, it is free enough to think of new, good ideas. The ideas are for both the moment of crisis and later when things are calm. The more ideas Debra can think of at this step, the better. She could:

☆ *Avoid the problem by shopping in the morning before Tami gets tired or restless.*

☆ *Respond to cooperation by saying, "You remembered to blow the mad feeling out," or by giving Tami stickers for calming down.*

☆ *Acknowledge Tami's feelings by saying, "You're disappointed we can't buy the big card."*

☆ *Set a limit by saying, "It's okay to be upset, and I won't let you hurt anyone."*

☆ *Teach new skills by showing Tami how to calm herself by taking three deep breaths, or singing a "Mad" song.*

A—*Act effectively.* Choose several ideas, make a plan, and use it. A wonderful plan will not help if you don't follow through. Get the support you need from family or friends to carry out the plan.

At the store, Debra might decide simply to acknowledge Tami's feelings and take her home. Once she is home, Debra needs to plan for how to deal with the problem in the future. For example, she might think, "I want to teach Tami to calm herself. I will model taking deep breaths. When Tami tries to calm herself, I will give her stickers. When she has five stickers, we will make cookies. I need to make sure both Dad and the babysitter are watching for her effort. While she is learning, I will try to reduce our stress by taking Tami to the park each afternoon."

R—*Review, revise, and reward.* What is working? What needs to be changed? Few plans work completely the first time. Most successful parents tweak their plans several times before the situation is satisfactorily resolved. When you review the situation, reward yourself for your effort. It is important to acknowledge effort as well as success.

A week later Debra could review what has happened. She might say to herself, "I did remember to model taking deep breaths when I was angry and Tami is beginning to do it, too. But I only went to the park twice. This week we can dance together in the afternoon if I don't have time to go to the park. Next week, if I exercise with Tami five days, I will buy myself a long-stemmed rose."

For most situations you can use the STAR Parenting process either deliberately or spontaneously. However, if you have a problem that's *really* bothering you, set some time aside and go through the process step by step.

STAR Parenting points and tools

STAR Parenting also offers you five groups of tools—one for each point of the star (see illustration). Each point focuses on a different aspect of child guidance. Each point has three tools, as you can see on the back cover. (See Part Two for a more complete description of the points and tools.)

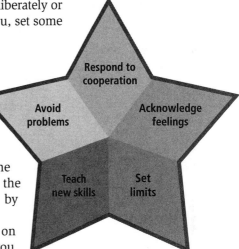

Avoid problems. The purpose of avoiding problems is to reduce the number of hassles with kids so that you can work more effectively on the important issues. Many problems can be avoided by reducing stress, by changing the environment or schedule, or by offering children choices.

Respond to cooperation. The behavior you notice and comment on is the behavior you get more of. This is true regardless of whether you praise or nag. (The more you nag children to hurry, the slower they seem to move.) You can encourage behavior you want by looking for it, giving the child time to cooperate, and encouraging him or her. The encouragement can be as simple as a smile, or as complex as you wish.

Acknowledge feelings. Many problems arise from children's feelings. Children need to know that feelings are different from actions. And they need to know that their feelings are accepted (not judged or changed). Often, simply acknowledging their feelings reduces objectionable behavior.

Set reasonable limits. Provide clear, reasonable rules. Tell the child what *to* do, rather than what not to do. For example, "No hitting" becomes "Touch gently." "Stop throwing" can become "Roll the ball" or "Throw balls outside." You don't need many rules, but they need to be clear, age-appropriate, and consistently enforced.

Back up rules with consequences and dependable follow-through. Children learn more from what you *do* than what you *say*. If the toddler hits you, put her down and move away. If the 4-year-old throws a toy, pick it up and put it away. Clear limits give kids security and strength, so respond gently, firmly, and consistently.

Teach new skills. Some problems arise because parents expect children to have

Children learn more from what you do than what you say.

The more points you consider, the more likely you are to resolve the situation.

skills they do not have. You can teach new skills such as sharing, speaking quietly, or managing anger by modeling, dividing the task into small pieces, and asking the child to re-do it right.

Look at Table 1–1: Around the STAR with temper tantrums below to see how to apply the tools and points.

With so many ideas, how do you decide what to do? If your problem is not serious, you can experiment with different ideas. If the problem is serious or really bothers you, use the four-step process on pages 12 to 13 to guide you. For the most success, develop a plan that involves all five points of the star we have just looked at.

Table 1–1: Around the STAR with temper tantrums

Problem: Whenever Tami, 3, can't have what she wants she has a fit. For example, yesterday afternoon we were at a toy store to buy a birthday present. After we chose a present, she wanted to buy a large, fancy birthday card. I told her that it was too expensive and she started yelling. When I said it was time to go home, she tried to hit me, saying, "I won't go home. Sally **needs** the card."

Point/purpose	Tools and examples for Debra and Tami
Avoid problems To reduce the number of problems so you can work on what is important.	☆*Reduce stress* of parent and/or child so situation does not become a problem. Two common ways are getting exercise and allowing *enough* time. For example, taking a brisk walk or allowing fifteen minutes to do a task instead of five. ☆*Change things or schedule.* Go shopping in the morning while Tami is still fresh. Explain to her in advance where you will go and how much money you can spend. ☆*Offer two yeses* for every no. You could say, "You may buy a small card now or make a big card when we get home."
Acknowledge feelings To accept children's feelings (not judge or try to change them).	☆*Use simple listening.* Noncommittal acknowledgment like: *"Uh-huh," "okay," "really?," "oh, yeah," "hmm," "tell me more,"* etc. ☆*Active listening.* Say, "You're disappointed we can't buy the big card." ☆*Grant in fantasy.* Say, "Wouldn't it be fun if we could buy *all* the birthday cards in the store? . . . if we could buy all the birthday cards in the *whole town?!*"
Teach new skills To give children the information and skills they need to cooperate.	☆*Model desired behavior.* For example, "I'm so mad, I'm going to take five deep breaths before I decide what to do." ☆*Shaping.* Divide the skill into "mini-steps" that are easier for Tami to do. First, practice breathing deeply when calm. Second, pretend to be angry and use deep breathing. Third, remind a grown-up to "take five" deep breaths when upset. Fourth, take deep breaths yourself when you're upset. ☆*Re-do it right.* Notice the "old behavior" and return *with* the child to re-do it right. For example, say, "Oops, you forgot to take five deep breaths." Then put your arm around her gently and breathe with her.

Respond to cooperation To encourage behavior you want by acknowledging it or rewarding it.	☆*Give attention.* Smile at her when she is playing well. ☆*Give effective praise.* Praise is specific, sincere, and immediate. "I'm impressed you remembered to take five deep breaths." Or, "I'll bet you're proud of the way you calmed yourself." ☆*Reward behavior.* Tell Tami, "Each time you use your words or take five breaths instead of screaming, you may choose a star sticker. When you have five stickers, we will make cookies together."
Set reasonable limits To establish clear boundaries for kids to test	☆*Clear, reasonable rules.* "Use your words or cry in your room or the car." ☆*Give and carry through with consequences.* Carry Tami to her room or the car if she continues to disturb others. ☆*Find a better way.* A better way is an idea both parent and child like. Say, "Tami, my way is we buy a gift for Sally. Your way is to buy her a big card. What is a better way?—something we will both like?" Tami might reply she could make a big card at home or that you purchase the card and a less expensive gift.

The more points you consider when dealing with a problem, the more likely you will be to resolve the situation satisfactorily. Most effective parents find they need to revise their plan several times.

In our example Tami is 3 years old. When you understand how the tools work, you can apply them to kids of any age.

In this chapter we have looked at an overview of the STAR Parenting process and illustrated how it could be used with a challenging situation. In chapter two we'll explore in greater depth how the STAR Parenting process works.

Chapter 2

The STAR Parenting Process

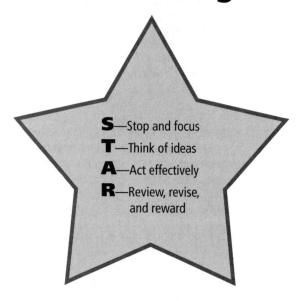

S—Stop and focus
T—Think of ideas
A—Act effectively
R—Review, revise, and reward

Parenting is easier with a plan

Parenting is a little like building a house. It is easier if you have a plan, a variety of tools, and a bit of skill. You could go to a store and buy a hammer, a bunch of nails, and some wood, then begin to build a shelter. The shelter might protect you from the wind and rain, but without a plan or helpful tools it won't be the cozy, airtight structure you wanted.

On the other hand, you could decide what you want, make a plan, and get a saw, ruler, and level, in addition to the wood. With a plan, more tools, and a bit of experience, the house you build will be more comfortable.

Parenting is similar—with a realistic plan, a few tools, and a bit of practice, parenting can be enjoyable much of the time. In this chapter we will look at developing a plan using the STAR Parenting process.

To review, the STAR Parenting process has four steps:

S—Stop and focus
T—Think of ideas
A—Act effectively
R—Review, revise, and reward

The STAR Parenting process can be used formally to make a plan for solving a problem that really bothers you. You can also use it informally, to respond to the day-to-day hassles you face. As you get more skilled, you may find yourself using the STAR Parenting approach for more routine problems as well. We will begin with *Stop and focus.*

STAR—**S**top and focus

The first step in STAR Parenting is to *Stop and focus.*

Written on one side of a grocery bag was the question, "What is the difference between discipline and abuse?" The reader was invited to consider the difference.

The other side revealed the answer: "Ten seconds." I like to think that the ten seconds referred to taking a calming breath and engaging your brain, rather than responding impulsively.

When faced with a challenging situation, effective STAR Parenting parents take a moment to stop and focus before they act. They focus on themselves, their expectation, and the problem. Their focus may be brief or substantial, depending on the nature of the situation. We will look at each of these elements.

Focus on yourself

Calm yourself. When a person is angry, frustrated, or scared, he or she rarely thinks well. The feeling dominates and the person may do something impulsive. When you calm down a bit, you can engage the problem-solving portion of the brain, review what has happened, and make a better long-term decision.

Different people have different ways of calming themselves. Some common ways are:

- Take a couple of deep belly breaths.
- Say to oneself, "This too will pass."
- Look out the window at trees or off in the distance.
- Visualize the child as sweet and cooperative.
- Take a step back and remove oneself from the situation.

You may have a different technique that helps you calm down. Some people get relief with one approach, others combine several.

Ask, "Is this really important?" Will this situation make a difference in five years? Sometimes the child's behavior is serious and must be addressed immediately. Other times parents are reacting out of personal frustration in the moment. Sometimes they may be responding as their parents did, even if they have different values.

Frank and his wife had recently adopted 4-year-old twins, Andrew and Alexis. Frank's new son did something that infuriated him. He grabbed Andrew and was running upstairs to spank him. On the way up, Frank realized two things. First, that his son's offence really didn't bother him, although it would have infuriated his own father. And, second, that he didn't believe in spanking. He realized he was taking Andrew upstairs because he had always been spanked upstairs as a child.

Assess your needs for the moment. Sometimes a parent's anger reflects the parent's unmet needs or expectation rather than the child's behavior. Take a moment to review if your feeling is really about the behavior. Would you feel just as upset if it were another person's child, or are you at the end of your physical and emotional resources?

Parental exhaustion often happens at the end of the day when you are trying to make dinner or put the child to bed. Sometimes a mini-break can help. Sometimes you have to get through as best you can and then look for ways to take care of yourself physically and emotionally.

Lynnette was trying to get a simple meal on the table. Her older son was continually whining about one thing or another. And her toddler was underfoot, demanding to be picked up no matter where she stepped.

She could feel her emotional steam building and was about to "blow" when she realized she needed a break. Her son was trying to do his homework and was having trouble. Her toddler just wanted a hug. There was nothing wrong with either behavior, it was simply that the behavior was inconvenient at that time.

She decided to set the food aside for the moment and take her toddler and older boy over to the couch and give them (and herself) a group hug.

Ask, "What am I contributing to the problem?" Children often reflect their parent's emotional state. When the parent is happy, they are cheerful. When the parent is stressed, they are demanding, as you saw in Lynnette's experience above.

Focus on your expectations

We all have expectations of how things will go. Sometimes they are realistic, sometimes they are not. When you have a problem, consider how it might be affected by your child's temperament, developmental stage, or experience. Further, look at how your values impact your expectations. We will look at each of these briefly in this section and in more detail in the next chapter.

Child's temperament. Research has identified ten temperament traits that are consistent up into adulthood (see box).

One of the traits is *activity level.* This means that if your baby is active compared to his peers, he will usually be more active than peers as a toddler, a preschooler, and a school-aged child. Conversely, if your child is physically quiet as a baby, she will probably be quieter than her peers as she grows.

Temperament traits are not inherently good or bad, but they are frustrating in some situations and helpful in others. For example, a trait of high activity can be helpful on the soccer field and a handicap in the classroom.

Consider the child's temperament when establishing your expectation. If the child has a high level of energy, it is not reasonable to expect him to sit still in church or stand patiently while you talk to a friend, even though some children do.

Temperament traits

Activity level

Intensity

Adaptability

Mood

Approach

Persistence

Distractibility

Regularity

Emotional connection

Sensitivity to physical world

(See chapter three for more information about temperament.)

We will talk more about temperament traits, how they impact child guidance, and strategies for coping with them in chapter three.

Child's developmental stage. A long time ago when families were larger and lived closer to each other, it was easier to observe what children were like at different ages. In our time, it is harder to know children and easier to develop unreasonable expectations.

Development affects children's behavior two ways. First, there are the developmental milestones like sitting, walking, and talking that influence parenting. Second, there are developmental tasks that children struggle with. The box on the right lists common age-related challenges.

When you understand the developmental purpose (or task) behind a child's behavior, it is often easier to deal with the behavior.

For example, knowing that young toddlers are wired to explore their world makes it easier to remove precious or dangerous items from their reach, rather than trying to insist that the child leave the items alone.

Similarly, understanding that older toddlers are beginning to learn how to handle frustration and disappointment makes it easier for many parents to focus on teaching them the skills they need to calm themselves, rather than getting angry in return or telling the child to "just deal."

Understanding development helps parents develop reasonable expectations for their child and helps the parents learn to pace themselves.

Child's life experiences. Major events in a child's life influence his or her behavior. For example, if a *parent has been ill or traveling,* the child may feel abandoned and be angry or hostile when the parent returns. If the *child has been ill,* he may have come to expect continuing attention to his wishes. If the *family has moved or there is a new sibling,* the child may feel very insecure or angry and need a lot more support or attention.

Children's day-to-day experience also influences their behavior. For example, if Mom says, "You guys must pick up the toys before dinner," but lets them eat with the mess still there, the children learn to disregard what she tells them. If Dad takes the time to show his son how to look at a puzzle piece and figure out where it goes, the child learns a life-long skill of observation and problem solving.

Values. Values provide a road map for parenting. They clarify the goal. When you know what characteristics you would like your grown child to have, it can make handling some of the day-to-day situations easier. You can see how understanding her values helped Annika decide how to respond to her son's fascination with vacuuming.

When Jiro was 2½ he wanted to vacuum. Annika, his mom, was delighted since she valued cooperation and "doing one's share." Unfortunately, Jiro was not coordinated enough to do the job well, and he got frustrated when he couldn't make the vacuuming wand go where he wanted. Every time he tried, he would dissolve into crying and flailing.

Annika was tempted to distract him with other activities until he was physically more skilled and able to manage his feelings. However, she valued cooperation and independence, and she was concerned that if she delayed teaching him until he was more skilled, the interest might be gone.

After considering her values and the probability that her son would not still be interested in six months or a year, Annika decided to take the time to "teach him

Challenging characteristics of different ages

Babies cry and most of them have irregular schedules.

Young toddlers explore their world. They get into everything—it is their job.

Older toddlers struggle with understanding their emotions. They have tantrums when they can't have (or do) what they want immediately. Their job is to learn to deal with feelings and to problem solve.

Preschoolers are interested in power. They watch the grown-ups and they experiment with different ways of being powerful— being bossy, acting helpless or sick, ignoring what others say, being helpful, or being a superhero.

School-agers are developing their own structure or rules for life. They collect information. They compare, disagree with, test, break, and experience the consequences of rules.

how to vacuum." She began by using the upholstery attachment which was lighter weight, shortening the wand so it was closer to his size, and vacuuming for only a couple of minutes at a time.

Gradually, she helped build the skills he needed and increased the length of time they worked. Six months later she had a three-year-old who was both capable and willing to vacuum!

When Annika recognized the seeds of adult behavior she wanted in Jiro's fascination with the vacuum, it was easier for her to think and act effectively with the long view in mind. In chapter three we will look at values in more detail and help you identify what characteristics you want for your child or children. Now let's look at how to focus on the situation.

Focus on the situation

When you consider a situation, it helps to clarify what the child says or does, collect data on how frequently the behavior happens, clarify who owns the problem, and decide what you want to have happen instead.

> *A behavior that is considered aggressive by one person may be seen as assertive by another.*

Describe what the child actually does or says. The goal is to make a *behavioral* description of the unwanted behavior. When someone says, "My child is rude" or "My child is aggressive," those are labels and the meaning may be unclear. A behavior that is rude for one person may not be considered rude by another. A behavior that is considered aggressive by one person may be seen as assertive by another. However, if one says, "My child covers her ears and closes her eyes when I speak," there is no ambiguity.

You want a description so clear that several people can watch the same situation, count the number of times the behavior occurs, and come up with the same number. That is important because your next step is to observe how frequently the behavior happens.

Collect data. Record how frequently the unwanted behavior is happening. You can note the frequency, the length, or the intensity of the behavior. Some people record on a calendar, others log events on a piece of paper, a file card, or on the computer.

Make a baseline. A baseline is important because our perceptions of how frequently a behavior occurs are sometimes incorrect. The record can help you determine if the situation is getting better, worse, or staying the same.

Bev was attending a sibling class because she believed her 4-year-old daughter, Hannah, was continually harassing Martin, her 2½-year-old son. The first class assignment was to watch your children for twenty minutes and log their interaction.

When Bev watched her kids, nothing happened, so she watched again. The second time Martin grabbed a toy that Hannah was playing with twice, and Hannah did nothing. Still convinced that her daughter was the aggressor, Bev continued to watch. The third time, Martin grabbed the teddy bear Hannah was reading to, knocked down the tower she was building twice, and pulled Hannah's hair once.

Bev shared her experience with her class, concluding that Hannah showed great patience rather than being aggressive as she had believed. Now Bev has a baseline for dealing with her son.

Notice the context. When you make a baseline, notice the context of the behavior—who was involved and what was happening prior to the behavior. The context often gives a clue on how to handle the situation.

Ashley shared in a parenting class that she was frustrated because her 14-month-old son, Robert, was throwing food "all the time, all the time, all the time." When asked if he threw food at breakfast, lunch, and dinner, she paused and replied. "No. Only dinner."

When asked if it was the same on weekdays and the weekend, she answered that it was. Then when asked if it happened both when her husband was home and when he traveled, she paused and said with a curious look on her face, "It only happens when he's home. And it only happens when we are talking."

The problem Ashley thought she had is quite different from the one she really has. If her son only throws food when his parents are talking, she might handle the problem differently than if he threw food all the time, regardless of who was present.

Decide "who owns the problem." The person whose needs are not being met is the person who owns the problem. Let's see what that would look like.

Child owns the problem. Stefan, 2½, is in his room crying because he cannot make a dump truck work as he wishes. His door is closed, and Mom is in the kitchen cleaning up, so his distress does not bother her.

No problem. Stefan has figured out how to work the dump truck. He is carrying a load of blocks from one room to another. There is no problem. He is content and so is Mom.

Parent owns the problem. Stefan has tired of moving blocks from one room to another. He went out back for a load of gravel, put it in the truck, then dumped it on the living room rug. Now Mom has a problem. Stefan is content to move the gravel from one place to another, but the gravel and dirt are not good for the carpet.

It is helpful to consider who owns a problem. Sometimes parents are tempted to act when nothing is needed, as Morgan discovered.

Morgan had taken her daughter, Abby, 7½, and her petite friend, Sophy, to swim lessons. The girls decided to trade swimsuits. Abby squeezed into Sophy's suit with effort. When Sophy put on Abby's suit, it sagged around her and she said, "Abby, you're fat!"

Morgan cringed at Sophy's comment and began to think about how she could help Abby deal with Sophy's unkindness. Before Morgan had devised a plan, Abby came and asked if her mom had some rubberbands. Morgan gave several rubberbands to Abby and watched as Abby used them to wrap around fabric and make the suit fit Sophy better. In spite of Morgan's original reaction, this was a "no problem" situation.

Later, as she was thinking about the situation, Morgan realized that she had been much more upset by Sophy's remark than Abby had been. She decided she would have to be careful to keep her feelings separate from her daughter's, so she did not create a problem where there was none.

How you respond to the situation depends on who owns the problem.

How you respond to the situation depends on who owns the problem. If the child owns the problem, the most helpful thing to do is active listening. This gives the child support, and still lets him or her solve the problem. This approach is especially useful if you value responsibility or independence for your child.

If the parent owns the problem, there are three alternatives. First, you can change your reaction. To do this you can review your values, your developmental expectation, and your child's experience to see if you can view the situation differently. Second, you can try to avoid the problem by changing things (using tools in chapter four) so the problem does not occur. The third alternative is to modify the child's behavior. To do that you can use the STAR Parenting process and all the points and tools.

Make a behavioral goal. Decide what you want the child *to do* instead of the unwanted behavior. When you say, "Don't hit your brother," it doesn't tell her what to do when he is annoying her. Do you want her to poke or push him instead? Do you want her to move away or get help? Do you want her to suffer in silence and let him destroy all her plans?

The idea here is to create a goal that you can use when brainstorming for ideas to solve the problem, and then to state that goal in positive language. For example, "Touch gently" rather than "No hitting" or "Speak in a pleasant voice" rather than "Stop whining."

The first step in the STAR Parenting process is to *Stop and focus*. We have looked at focusing on yourself, your expectation, and the situation. Once you have an idea what the problem is, then you can generate ideas.

STAR—**T**hink of ideas

The second step in STAR Parenting is to *Think of ideas*. Some parents come to parenting classes because they have no idea what to do. They may say, "I've tried everything and nothing works." This usually means they have tried a couple of things that did not work.

Fortunately, the more ideas you have, the more likely you are to find something that works well. Sometimes knowing you have enough ideas changes the situation without having to do much else.

Mario and Maria were attending the first evening of a parenting class. They were desperate for help. Every time Maria stood at the kitchen sink, their son, Tomás, 18 months, would come up and bite his mother on her calf. This had been going on for six weeks and they didn't know what to do.

Parents in the class chose to use the tools they had learned the first night to generate ideas for Mario and Maria. The group came up with forty-eight ideas! Some of the ideas were silly, but many were practical.

Mario and Maria were so hopeful of solving the problem that when they got home, Mario went into Tomás's room, bent over his crib, and spoke softly to Tomás as he slept, "Tomás, you can forget about biting your mom, because we have more ideas than you do. The biting simply must stop."

The amazing thing is that Tomás never bit his mother again! His parents reported that they were partly pleased the biting stopped and partly disappointed that they didn't have an opportunity to use some of the ideas. I wish I could say that their experience was common, but it is not. However, many people report that things are easier than they expect, perhaps because they feel more confident when they're armed with lots of good ideas.

Finding ideas

When you think of ideas, be creative. Be playful. Be flexible. Separate yourself from your situation and think what might work for someone else. When you list ideas, look for both quantity and quality.

Where can you get ideas? You can get ideas from the STAR Parenting points and tools, books, parenting classes, professionals, Internet, friends, and relatives.

STAR Parenting points and tools. Apply each of the STAR Parenting tools to your problem. There are five points with three tools on each, giving fifteen tools. These tools are discussed in chapters four through eight. You can use the chart on the back cover to help.

Books. In the Resources section are a number of books that have ideas. Two books parents find particularly useful are *365 Wacky, Wonderful Ways to Get Your Children to Do Want You Want* by Elizabeth Crary and *Is This a Phase?* by Helen F. Neville.

Parenting classes are a good source of ideas. They are often sponsored by community colleges, churches, mental health associations, or children's hospitals.

Professionals can offer ideas. These may be parent educators, teachers, childcare directors, pediatricians, nurses, or pastors.

Internet. Parenting Science (parentingscience.com) and The Informed Parent (informedparent.com) are two thoughtful sites that some parents like. Remember that with ideas from the Internet as with other sources you need to decide if the ideas make sense for you, your child, and your values.

Friends and relatives may be helpful. However, if you ask for help and then don't take their advice, some people may be insulted. You can get around that by saying you are making a list of twenty things you can do when your child does something unwanted and ask others for ideas to add to your list.

Deliberately generate silly ideas. When your mind is free enough to think of silly ideas, it is free enough to come up with new good ideas. Also, if you are generating ideas with someone else, one person's silly idea may stimulate a really good idea in someone else.

Avoid judging ideas as you generate them. The process of evaluating ideas stops the process of generating them. When you judge the ideas as you think of them ("Oh, that won't work," or "That's too hard"), you may reject the perfect idea without even considering it.

How many ideas are enough?

When I work with parents, I try to come up with at least twenty-five ideas when we brainstorm. In STAR Parenting classes, we usually come up with forty to fifty ideas. When I ask parents to think of ideas for their problem, I ask them to come up with at least fifteen.

In the beginning, most parents find that it takes three or four revisions before they find a solution for a problem, so they need many ideas. If you have ten to fifteen ideas, you probably have enough ideas to solve the problem. Once you have enough ideas, then you need to evaluate them, make a plan, and act effectively.

Crazy is doing the same thing over and over and expecting a different result.

STAR—**A**ct effectively

The third step in STAR Parenting is to *Act effectively.* To do this, you make a plan, anticipate difficulties, and follow through.

Make a plan

Making a plan involves selecting an approach, developing a strategy, and following through. Your final approach may incorporate several ideas.

Choose an approach. Now is the time to evaluate the ideas you brainstormed earlier. Ask yourself:

- Is this idea reasonable for my child's age and temperament?
- Does it strengthen my long-term goals for my child?
- Will I follow through (do I have time and energy)?

Develop a strategy. Think about when is the best time to start. List what supplies or equipment you need. For example, if you decide to make a push to toilet train your 3-year-old son, when will you start? Will this be a joint venture with Dad's help or something Mom will do herself? If Dad helps, how will you split the duty? Also, how will you motivate your child? If you decide to use stickers with pictures of cars and trucks for your son's effort, and little cars and trucks for success, who will buy them? If you want a chart, who will make it?

Decide how long to continue. Few plans work exactly as expected. Choose a specific date to review your progress and decide whether to continue, revise your plan, or make a totally new plan.

Anticipate difficulties

Consider when you might have problems and how you can cope with them. For example, if you tend to give in when your child resists your instructions, how will you help yourself remain firm? The plan should include support for yourself. You can see this in Sally's story.

My 3-year-old daughter, Sasha, was having more and more tantrums and I decided to ignore them. Since I usually give in when she cries, I needed to find some way to cope with the crying. I devised a three-step plan. First, I would use ear plugs to reduce the sound. If she was too loud, I would put on head phones and listen to music. If she was still too loud, I would go into my room and close the door.

Set the stage. Once you have made a plan and anticipated the problems and possible solutions, you are ready to set the stage. Get the tools and material you need. Inform others—partner, daycare, friends—of what is happening and what you need from them. You can see this in Beth and Bob's experience.

When Chase was about 19 months old, he had a bad ear infection. He was in the habit of waking in the night and receiving care. Once the infection was gone, his desire for late night attention continued. After trying several unsuccessful things, we decided to let him cry it out. We lived in a small apartment and were concerned that Tammy, our neighbor who shared the wall with Chase's room,

The more STAR Parenting points you use, the more success you'll have.

might be disturbed by his crying. We were also unsure how we would manage if he cried for a long time.

After talking about it, we decided to wait for a three-day weekend. We told Tammy what we planned. She chose to go camping that weekend, which is what we hoped she would do.

Fortunately, the bathroom was between our room and Chase's, but we were still concerned about sound. Bob hung some old heavy wool blankets on Chase's wall to deaden the sound and moved the stereo into our bedroom.

All our effort paid off. The first night he cried a long while, the second night he cried for fifteen minutes, and the third night he cried for only a couple of minutes.

Follow through

DO IT and follow through. An excellent plan with no follow-through gets you nothing. One woman in class described it this way.

Follow-through is essential. It is the gas that fuels the plan. Without follow-through you have nothing. In some cases you may teach your child to disregard you by lack of follow-through. For example, if you tell your son to "Talk pleasantly," but give him what he wants to stop his whining, he will continue to whine.

How long do I need to continue? It all depends—three days, three weeks, three months? There are no clear answers. You need to continue long enough for the child to learn, but you also need to stop or revise if the plan is not working.

In my experience, if your plan is realistic and you remain firm, usually three to five days is long enough to see a change with young children. Many professionals say that it takes twenty-one days to change a behavior. If you are working against a child's temperament or against her developmental stage, it may take three to six months.

If change takes longer than that, you may be dealing with a physical or psychological problem or an addictive behavior, and it would be helpful to work with a professional. If no change is happening, check to be sure you aren't inadvertently encouraging the unwanted behavior in some way, thus sabotaging your own good plan.

How can I tell if I'm making headway? The simplest way to know if you are making progress is by charting the unwanted behavior. You can chart the frequency or the duration. Charts are useful because our perception of what is happening is often colored by our feelings at the time. If the behavior is decreasing, then what you are doing is helping, even if it is not as fast as you would like. If the frequency of the behavior is increasing, then something is encouraging the unwanted behavior. If there is no change, what you are doing has no impact.

> ### Possible problems with a plan
> - Child's anger
> - Child's persistence
> - Your fatigue
> - External stresses
> - Unintended consequences

STAR—**R**eview, revise, and reward

The last step in STAR Parenting is to *Review, revise, and reward.*

Review

After you have been working on a problem for a bit, take time to reflect on where you are and what you have done. If things are going well, continue with your plan.

If not, then revise your plan. Most people find it takes several revisions to reach their goal.

Tiffany was concerned that her daughter, 26-month-old Zoe, had turned mean. Zoe would hit her parents or friends without provocation. Tiffany and Peter's effort to teach her to touch gently had no effect. They told Zoe firmly that it hurt when she hit them. And nothing changed.

Tiffany related her frustration to Kathy, the parent educator assigned to her mom-and-tot group. Kathy explained that sometimes the attention you give while scolding a child can encourage the behavior you don't want. She suggested they distance themselves and give Zoe no attention whatsoever when she hit them, and then give her lots of attention when she was appropriate. This would mean to say nothing about the hitting, to look away from her, and to put her down or move away if she was near them. And then get close, and both look at and talk to her as soon as she was kind or gentle.

Although it was difficult for them to distance themselves, they decided to try it for three days. At first, Zoe was angry and would scream when they didn't respond. However, by the end of the second day she was hitting less. The third day, she did not hit her parents at all; however, on reflection, Zoe still hit her friend. So they had solved half the problem and had the other half to go.

Revise

Most plans need to be revised a couple of times before the problem is solved. If your plan is not working, you can:

- Reflect on the problems and adapt your current plan.
- Go back to your original list of ideas and make a new plan.
- Review the dark side of the STAR (chapter ten) and see if you are unknowingly sabotaging yourself.
- Generate more ideas.
- Get help.

Reward yourself

Good parenting can sometimes feel lonely. Children rarely, if ever, turn to their parent and say, "Thank you so very much for remaining firm with me on this. I know it will help me when I'm older."

One way to acknowledge your parenting is to reward yourself—either for your effort or for success. You could put a star on the calendar, call a friend and brag, take a bubble bath, treat yourself to a latte, or get a babysitter and go out. Do something you enjoy to celebrate your success.

If you are uncomfortable with the word "reward," use a different one: celebrate your success, recognize your work, acknowledge your effort (even if not successful), or affirm your progress. The goal is to notice your success and/or your improvement.

In order to resolve a parenting challenge, it helps to have a clear long-term view for your child. We have looked at the STAR Parenting process—*Stop and focus; Think of ideas; Act effectively;* and *Review, revise, and reward.* In the next chapter, we will go into more depth on identifying your values, your child's temperament, and your child's developmental task so you can take a long view.

Summary of
The STAR Parenting Process

★ **S—Stop and focus**—Focus on yourself. Focus on your child. Focus on the situation (and decide who owns the problem).

★ **T—Think of ideas**—Generate at least fifteen to twenty ideas. Apply each STAR Parenting tool to your problem. For more ideas, check books, parenting classes, friends, and professionals for ideas.

★ **A—Act effectively**—Make a plan, decide on your approach, and anticipate possible problems. When your plan is complete, set the stage, do it, and follow through.

★ **R—Review, revise, and reward**—Reflect on how things are going. If you have a problem, revise your plan and try something different. If things are going well, acknowledge your effort and reward yourself.

STAR in Action Story[1]

Patience, Please

My daughter, Andrea, 4, is very impatient. When she wants something, she wants it NOW. Last week, while I was making biscuits, she sat on the kitchen floor doing a puzzle. When she got stuck, she asked for help. I explained I was in the middle of kneading and could help her in a couple of minutes. Apparently that was not soon enough, and Andrea started yelling at me to do it NOW. Then I tried to tell her that my gooey hands would ruin the puzzle piece, so she would have to wait until I washed my hands. She just screamed, "NO, NOW!" By then I was losing patience and raising my voice, telling her to be quiet. The whole interaction was horrible.

S—Stop and focus

I realized there needed to be a change. These battles with my daughter were so stressful for us and were not teaching her the values we wanted her to have: Respect for others and the ability to take care of herself. I also realized that I wanted to do something that would help the underlying problem (impatience) rather than simply fixing the problem of the moment. So each day this week during Andrea's nap time, I have been working on a plan for change.

First, I set up goals for the desired behavior: 1. To ask pleasantly; 2. To learn four ways to occupy herself while she waits; 3. To teach her ways to measure the passage of time.

T—Think of ideas

Then I used the points on the STAR Parenting star to list my options.

Avoid problems

☆*Change things:* ①Use a timer. Set it for two minutes. When it rings, go help her. ②Show her how to use a clock. Tell her that when the fast hand (second hand) gets to the top (12), I will help her. ③Say, "I will help you when I have washed and dried my hands." As I wash and dry, I'll keep up a running monologue of my progress. ④Say, "I'll help you after I fix the biscuits. Do you want to help mix the dough so I'll be done quicker?" ⑤Tell her, "I'm going to be busy fixing dinner for a bit. Do you need any help before I start?"

☆*Reduce stress:* ⑥Give her a light snack before I start something that I can't stop easily. ⑦Make sure she gets some active play (run, dance, etc.) before I start something that I can't stop easily.

☆*Two yeses:* ⑧"You are having trouble with the puzzle. You can continue to work on the puzzle yourself until I'm done, or you can help me knead the biscuits so I am done quicker." ⑨"You can help me in the kitchen or read to your baby doll."

Teach new skills

☆*Modeling:* ⑩Demonstrate different ways to occupy oneself while waiting.

- Count the number of—tiles on the wall, lights on the ceiling, people in line.
- Talk to the person next to me in line about—weather, current events, etc.
- Play mind games—doubling a number, $1 + 1 = 2$, $2 + 2 = 4$, etc.
- Close my eyes and listen to sounds around me.
- Play "I Spy"
- Practice relaxing different parts of my body
- Sing quiet songs
- Practice a breathing exercise
- Make up silly stories
- Plan my shopping list
- Bring a book and read

---

1 There is a STAR in Action Story at the end of each chapter. Each story is written by a parent in his or her own words and shows how that person adapted the STAR Parenting process to his or her own life.

These stories use tools from all points, so some may be unfamiliar until you have read the appropriate chapter. You can see how different parents, with different values or with kids of different temperaments, might make different choices.

☆*Re-do it right:* ⑪When she demands "Do it now!" go to her and say, "Oops, that was an unpleasant voice. Try a pleasant voice."

☆*Shaping:* <u>*With tasks.*</u> ⑫Gradually increase the length of time I ask her to wait. 1. Dry hands. 2. Wash and dry hands. 3. Measure ingredients, then wash and dry hands. 4. Measure ingredients, knead, wash and dry hands.

<u>*With time.*</u> ⑬Gradually increase the length of time she needs to wait. Start with one minute, then one and one-half minutes, two minutes, three minutes, five minutes.

Respond to cooperation

☆*Attention:* ⑭I could smile at her when I notice her speaking pleasantly.

☆*Praise:* ⑮When I notice her asking pleasantly, say, "Wow. You asked pleasantly." ⑯When she waits, say, "You occupied yourself until I was ready." ⑰When she waits, say, "Thank you for waiting. You are getting better control of yourself."

☆*Reward:* ⑱Give her an "Instant Help" card. Tell her every time she asks pleasantly and waits until I am ready, I will give her a star. When she has five stars, I will give her an Instant Help card, which she can give me when she needs instant help. Having an Instant Help card can help her learn to rate the urgency of her needs.

Acknowledge feelings

☆*Simple listening:* ⑲Respond with "Hmm," "Oh," or "I see" when she is upset.

☆*Active listening:* ⑳"You're disappointed that I can't come right now." ㉑"I'll bet you're double frustrated. Frustrated you can't fit the piece in, and frustrated I can't come right now."

☆*Grant in fantasy:* ㉒"Do you suppose we could make a machine that would do whatever you want? Put puzzles together? Bring you a glass of water?" ㉓"Wouldn't it be fun if you had three mommies? One who could cook, one to clean the house and wash the clothes, and one who could play with you and help with the puzzle?"

Set limits

☆*Clear rule:* ㉔"Ask pleasantly." ㉕"I will come when I finish my task."

☆*Consequence:* ㉖"When you yell, the answer is no." ㉗"When you yell, it distracts me and takes me longer to complete my task."

☆*A better way :* ㉘"You want me to help with the puzzle now. I want to finish making biscuits. What can we do so we can both be happy?" (Let the child offer ideas.)

A—Act effectively

It is surprising how many ideas I found when I worked at it systematically, point by point and tool by tool. I narrowed the ideas to four options to try: #11 (☆*Re-do it right*), #19 (☆*Active listening*), #1 (☆*Change things*), and #9 (☆*Two yeses*).

- Introduce ☆*Re-do it right*. Today I was making biscuits again. Andrea was playing on the floor of the kitchen with her doll. Suddenly she decides she wants to change the dolls's clothes and I MUST snap the tiny snaps, "NOW." I took a deep breath, and then I said, "Oops, that was an unpleasant voice. Try a pleasant voice." She looked at me funny then said, "Snap the dress, NOW!"

  I responded, "I'm still listening for a pleasant voice." Andrea said softly, "Mommy, can you snap Dolly's dress?" I told her, "Yes. Thanks for asking pleasantly," and I snapped Dolly's dress. We both went back to our activities.

  In the middle of kneading dough, my hands all covered in flour, Andrea wanted me to snap Dolly's dress again. "Right now!"she demanded. "You need Dolly's dress snapped right now, please?" I said in a pleasant voice. *(Clarify expectation)* "I have to wash off my hands first." Andrea didn't like that. She started to scream, "DO IT NOW!"

- Reflect her feelings. I squatted down to her and said, *(Active listening)* "Wow. You are really frustrated that I can't do it immediately. I do need to wash my hands first. *(Two yeses)* You may read a book or brush Dolly's hair while you wait." Andrea stopped fussing, picked up her doll and began brushing. I was pleasantly shocked and hurried to wash my hands. "May I snap Dolly's dress for you now?" I asked. "Yes," she answered."

- Introduce the timer. "Thanks for keeping yourself busy and calm while you waited for me. I know it can be hard to wait." Then I said, "I want to show you this timer. If you press this button, it will count for two minutes." (We practiced starting

and stopping the timer). "Next time you have asked pleasantly for help and have to wait for me, press the timer and when it rings, I will be ready to help you." We both went back to our activities again.

Just as I was opening the oven to load the biscuits, Andrea screams, "Snap it NOW, Mommy!" I said, "In two minutes." She looked at me, ran to the timer and pushed the button. She watched the timer as I finished loading the trays into the oven and put dishes in the sink. When the alarm went off, she shut it off; I sat down and snapped the doll dress. Then we played for ten minutes.

R—Review and revise

We are making headway. She can speak in a pleasant voice if she tries. She also seems to like the timer. I think it gives her a sense of hope and power.

She still reverts to demanding occasionally, especially in the late afternoon. I think I may need to teach her some strategies to calm herself so she can speak pleasantly. And I might try rewarding her with the Instant Help tickets.

Chapter 3

Consider Your Expectations

~~~~~~

Reasonable expectations
make parenting easier

~~~~~~

Why would you want to spend the time to clarify expectations? The answer—realistic expectations make parenting easier.

Often before a child is born, parents may believe that their child will always be "good" because they will love the child, treat the child right, or provide sensitive parenting. Comforting as these expectations are to the parents, they may have unexpected consequences, as Marta discovered.

I read tons of parenting books. I decided to raise my daughter with sensitive parenting. I would be responsive to her in every way. I would not need rules or punishment because she and I would be so attuned. She would intuitively know what I wanted her to do and do it.

This plan worked pretty well for the first year. I made the house safe so Tessa rarely ran into any restrictions. As she approached 2, she began to have tantrums. I had heard that was common, so I tried to sidestep the tantrums by anticipating her demands. I wanted her to feel loved and cared for. The tantrums continued and grew more intense, but I wasn't concerned.

By the time Tessa approached her fourth birthday, she was very bossy. If she couldn't get what she wanted she had a fit, and it was a doozy. I began to worry about kindergarten the next year. What if Tessa had a teacher who didn't love her as much as I did? Would the teacher give her the support she needed? What if there were twenty kids like Tessa? There would be no way the teacher could accommodate all of them! It was then that the thought crept into my mind, "Had I created a very selfish child rather than a very secure one?"

Gradually, I came to realize that children need limits, which provide structure, as much as they need love and sensitivity. So if I wanted her to be a pleasant, capable adult, I had some work to do.

When you know where you are going, that is, what you want your child to be like as a grown-up, it is easier to get there. When you understand your child's temperament, you can adjust your plans so they are realistic. When you understand what is typical for different ages, you can determine if you are on track or off. Finally, if you take good care of yourself, you will have more energy for the job.

We will look at parents' values, children's behavior and temperament, and the vision you have for your child's future.

Values

Your values consciously or unconsciously influence your expectations.

Your values consciously or unconsciously influence your expectations. Everyone wants nice children, but people's ideas of "nice" are very different. Some people want quiet, courteous, compliant children; others want active, curious, athletic children. It is helpful for parents to identify what characteristics they would like their child to have so they can parent in a way to make those traits possible, although there are no guarantees. It is also helpful for parents to identify their values so they can choose a method of dealing with situations that is compatible with them.

For me, a classic conflict of values and implementation occurs when a parent spanks a child for hitting a sibling. Presumably, the parent objects to hitting a sibling because she is opposed to violence or hurting people; however, by spanking the child, she models the very behavior she is objecting to. The child is left to figure out whether hitting is really okay, or if hitting someone much smaller than oneself (as adult hitting a child) is okay.

How you respond to challenging situations conveys a message about what you believe is important. There are many ways to deal with unwanted behavior. The task of the parents is to respond in a way that models their long-term values, as Lynn's experience shows.

Lynn was a single parent. During the summer her 7-year-old son, Joseph, was in a daycare program that provided interesting field trips and allowed the kids a fair amount of freedom. In return, children were expected to act responsibly.

Two days before a trip to the circus, Joseph and another boy, Nick, got into a fight during swimming lessons. The boys were told their behavior was unacceptable and they were expected to work things out together or ask an adult for help. Further, they could only go to the circus in two days if they were pleasant during swimming lessons the next day. The daycare staff explained what had happened and what was needed to go to the circus to each boy's mother when he was picked up.

Lynn used the conflict to talk with Joseph about ways to cope with different situations that might occur with Nick. They even role-played a couple of the more likely scenarios. Lynn was cautiously optimistic that Joseph would manage better.

When she picked up Joseph, she asked the staff how things went at swimming lessons. The teacher told her that Nick's mom gave her son permission to skip swim lessons to guarantee he could go to the circus.

Lynn valued problem solving and personal responsibility. Without more information, we must speculate about Nick's mother's values. From her behavior, one might conclude that she valued either having fun, avoiding conflicts, or expedience. While skipping a swimming lesson was simple and avoided the problem for the day, it did not teach Nick how to handle situations or how to avoid them in the future. One challenge of parenting is balancing the present and the future, or long view. Notice how Anita rebalanced her expectations.

Anita had three children—George, 13, Ellen, 11, and Toby, 8. While at work, she received a phone call that guests she expected at the end of the week would arrive that evening. She phoned home and asked George to clean the bathroom. She also gave him instructions to relay to the others.

George balked, "Why do I always have to clean the bathroom?"

"Because you do such a good job," Anita responded.

"You mean if I didn't do such a good job, I wouldn't have to clean the bathroom?" George asked.

His complaint caused Anita to stop and quickly reflect on her values and actions. She affirmed that she valued competence in her children and she did want them all to be able to clean well. However, she had gotten in the habit of assigning kids jobs they already did well, so George's complaint was justified. She replied, "Please clean the bathroom well this afternoon, and we will discuss reassigning chores when our guests leave."

Part of the power of STAR Parenting comes from helping parents understand the values they want for their children in the long term, so they can more effectively balance the present and future needs and wishes of their children. Let's look a bit at the nature of values.

Nature of values

Values are the principles upon which you base your behavior. They may be conscious or unconscious. They may conflict with one another. They vary between individuals and between cultures. And they affect your parenting decisions.

Values may be conscious or not. Some parents are very clear about their values. They know what they want, and they measure their behaviors against that standard. Other parents may not have thought much about what they want and even less on how their behavior reflects that. Here's how two parents fell into that trap.

Marilyn espoused honesty, but frequently asked her 5-year-old daughter to tell

Q What values were demonstrated?

What messages might Joseph and Nick have received about how to deal with conflict?

the person on the phone that she wasn't home. Joshua urged his children to be responsible and keep their promises, however, when he was tired he would ignore his promises to read a story or play a game.

The problem is that children learn more from what you *do* than from what you *say*. So when a parent asks a child to lie, that calls the value of honesty into question.

Values may conflict with one another. Most people hold conflicting values—polite *vs.* honest, independent *vs.* dependent, happy *vs.* healthy are just a few.

Polite vs. honest. A common conflict between values occurs when someone asks a child a question and he or she gives an honest answer. It could be, "Did you like the book I sent you?" ("It was dumb.") "Do you like Grandma?" ("No. She smells funny.") The answer the child gave was honest, but tactless, and then the parent gets upset.

Independent vs. dependent. There is a constant tension between what the child may do and what he or she wants to do. The child is:

• too big (old) for a bottle, but too young for a glass
• too old for baby toys, too young for marking pens
• too old to be carried, too young to walk ahead by himself
• too old to jump on the sofa, too young to walk to a friend's house

Happy vs. healthy. Some parents want the child to develop healthy habits and at the same time are tempted to give in when the child resists because they want their child to be happy. You set yourself up for this dilemma when you:

• Ask, "Do you want to go to bed now?" and the child says "No!"
• Offer carrots for dinner, and your child refuses and turns away.
• Accept a child's statement that she brushed her teeth when she obviously did not.

Responsible vs. popular. Some parents feel torn when the child's irresponsibility may cause difficulties with his friends. For example:

• Tony was to do his chores before he went out to play with his buddies, but he forgot them. Now his friends are at the door.
• Samantha is supposed to finish her homework before she talks on the phone with her friends. Her homework is not finished, and one of her friends "needs" to talk right now.

Values for your child may conflict with what you want for yourself. A common conflict is independence for child versus expediency for parent. For example, carrying kids who are too slow, pouring juice for the child who wants to do it alone because it may be messy, or putting shoes on a child because he takes too long to do it himself.

Why clarifying values is helpful

Knowing your values helps you detach from conflicts, gives you direction, and helps you notice desirable behavior. How can a clear vision help you parent well?

Help you detach. Sometimes parents are sucked into conflicts with their children and respond without thinking. Values can help you stop and focus on what is important in the long run. If the wind is biting cold and your 4-year-old is whining that her hands are cold, you can tell her to put them in her pockets, or ask her if she would rather put them in her pockets or pull her sleeves down over her hands, or say, "Your hands are cold. What can you do to help them get warm?"

Give you direction. When you pause before responding to unwanted behavior, you can ask yourself, "How can I use this situation to encourage the behavior I want?" For example, when your child has grabbed a toy from a friend, you can say, "Oops, José, you forgot to ask Roberto if you could have a turn. Let's try again." Then give the toy back to Roberto so José can try asking for a turn. If Roberto says, "No," then teach José what he can do. For example, "Do you want to look at a book or build with the blocks while you wait for your turn?"

Increase consistency. When you identify what is most important to you, it is easier to make clear rules and be consistent with your children. When you are consistent, the children do not need to test as much because they know what is important.

For example, education was important to Becky. When she kept that thought in her mind, it was easier for her to take the time to help her son build good study skills and teach him strategies to motivate himself when schoolwork got boring.

Help you notice desirable behavior. Unfortunately, our society focuses on the negative and often misses the positive that exists. This attitude carries over into parenting. If Robbie asks his mother pleasantly to read to him, she may disregard it. However, if he hits his sister, he gets attention immediately.

When you know what you value for your child, you can look deliberately for those behaviors and encourage them. For example, if Robbie knelt down and made faces at the baby, Mom could say, "Wow! You made Fen smile. That is very kind," thereby labeling the behavior she values and giving him attention for being appropriate.

Enable long-term planning. Mark grew up in a family that valued charity. When his kids were little, he subscribed to the share-save-spend philosophy. He would give his young children three quarters each—one went in a jar for sharing, the second in a jar for saving, and the third could be spent. In January the children would count the money in the "share jar" and give it to their Sunday School charity.

When his children were school-aged, the amount of allowance increased and the process changed slightly. In January the children were given a choice of the charities they could donate their "share" money to and were to explain why they chose the one they did.

As they grew, the process continued to change until, when they were in high school, Mark's teens were expected to research several charities and choose one to investigate more. They would review the charity's annual statement and visit the charity to talk to the people to see how they worked. The goal was not just to donate money, but to understand the work the charity did, and to distinguish genuinely helpful programs from superficial ones. Mark valued not only charity, but responsible stewardship as well.

With understanding why we clarify values in mind, we will look at two ways to identify values.

Identify your values

Harriet Heath, in *Using Your Values to Raise Your Child to Be an Adult You Admire*, offers three ways to identify your values: the attribute (word), the definition, or the behavior. Below are five examples. She has many more in her book.

> *Ask yourself, "How can I use this situation to encourage the behavior I want?"*

Table 3–1: Examples of values

Value name: Definition	Example of adult behaviors reflecting the value
Compliance: Yields or conforms to others	Follows partner's vacation plans without comment. Allows another to break in line ahead of her.
Courage: Stands up for convictions	Speaks out about illegal or immoral practices. Intervenes when someone is being bullied.
Empathy: Feels as others are feeling	Feels the pain of a young child who loses at "Fish." Sends money to the Red Cross to help flood and earthquake victims.
Ethics: Acts from a personal moral code	Does not take supplies home from the office. Tells child when she is leaving, instead of sneaking out.
Flexiblity: Responds according to circumstances	Is willing to bike or take the bus to work if the car is in use. Enjoys fancy parties as well as camping trips.

Getting started. This chapter provides two activities about values for you to use. Activity 3–1: Desirable children's traits focuses on children's behavior, and Activity 3–2: Ranking children's traits asks you to rank twenty-five traits. For those of you who would like more values to work with, there is a list of 225 desirable attributes in the appendix, page 243.

Activity 3–1: Desirable children's traits

Directions: Imagine that you find that the preschool child you are planning to adopt has the characteristics listed below. Check your reaction to each statement listed below under the appropriate letter.

O *= outraged,* ***C*** *= concerned,* ***N*** *= neutral,* ***P*** *= pleased,* ***E*** *= elated*

Your new child:	*Your response:* O C N P E
1. is very active, always on the go.	__ __ __ __ __
2. takes whatever she or he wants.	__ __ __ __ __
3. can throw and catch a ball very well.	__ __ __ __ __
4. is a very beautiful child.	__ __ __ __ __
5. has a smile for everyone.	__ __ __ __ __
6. doesn't want to be dirty or messy.	__ __ __ __ __
7. can do "physical" things easily (*e.g.,* run, climb, ride a trike).	__ __ __ __ __

Your new child:	Your response: O C N P E
8. faces unpleasant situations (*e.g.,* doctor's shots) without flinching.	— — — — —
9. asks questions about everything.	— — — — —
10. can do things a variety of ways.	— — — — —
11. always turns out lights when leaving a room.	— — — — —
12. gives toys away to anyone who asks.	— — — — —
13. sees what needs to be done and helps without being asked.	— — — — —
14. tells the truth even when it is to his or her disadvantage.	— — — — —
15. always wants to do things by him- or herself.	— — — — —
16. is tested as academically gifted.	— — — — —
17. does what anyone says.	— — — — —
18. lets another child bite him or her.	— — — — —
19. doesn't like activities interrupted.	— — — — —
20. always thanks people.	— — — — —
21. is always sought out by playmates.	— — — — —
22. says prayers every night.	— — — — —
23. can be trusted to leave tempting items alone.	— — — — —
24. comforts a sad child at preschool.	— — — — —
25. gets own snack whenever hungry.	— — — — —

When I teach a STAR Parenting class with eighteen or more people, almost always one person is elated by a trait that outrages someone else.

Each of the traits in the activity is seen as desirable by some people and not desirable by other people. This difference arises in part from different interpretations of the traits and in part from different life experiences that cause us to value different things.

Responses to the questions in the activity vary. On particular questions, some people feel positive, while others do not. For example, some people are concerned when a child "doesn't want to be dirty or messy," while others are pleased. Similarly, some are pleased when a child would "give toys away to anyone who asked," and others are concerned.

Janet and Sandra had been friends since grade school. They were taking a STAR Parenting class together, and the group was sharing their answers for Activity

3–1: Desirable children's traits. They were startled to discover that they were polar opposites on question 19. Sandra checked that she would be very concerned if her son didn't like activities interrupted, while Janet checked she would be elated.

The friends conferred to discover why they were so far apart. As it turned out, Janet's son was easily distracted and she was concerned that he was not persistent enough, so she would be pleased if he didn't want his play interrupted. Sandra had a younger brother who was autistic; she worried that if a child didn't want his play interrupted, his behavior might fall somewhere on the autism spectrum. So, each woman's values made sense in terms of her experience.

Some people find it difficult to rank the traits. If you have trouble, you can circle the ones that are most important to you, and cross out the ones that you don't want or don't care about. Then look at the ones you circled and rank them.

You may want to rank the traits twice—once for where your child is now and once as you would like him or her to be ten or twenty years from now.

Activity 3–2: Rank children's traits

Directions: Rank the personality traits listed below. Begin with 1 as the most important to you.

Note: The traits are the same as were presented in Activity 3–1. The numbers in parentheses indicate the corresponding statement in Activity 3–1.

____ **Active,** lots of energy, always moving (1)
____ **Aggressive,** competitive (2)
____ **Athletic,** does well in sports (3)
____ **Attractive,** physically nice looking (4)
____ **Cheerful,** pleasant, friendly (5)
____ **Clean,** neat, uncluttered (6)
____ **Coordinated,** physically coordinated (7)
____ **Courageous,** stands up for own beliefs (8)
____ **Curious,** inquisitive (9)
____ **Flexible,** resourceful, innovative (10)
____ **Frugal,** conserves resources and energy (11)
____ **Generous,** shares with others (12)
____ **Helpful to others,** altruistic (13)
____ **Honest,** truthful (14)
____ **Independent,** self-reliant (15 & 25)
____ **Intelligent,** intellectual (16)
____ **Obedient,** compliant (17)
____ **Passive,** not aggressive (18)
____ **Persistent,** has "finishing power" (19)
____ **Polite,** well mannered (20)
____ **Popular,** liked by peers (21)
____ **Religious,** respects God (22)
____ **Self-controlled,** self-restrained (23)
____ **Sensitive,** considerate of others' feelings (24)

List your values. In the activity below, choose an age (12, 18, or 25) and think about what you would like your child to be like at that age. Write down several characteristics you would like him or her to have.

After you have made your list, look at your child. Which traits does he or she already have? Which traits will you need to work on? When you have a clear vision of what you want your child to be like as an adult, it can help you notice and nurture the seeds of that behavior when the child is young.

Activity 3–3: Identify your primary values

Choose an age sometime in the future—12 or 18 often works.
Think about what you would like your child to be like at that age.
List three to five characteristics you would like your child to have.

1. _____

2. _____

3. _____

4. _____

5. _____

Working as a team. When two people are raising a child, it is interesting for them to rank their values separately and then compare them. When you do, remember values are neither right nor wrong. Each person has a right to his or her own values.

In a couple's class I taught, people were sharing behaviors they were most pleased about and most concerned about. One woman shared that she would be elated if her son "always turns out lights when leaving a room." Her husband was shocked since he would be very concerned about the same behavior. The couple withdrew from the group to discuss why they were so far apart. After a brief discussion, they realized that Dad thought that always turning off the lights was a compulsive behavior (which concerned him), while Mom was concerned about conserving resources.

Sometimes the differences are more fundamental, as you can see in John and Marianne's story.

John grew up with a single working mom where money was very tight. Most of his childhood they struggled to cover basic needs. He wanted his children to have a sense of abundance. His wife, Marianne, grew up in a family that had money, but no money management skills. She wanted their children to be frugal and thoughtful about their expenditures. Over time, John and Marianne were able to come to agree that they both wanted the children to have good money management skills and a few luxuries. So they developed a procedure for deciding how and when to spend money on their children.

We have looked at the nature of values, why they are important, and how to identify yours. This is a good start. It is also helpful for parents to consider the child's temperament and age or developmental stage before responding to challenging behavior.

Age-appropriate behavior

Children's behavior is influenced by their age. When parents and caregivers are unaware of behavior typical for different ages, they may have unrealistic expectations. When you have realistic expectations, it is easier to deal with the developmental behavior in ways that encourage your long-term values.

- *Noah, 15 months, is fascinated with the light switches and keeps turning them on and off. At first it was cute, but now it is really annoying.*
- *Jackson, 28 months, whines when he can't have what he wants. We are out of cereal and he keeps asking like we are deliberately starving him.*
- *Vanessa, 4, appears to have developed a case of intermittent deafness. I have asked her three times to set the table and she pretends she doesn't hear me.*

There are many approaches to looking at child development. My favorite approach clarifies developmental tasks for six stages.

In the ideal world, children would learn the skills needed during the initial stage. However, sometimes they do not. Fortunately, the stages repeat themselves throughout the life span, so if a child does not learn what he or she needs at one age, the child has the opportunity to learn it later.

When I look at a child's behavior, I usually find that the behavior makes sense in terms of the child's developmental tasks. It is often easier in the long run to help the child learn the skills needed for his developmental task than to try to stop unwanted behavior. Let's look at the developmental tasks and then see how they relate to the situations above.

Behavior makes sense in terms of the child's developmental tasks.

Developmental tasks

Birth to six months—being. The task is to grow and trust. When a baby cries and the parent or caregiver comes to offer comfort, the baby learns to trust he will be taken care of. If the baby cries and no one comes, then he learns that he is alone in a scary place. He must depend on himself because there is no one else he can depend on.

Six to eighteen months—exploring. The task of the young child is to explore the world. This begins with exploring her hands and feet, and moves to the wider world when she begins to crawl and walk. When her space is safe and she can explore her surroundings, she learns that the world is safe. When her space is unsafe or the adults angry or hurtful, she may learn to distrust the world.

A young toddler typically repeats the same behavior (dropping food on the floor or hammering a block on the wall) over and over again. She may even look at you gleefully before she repeats the behavior you

Developmental tasks

Birth to 6 months—Being

6 to 18 months—Exploring

18 to 36 months—Thinking & feeling

3 to 6 years—Power & identity

6 to 12 years—Structure & skills

12 to 18 years—Separating & sexuality

have told her not to. This is not because she is out to get you, although it may feel that way. It's because she is *programmed* to explore and she has not yet developed self-restraint or is checking to see if her parents will respond the same was as they did before.

The simplest way to help her is to make it impossible for her to do the unwanted behavior. If she is dropping the food on the floor, simply take the plate away or put her on the floor. Over time, with consistency on the parent's part, she will stop trying the behavior. The length of time that this will take depends on the child's temperament. We will talk about temperament later in this chapter.

Eighteen months to three years—thinking and feeling. The task is to learn to think and to deal with feelings. Toddlers have tantrums—whether it is because the square puzzle piece will not fit in the round hole or the pajamas he wants to wear are in the washing machine.

It is helpful to show toddlers how to think about their problems *and* how to deal with the feelings, rather than to simply solve the problem for them. You can help a child see that the puzzle hole is smooth all around and the square piece has sharp corners. Then help him hunt for a piece that is smooth all the way around—running his finger on the edge to check if it is smooth. You can teach him to calm himself by "shaking out his mads" or taking deep breaths, rather than throwing the puzzle across the room.

One of the benefits of problem solving is that it permits the child to consider alternate paths of behavior, thus beginning to develop self-control.

Three to six years—power and identity. The tasks are to decide how to be powerful and who he or she is. This often takes the form of resisting requests, bossing people, and being outrightly defiant. Some different kinds of power people may try are:

Physical power—taking things they want or hitting. Using their size or strength to get what they want.

Manipulative power—taking advantage of others by unfair means. "If you don't give me the book, I'll tell Mommy you hit me."

Passive defiance—deliberately declining to hear or respond to statements or requests they don't like.

Acting helpless—looking woebegone, crumpling on the floor, or whining "I can't do it."

Active defiance—deliberately doing (or refusing to do) what is right or requested, in a confrontational way—"You can't make me," or "You're not my boss."

Endless negotiation—always trying to make a deal or change the terms set down by the parent.

Cooperative power—looking for solutions that meet both people's needs.

A challenge for parents is to decide what they want their children to know about power. You can see two different types of power displayed by the parents in the scenarios below.

Brian's son, Matthew, hit his sister because she wouldn't give him her book. Brian wanted him to understand that behavior was totally unacceptable, so he spanked Matthew for hitting his sister.

Danielle's daughter, Alyssa, wanted a cookie before dinner, and her mother did not want Alyssa to spoil her appetite with sweet food. Instead of arguing with Alyssa, Danielle said, "Your way is to have a cookie now. And I'm afraid you'll spoil your appetite for dinner. My way is for you to wait until after dinner for a cookie, but you are hungry now. What can we do that might work for both of us?"

Activity 3–4: Identify the type of power

Read the examples above and notice the type of power the parent used.

1. Brian used _____ power with Matthew.

2. Danielle used _____ power with her daughter Alyssa.

Answers: **1.** Brian modeled physical power by spanking Matthew. Further, Dad demonstrates that it is okay for big people to hit little people, even though children hitting each other is not okay. **2.** Danielle shared power (cooperative power) with Alyssa by using problem solving and negotiation. She clarified the problem and asked Alyssa for a solution that met the criteria.

Six to twelve years—structure. The task is to understand structure, or how the world works. This involves gathering information about the world and understanding rules, the relevance of rules, and the consequences of breaking them. Children check the structure or rules at home, school, church, youth groups, etc.

A child might come home from a friend's house and say things like, "Why do I have to set the table or help with the dishes? Cody doesn't have to," or, "I wish I lived at Peter's house; his mom lets him watch all the TV he wants." Your daughter may want to find out if she really has to do all the work her teacher says.

A dilemma with schoolwork is if you insist your child does all her schoolwork, she may not learn to motivate herself or develop her internal structure. On the other hand, if you let her continue to fail, she may conclude schoolwork isn't important. This again is why we have the *Review, revise, and reward* step of the STAR Parenting process.

It often helps school-aged kids when you can explain the purpose of the rule or the value it is based on. For example, one might say to the child who doesn't want to set the table, "Different families have different rules. In our family we each contribute to the family, and each member receives from the family. If there is something else you would rather do to contribute to the family, let me know and we can talk about it." In this response Mom conveys the value of both cooperation and problem solving.

Twelve to eighteen years—identity, separation, and sexuality. The task is to work on identity, separation, and sexuality. The question for the teen is, "How can I become a separate person, with my own values, and still belong?" This task needs to be dealt with in different areas—at home, in school, with friends.

Adolescents make some of their identity and separation choices by revisiting earlier developmental tasks with the new information and the sometimes confusing pressures of emerging sexuality. This is why they may seem very grown up one minute and very immature the next.

A challenge when raising adolescents is to accept and affirm the teens' growing independence, and at the same time keep them safe by confronting unhealthy or self-defeating behaviors. Sometimes the relentless, frustrating behaviors of teens help them separate from their parents, and help the parents anticipate their departure with some relief.

The way developmental tasks can influence a child's behavior is summarized in the following table.

Table 3–2: Age and developmental task summary	
Birth to 6 months	**Being:** The task is to grow and trust. When a baby cries and the parent or caregiver comes to comfort him, the baby learns to trust he will be taken care of.
6 to 18 months	**Exploring:** The task is to explore the world. This begins with exploring her hands and feet, and moves to the wider world when she begins to crawl and walk.
18 to 36 months	**Feeling and thinking:** The task is to learn to think and to deal with feelings. Toddlers need to learn how to calm themselves and how to make decisions about the difficulties they face.
3 to 6 years	**Power and identity:** The task is to decide how to be powerful and who he or she is. This often involves kids resisting requests, bossing people, and acting outrightly defiant.
6 to 12 years	**Structure and skills:** The task is to understand structure and how the world works. This involves gathering information about the world, and understanding rules, the relevance of rules, and the consequences of breaking them. If there is no consequence, there is no learning.
12 to 18 years	**Separating and sexuality:** The task is to separate and accept one's sexuality (what it means to be male or female). Particularly, "How can I become a separate person, with my own values, and still belong?"

Clues for identifying developmental tasks

There are three clues for deciding what purpose a behavior serves for the child: (1) the child's age, (2) what preceded the child's conflict, and (3) your feelings. First, we will look at Megan's story and discuss the three clues, and then apply them to her behavior.

Right now I'm having a really tough time with my daughter, Megan, who is 8. Sometimes she is a delight and fun as can be; other times, she is ornery and provoking. This morning I was watching a friend's children, so the house was full of kids. Megan walked up to her older brother, who was reading on the sofa. She looked at me to make sure I saw what she was doing and then hit him—not enough to hurt, but enough to be a clear violation of family rules.

I went to her and asked her to apologize. She said, "No," loud and clear, as though to an audience. I reminded her she had broken a family rule and she needed to do a "kindness." Again she said, "No." By now all the eyes are on our confrontation.

I had no idea what I wanted to do, but I was sure I didn't want everyone watching. So I picked her up and carried her to the next room. All the kids trailed along behind. When I closed the door, I heard the buzz of quiet conversation in the hall. Megan could hear it too and was grinning from ear to ear.

Q

What could be the developmental task?

What developmental task might be driving Megan's behavior?

I opened the door and told the kids that Megan had broken a family rule and would be out as soon as she was willing to do a kindness for her brother. When I closed the door again, I could hear the footsteps of the children retreating. As soon as the steps faded, Megan hopped off the bed and said, "I will set the table for Rick when it is his turn. You can get the calendar and I'll cross his name off and put mine in."

So the storm was gone as fast as it arrived. I'm not sure what it was about. Did she want a power struggle? Did she want my attention?

Clue 1—the child's age. Children's age can give a clue to their motives. This is the simplest clue and sometimes can be misleading. In general, a child's behavior will reflect either the child's age-appropriate task, or a previous task he or she is still working on.

For example, toddlers get into things as they explore and 2-year-olds fall apart emotionally if they can't have what they want. Four-year-olds challenge adults' authority. An 8-year-old promises to start his homework "in a minute," but somehow never gets around to it because he is waiting to see what will happen.

These behaviors are age appropriate. However, it is common to find a child revisiting an earlier, but incomplete task. This is when you see an 8-year-old still dealing with power, or a 4-year-old who is working on dealing with feelings or struggling to find suitable ways to connect. Age gives you a place to start as you consider the other clues.

Clue 2—what preceded the conflict. Often when children are difficult, parents focus on the precipitating event, the "straw that broke the camel's back," as it were. You can see this in the following example.

Bonnie asks her dad to read her a story. He says, "Later." She asks again later. He declines again. She turns on the TV and he gets up, turns the TV off, and says, "How many times do I have to tell you? No TV after supper."

If you focus on the last behavior, you might think the child's purpose was power, but if you look at the whole exchange you can see that it began when the parent ignored her request for a story (connection or attention). When she could not get attention constructively ("Please read me a story"), she changed tactics to one she knew would work (breaking a rule).

Clue 3—your feelings. Some people believe that you can tell the motive of a behavior not by what the child did, but by how you, the adult, felt about the child's behavior. The two motives that are most relevant for parents are the desire for attention and the desire for power.

Attention. When a child does something for attention, the parent feels annoyed, irritated, put upon. Bids for attention:

- often come when the parent is tired or otherwise engaged
- are made when the parent seems emotionally unavailable
- build over time (It's not the first request that is upsetting—it's the repetition.)

Power. When a child does something to assert power, the parent may feel proud or another time angry, threatened, powerless, or enraged. Power-seeking moves:

- are often, but not always, made when there is an audience to increase the parents' discomfort
- tend to be created for a specific person, or to collect specific information
- are often a single unanticipated thrust

You can use these three clues to figure out what the purpose of Megan's behavior might have been. Note, seeking attention or power is not "bad"—only appropriate or inappropriate. When a child asks for a hug when waking up in the morning, parents are often delighted. When a child uses her power to defend a friend, parents usually feel proud.

Activity 3–5: Understanding Megan's behavior

Read Megan's story above (page 43) and decide what you think about her behavior.

1. Megan's age is _____. Her developmental task is _____.

2. Behavior preceding breaking the rule: _____

3. How Mom felt: _____

Megan's probable motive is _____,

because: _____.

Answers: **1.** Age 8. Developmental task is structure. However, Megan may still be working on power. **2.** Nothing was going on. **3.** Angry and confused. The motive probably is power because she wanted an audience to demonstrate her skills for.

Now, let's practice identifying the developmental task and what skills kids need by looking at the three children on page 40. I have done the first one. You can do the next two.

Activity 3–6: Identify the developmental task

Directions: Review the stories of the three children on page 40.
Look at how the questions are answered for Noah in part A. Use the same process to identify what skills Jackson and Vanessa need in parts B and C.

A. Developmental task for Noah	
Describe the behavior.	Turns light switches on and off all day.
Note the child's age and developmental task.	*Age:* 15 months *Developmental tasks:* to explore his world
Identify a possible motive behind the behavior.	Noah is exploring cause and effect by turning on and off the lights. Some children need to do it more times than others.
Skills child needs	Practice turning something on and off

B. Developmental task for Jackson	
Describe the behavior.	

Note the child's age and developmental task.	
Identify a possible motive behind the behavior.	
Skills child needs	

C. Developmental task for Vanessa	
Describe the behavior.	
Note the child's age and developmental task.	
Identify a possible motive behind the behavior.	
Skills child needs	
Answers below	

We have seen how the child's developmental stage can influence behavior. Another strong influence is the child's temperament. We will look at that in the next section.

Answers: Developmental task for Jackson	
Describe the behavior.	Whines when he can't have what he wants.
Note the child's age and developmental task.	*Age*: 28 months. *Developmental tasks:* to manage his feelings
Identify a possible motive (task) behind the behavior.	Jackson whines because he doesn't know how to calm himself.
Skills child needs	Several self-calming tools

Answers: Developmental task for Vanessa	
Describe the behavior.	Ignores Mom's requests to set the table.
Note the child's age and developmental task.	*Age:* 4 years *Developmental tasks:* to explore power and identity
Identify a possible motive (task) behind the behavior.	By ignoring her mother's request, Vanessa can do whatever she wants. She is *powerful*.
Skills child needs	Skills to negotiate. Information that you can still be powerful when you help others or do what others request.

Now you can think about your child's behavior and look for the developmental motive at work in Activity 3–7.

Activity 3–7: Your child's developmental task	
Child's name	
Describe the behavior.	
Note the age and developmental task.	Age: _____ Developmental task: _____
Identify a possible motive (task) behind the behavior.	
Skills your child needs	• • • •

We looked at the impact of a child's age on behavior by considering the child's developmental task and what skills the child might be practicing. Next, we will look at how a person's temperament affects his or her behavior.

Temperament

Children are different; even children in the same family can be very different.

- Allie is always cheerful; Jamila tends toward somber.
- Jayden screams when disappointed; Zhong merely whimpers.
- Emily continues to climb on the table when told not to; Vesta accepts the limit gracefully.
- Eli is always on the go; Austin would rather read a book.
- Taylor gets hungry like clockwork; Leila's appetite varies in both when she is hungry and how much she eats.

These differences reflect the child's temperament.

What is temperament? Temperament is the combination of inborn traits that influence how a child deals with the world. These inborn traits dramatically influence what a child will be like as an adult. When you set your expectations, you need to consider what your child is actually capable of.

Temperament is different from developmental stages. Development determines *when* a child walks. Temperament determines *how* a child learns to walk. Temperament traits tend to remain the same as the child grows. Developmental behaviors change dramatically as the child grows.

Nature of temperament

The classic research by Chess, Thomas, and Birch identified nine temperament traits. Since then a tenth trait has been added. These are listed in the sidebar on page 47.

Temperament traits are inborn. Temperament traits are present at birth, although they may be hard to notice until after 4 months of age. They are "hardwired" along with gender, hair color, and potential size. Some mothers notice traits before their

Temperament traits

Activity level

Adaptability

Approach

Distractibility

Emotional connection

Intensity

Mood

Persistence

Regularity

Sensory awareness

*Traits are described in table on page 51.

child is born. For example, some babies are very active even before they are born.

Traits are measured relative to the child's peers. For example, most newborns cry. However, intense infants cry longer and louder than other babies. One student of mine had a son who was very intense—so intense that the hospital nursery asked them to leave early because his crying disturbed the other mothers and newborns. On the other end, some babies are "very good" and cry softly. These differences are due to the inborn trait of intensity.

Traits are consistent through time. This means that if you have an active baby, you will probably have an active toddler, preschooler, and school-aged child. If you have a baby who cries a lot, you will probably have an emotional toddler, an intense preschooler, and a dramatic school-aged child.

What this means for parents is that if the behavior you are concerned about is driven by temperament rather than a developmental stage, the child won't "outgrow it." For example, if your young toddler is slow to approach (cautious) and doesn't initially like new food, he will continue to resist new foods as an older toddler, preschooler, and school-aged child unless you teach him some coping skills.

Traits only change with a traumatic event or consistent, long-term parenting. It is not surprising that some children change as a result of something traumatic like the death or deployment of a parent, a move, life-threatening accident, or abuse.

What some people find surprising is the impact of long-term parenting for good or for bad—especially how good intentions can backfire. Chess and Thomas describe the case of Pamela. She was a very engaging infant and child, cheerful, responsive, adaptable, fun to be with. Her parents' childhood experiences were unpleasant, so they tried to make her life perfect (see the story on page 49). By the time Pamela was 7, their well-intended support prevented her from learning needed social and academic skills.

Similarly thoughtful, consistent parenting can modify a difficult behavior. John was intense! He either howled long and loud, or beamed and laughed vigorously. His first reaction to new situations was negative. He screamed when there was a change of plans. John's internal schedule varied from day to day. No one could predict when he would nap or when or how much he would eat. His temperament was intense, generally negative, irregular, and slow to adapt.

John's mother had an almost inexhaustible store of patience. When John was upset in the grocery store, she would pick him up screaming and kicking, check out, and go home. When John was inappropriate, his mother removed him. John's demands brought firm, consistent, and quiet removal from the scene. His mother taught him self-calming techniques. Little by little John adapted. His tantrums diminished. By first grade, he was able to control his reaction to disappointment and had become a more social child.

Traits are neither good nor bad. They are helpful in some situations and difficult in others. For example, high persistence is a great trait if it helps a child continue to memorize difficult math facts, and a liability when the child persists in unwanted behavior. Low approach, resistence to new things or ideas, is helpful when resisting peer pressure, but a hindrance in moving to a new school.

The same trait can even be seen differently by different people. For example, high activity level could be seen as energetic (positive) or restless (negative); low activity level can be seen as calm and restful, or lazy and lethargic. So the traits are not inherently good or bad—only helpful in some situations and a hindrance in others.

One challenge for parents is to give children the skills they need to manage their temperament. We will talk a bit more about that later.

Some traits often come together. *Easy, flexible kids* amount to forty percent of the population. Easy kids are calm physically, adaptable, happy, easy going, and have regular habits. *Cautious, shy children* are about fifteen percent of kids. These kids are generally inactive, fussy, and resist new things and situations. *Spirited or difficult children* amount to ten percent of children. These kids are intense, may be upset by noise, may have irregular body rhythms, and have trouble with changes and new routines. They may be either extremely cautious (low approach) or extremely curious (high approach). *Temperament Tools: Working with Your Child's Inborn Traits* by Helen F. Neville and Diane Clark Johnson describes eight clusters of traits and how to deal with them.

Some combinations take more energy than others. If your child is active, intense, persistent, cautious, and slow to adapt, your life is going to be more difficult than if your child is physically and emotionally quiet, easy to distract, and adaptable.

Jessica was often exhausted. Her son Benjamin, 2½, was active, persistent, and intense. He kept Jessica on the run all day. Jessica received a lot of advice from her sister-in-law, Michelle.

Michelle felt that if everyone would parent as she did, they would not have so many challenges. For example, she told Jessica that all she needed to do to get through church with Benjamin was to bring a story book and a bag of Cheerios®, like she did for her daughter, Vesta.

Michelle got her chance to check her theory one weekend by watching Benjamin so his parents could go to a wedding. When his parents returned, Michelle greeted them with, "Jessica, I owe you an apology. Kids are different. Benjamin takes much more energy and persistence than Vesta does. I don't know how you manage as well as you do. The book and snack idea for church was a flop. Shortly after the service

Good Intentions Can Backfire

Pamela was a good baby. She slept well, accepted new foods, and adjusted to changes in schedule quickly. She was moderately active and enjoyed both running outside and sitting for a story. At 3 she got along well with her peers—she was usually charming, would share toys, and never threw sand in the sandbox.

At home her parents were enchanted. They would play with her for hours. They were reluctant to make demands like "Help put the toys away" or "Wait a bit while I finish this." When she showed her mother a picture, her mom would respond, "Wonderful!" When she performed a new trick, her dad would always say, "Awesome!" She got the impression that everything she did was charming.

When she went to kindergarten, she had trouble recognizing and following instructions. By second grade, she had learned so little about rules of play that other children were no longer interested in being with her.

By 7, although she was still amiable, she was beginning to be lonely. She wanted to please, but no longer knew how. Her parents' undiscriminating acceptance had prevented her from learning how to work and play when others made the rules, and how to master skills and responsibility.

This story is adapted from Chess, Thomas, and Birch's book, *Your Child Is a Person: A Psychological Approach to Parenthood Without Guilt* (1965) that introduces their classic work on temperament.

started, he was crawling around on the floor looking for Cheerios®. When I tried to pull him back, he screamed. It was so embarrassing.”

Goodness of fit. Some traits are easier for one parent to deal with than another. Megan was the most active toddler I have worked with. Fortunately her mom, Tracy, also had very high energy. In fact, Tracy exercised each morning before going to work so her energy (restlessness) would not bother her co-workers. Megan and her mom were a good fit.

Some parents are better suited to parenting a child with one cluster of temperament traits than another. This can be seen in the tale of two couples.

Steven and Donna were ivory tower scholars. They were quiet people both physically and verbally. They liked routine—you could almost set your watch by either of them. They liked nothing better than to sit with a book or play a quiet game of cards.

Tom and Kayla, on the other hand, were active. They liked to be on the move—hiking, biking, and skiing. They were a rowdy, fun-loving pair. They enjoyed doing things spontaneously and didn't mind changing their plans to accommodate a sudden whim.

Both couples became pregnant about the same time with their first child. When their babies were born, it was almost as though they had been switched—so different were the children from their parents.

Steven and Donna had an active, intense baby, Oscar, who had no schedule. One night he would sleep four hours; another night, ten. They couldn't predict when he would eat or sleep. As he grew he always wanted to move. His parents were exhausted by Oscar's intensity and frustrated by the disruption to their well-ordered life.

Kayla and Tom had a darling little girl, Mandy. She was dainty and quiet. Even as a newborn she was more likely to whimper than cry, and she quickly settled into a pattern of sleeping and eating regularly.

As Mandy grew, she preferred quiet activities like reading or drawing. When Kayla and Tom took her hiking, she annoyed them by walking slowly or asking to be carried. She further frustrated them by wanting to nap and eat on her internal schedule, regardless of where they were.

Neither of the families above had a temperamentally good fit. Even though they each loved their child, the child's temperament was difficult for them. However, if the temperaments of their children were switched, the fit would have been much better.

Variations within a family. Temperament varies within a family in the same way physical characteristics do. In some families, all the kids look the same. Similarly in some families, all family members share many temperament traits. In other families, each child may resemble a different ancestor, so the family may have a short dark child and a tall fair child. One child may be physically active, intense, persistent, and slow to adapt, while another may be only moderately active, mildly intense, very adaptable, and quick to approach new experiences.

When parents have children with different temperaments, parenting takes more thought. They need to look at the temperaments of each child and what skills each child needs to be a successful adult, and then blend that together to make a plan.

If your child's temperament is hard for you, it will increase your stress and decrease your energy. It might be helpful to get support and time off. We will talk a bit about that in the self-care section of this chapter.

How to identify temperament

When you've identified your child's temperament, you can teach him or her needed skills or modify your expectation. To identify your child's temperament, first familiarize yourself with the ten traits and then rank your child on each one.

Temperament traits. Ten temperament traits are briefly described in Activity 3–8: Identify your child's temperament traits. Once you have read them, you can practice identifying these traits in Activity 3–9: Identify the trait. This activity looks at the traits of the children mentioned at the beginning of this section (page 47). For more information about the traits, look at *Understanding Temperament: Strategies for Creating Family Harmony* by Lyndall Shick.

Activity 3–8: Identify your child's temperament traits

Directions: For each trait, read the description, and then mark where your child fits on the scale provided.

1. **Activity level.** How active is your child? If you were on a desert island, would your child be "on the go" or "laid back and idle?" Are her movements quick or slow?

   Physically active . . . . Physically quiet

2. **Adaptability.** How quickly does your child adjust to changes in plans? How quickly does she adapt to new places, foods, or things?

   Quick to adapt . . . . Resists change

3. **Approach.** What is your child's first reaction to new people, places, or experiences? Is he or she eager or reluctant for new experiences?

   Curious . . . . Cautious

4. **Distractibility.** Is your child easily interrupted by things going on around him? Does he continue to work or play when noise is present?

   Hard to distract . . . . Easy to distract

5. **Emotional connection.** How readily does your child understand other people's feelings? How much is your child affected by other people's feelings?

   Unaware of feelings . . . . Very aware of feelings

6. **Intensity.** How much energy does your child use to express emotions? Does she laugh or cry vigorously? Or, does she smile and fuss mildly?

   High intensity . . . . Low intensity

7. **Mood.** What mood does your child usually display? Does your child see the world as a pleasant or an unpleasant place?

   Somber/Grumpy . . . . Sunny/Cheerful

8. **Persistence.** How long does your child continue with a difficult activity? Can he continue when frustrated? Can he stop when asked?

   Very persistent . . . . Stops easily

9. **Regularity.** Does your child have a predictable internal clock? Does he or she generally get hungry at the same time everyday? . . . sleep at the same time? . . . have bowel movements at the same time?

   Irregular schedule . . . . Regular schedule

10. **Sensory awareness.** How aware is your child of his or her physical world? How sensitive to changes in sound, light, touch, pain, taste, and odor? Note: Kids can be sensitive to one sense and less so to another.

    Physically insensitive . . . . Physically very sensitive

Activity 3–9: Identify the trait

Read each description below and see if you can pick out the temperament trait it refers to.

Description/behavior	Trait	Strength (high or low)
Allie is always cheerful.	*Mood*	*Sunny/Cheerful*
Austin is only content curled up with a book.		
Eli is always on the go.		
Emily continues to climb on the table when told not to.		
Jayden screams whenever he is disappointed.		
Jamila tends toward somber.		
Leila's interest in food varies dramatically from day to day.		
Taylor gets hungry every day like clockwork.		
Vesta accepts limits gracefully and doesn't push them.		
Zhong merely whimpers when upset.		

Identify your child's temperament. Use Activity 3–8 to identify your child's temperament. When you are done, you can also consider your temperament and how well you and your child fit together.

It is interesting to have a partner or other caregiver rate your child so you can compare notes. Sometimes their opinions are different, sometimes similar. There is an additional copy of the chart on page 228 in the appendix.

Once you have identified your child's temperament, you can consider whether there are any skills your child needs in order to be successful in the adult world.

Activity 3–10: Summarize your child's temperament

Review the traits you marked in Activity 3–8. Record the five traits that you think most affect your child's behavior.

1. _____

2. _____

3. _____

4. _____

5. _____

Working with challenging traits

Working with challenging temperament traits involves both short-term and long-term strategies. In the short run, you need to respond to the current behavior driven by the temperament. In the long run, you need to plan how you will provide your child with the skills he or she needs to be a capable adult. The STAR Parenting process, points, and tools provide a structure for both of these.

Responding to current challenges. When you identify what part of a behavioral problem is based on temperament, then you can include that in your planning. For example, if you have a persistent toddler, it is easiest to avoid the problem and to work on developing self-restraint.

Greta was a bright, persistent 20-month-old. She could sit and do puzzles over and over and over. Eda, her mother, once counted her doing the same puzzle twenty-two times. However, Greta also persisted in repeating unwanted behavior as well.

Things went pretty well until Greta started standing on the dining room table. Eda explained to her daughter, "Feet on the floor, hands on the table." Mom would put her down and Greta would scramble back up. Mom took her to another room and Greta returned to the table. Mom moved the chairs away from the table and Greta pushed them up to the table. The only thing that worked was to take all the chairs to another room.

When children are persistent, parents need to carefully consider before they set a limit, "Will I really follow through if my child resists strongly?" If you're not going to follow through, don't make the rule. When you set a limit and then give in, you are teaching your child to be persistent in defying you by rewarding his or her persistence.

In the book, *Temperament Tools: Working with Your Child's Inborn Traits,* the authors offer strategies for dealing with different temperaments. For example, here are their keys to living with the intense, slow-adapting child.

- *Avoid the intensity spiral.* When the child gets intense, increase your calmness. If you yell "Stop that!" or "Be quiet," the child's intensity increases further.
- *Channel intensity to forms you can live with.* You might try singing, make-believe stories, or even running.
- *Expect difficulty with transition and change.* Everything from waking in the morning to wearing a new shirt is difficult for these children. Talk about transitions ahead of time. "After breakfast we will go to preschool." "After lunch will be nap time."
- *Expect strong emotions.* Tantrums are routine in the early years. Although unpleasant, they are not life-threatening. When the parent remains calm, they will subside. If the parents back down, the child will rule the family.
- *Mind pictures must change before behavior can change.* These children are natural planners. They have a picture of what they expect to happen. Before she can change her behavior, the child must change the picture. They need time to change the picture.
- *Rules and rituals are relaxing.* These children love the predictability of rules and rituals that are familiar.

The book has tips for dealing with other temperament traits. In addition to ideas for getting through the day, you need to consider what skills your child will need in the long run.

Consider what skills your child will need to thrive as an adult. If he has a very high activity level, then he will need outlets for his energy. If she has low energy, then she will need to learn to push herself to walk briskly to get the exercise she needs to maintain good health. Similarly, if she is intense, she will need self-calming tools to avoid alienating others. If he has low intensity, he will need to learn to speak strongly to be heard.

Table 3–3: Possible skills for different temperaments

Trait	High	Low
Activity level	*High*—Run off energy: Let some part of the body wiggle. Take breaks for exercise.	*Low*—Get regular exercise (go for walks together). Push self.
Adaptability	*Quick to adapt*—Reflect if activity is wise. Also, take care of herself, not just others.	*Resists change*—Self-calming tools
Approach	*Curious*—Ask, "Is this safe?"	*Cautious*—Ask, "What do I need to feel comfortable?" Or, use self-talk: "I will feel comfortable in a bit."
Distracti-bility	*High*—Identify and remove the distractions.	*Low*—Set a time to interrupt self and check surroundings.
Emotional sensitivity	*Self, high*—Ask, "How important is this?" *Others, high*—Separate others' feelings from yours.	*Self, low*—Ask, "How do I feel?" or "Does this bother me?" *Others, low*—Look for emotional clues in the face, tone, words, and body language.
Intensity	*High*—Self-calming tools	*Low*—Assertiveness skills
Mood	*Cheerful*—Be sensitive to other moods.	*Grumpy*—Look for the silver lining.
Persistence	*High*—Ask, "Is this reasonable/ best use of time?"	*Low*—Set goals and motivate (or reward) self. Break task into small easier pieces.
Physical sensitivity	*High sensitivity*—Strategies to reduce intense stimuli: ear plugs, sun glasses, etc.	*Low sensitivity*—Practice noticing surroundings and rating them on a scale of 1 to10.
Regularity	*High*—Step out of comfort zone.	*Low*—Carry extra snacks as needed for hunger.

How to encourage a shift in temperament. With each temperament trait comes opportunities and a liability. You cannot make an active child passive or an intense child mellow, but you can provide skills so they can shift a bit toward moderate.

The first step is for parents to identify their child's temperament. The next step is to determine what skills your child will need, and finally, to teach your child those skills. Keep in mind that changing temperament-based behavior takes months or years, rather than days or weeks.

Annette's son, David, was very reluctant to do anything new. She wanted him to be physically coordinated, but he was uninterested. She enrolled him in a preschool gymnastics class, hoping he would get excited, but he did not. He refused to join the other children and wanted to go home.

Mom reviewed her goals. She wanted David to be physically fit and comfortable in new settings. So she decided to divide the process of increasing activity into several small steps, and to teach him some skills for feeling comfortable in new settings. To do this she involved David's friend, Andy. Andy also had a low activity temperament, but he was more willing to approach new things. Annette's plan was to get the boys comfortable doing physical things together, so that next semester they could enroll in the gymnastics class together.

Increasing physical activity. *Annette created several small projects that she "needed" the boys' help with. The first project was moving a small pile of bricks from one corner of the garage to the fence. When they were done, she rewarded them by saying, "You boys worked so hard and were such a help, I think we should make some cookies." She gradually increased the difficulty of the tasks and removed herself from the projects.*

Self-comforting skills for new situations. *Annette decided that the two skills she would focus on were self-talk and going with a friend. She began by modeling self-talk. When they made the cookies she said, "This new recipe is a bit scary, but I know it will be comfortable after I have made it a couple of times," or "This is only scary since it's new. When I have done it a couple of times, it won't be new or scary anymore. It'll be familiar and easy."*

Annette also modeled going to classes with a friend. "I'm going to start knitting lessons. I've always wanted to take lessons, but I was afraid to go alone. This time my friend Sharon and I are going together." By the time next semester arrived, David was almost looking forward to gymnastics class.

Activity 3–11: Identify skills David needs

Directions: Read Annette's story (above). Record David's strong temperament traits and the skills Annette might teach him.

Trait and strength	Skills needed to flourish
•	•
•	•

David's temperament and skills needed.
Trait: low activity level. *Skill needed:* to enjoy physical activity
Trait: low approach (cautious in new situation). *Skill needed:* to be comfortable in new setting. At least three self-comforting strategies (for example, self-talk, deep breathing, go with a friend)

Annette decided what skills David needed and then began to create experiences so he could learn those skills. You can use Activity 3–12 to list the skills your child may need for his or her temperament.

Activity 3–12: Skills for your child's temperament

Directions: Record your child's dominant temperament traits and the skills you might teach your child.

Trait and strength	Skills needed to flourish
•	•
•	•
•	•

Now that you have clarified your expectations using values, and your child's stage of development and temperament, you can create a long view for your child's future. This will save you time and energy: with a goal, you can ask yourself at any time, "How can I handle this situation to further my goals for my child?"

A Long View

What is a long view?

A long view is your vision for your child some time in the future, when she enters school or high school, goes to camp, leaves home, goes to college, or gets a first job.

Why create a long view? The simple answer is that it makes your life easier in the long run. When your vision for your child is clear, you are less likely to succumb to the temptation to use an easy idea that sets a bad precedent, and more likely to keep looking for ideas until you find one that furthers your goals for your child.

Create a vision

Identify your values. In Activity 3–3, you wrote the characteristics you hope your child will develop.

Consider temperament. Look at your child's temperament traits (Activity 3–10) and see if they will make it easy or hard to achieve the characteristics you value.

Consider the child's age. How can you support your child's developmental tasks (Activity 3–7) in a way that encourages your long view?

Write a long view for your child. You can see the long view Amy created for her son Eric in the box, and the worksheet she used to create the long view is illustrated on the following page. You can use Activity 3–13 to gather your thoughts.

The vision for each child is different. What you want for your older son with his unique temperament may be different from what you want for your younger son or daughter with a very different temperament.

Amy's long view for Eric

Responsible—

People can trust his word, depend on him to complete tasks and to do what is right.

Caring—

He recognizes how people feel and acts kindly toward them.

Flexible—

He sees things from different viewpoints and adapts to the unexpected changes life brings.

Long view worksheet for Eric

Below are thoughts that Amy collected when her son, Eric, was 5.

Values: I'd like my son to have these characteristics.

- *Responsible*
- *Caring*
- *Good decision maker*
- *Flexible*
- *Generous*

Temperament: Traits my son has that may affect (either support or hinder) my vison for him.

- *High persistence—can stick with a task until he completes it.*
- *Moderate adaptability—a little difficulty adapting to circumstances, but can do it.*
- *Low sensory awareness—not aware of the presence of people and noise, hard to pick up on social cues.*

Developmental task: How my son's current developmental task relates to my vision for him.

Child's current age is: *5 years*

Developmental task is: *Understanding power and identity*

Possible influence of developmental task on my long-term goals:

- *Needs to see himself as caring (identity).*
- *Needs to find ways to use his power that are respectful of others.*

What do you do with the long view?

Make a plan for yourself. Think about what kind of parenting your child will need to grow as you wish. Then review your strengths and weaknesses and see where you need to grow. For example, if you want your child to be comfortable with new people and places (high approach and high adaptability temperament traits) but you and your child are both shy (low approach), you will need to move out of your comfort zone and discover what strategies your child will need to be successful.

Activity 3–13: Create your long view worksheet

Child's name: _____

Values: I'd like my child to have these values (from Activity 3–3).

- _____
- _____
- _____
- _____
- _____

Temperament: Traits my child has that may either support or hinder my vison for him or her (from Activity 3–10).

- _____
- _____
- _____

Developmental task: How my child's current developmental task relates to my vision for my child (from Activity 3–7).

Child's current age is : _____

Developmental task is: _____.

Possible influence of developmental task on my long-term goals: _____

_____.

Notice your day-by-day decisions. When life gets chaotic or difficult, parents sometimes slip into unproductive habits. Anita helped her son with his homework because she did not like to see him frustrated. Angie got in the habit of taking her daughter Emma to school rather than requiring her to walk the three blocks. Andrew let his kids go out and play even though they had not finished their chores. Certainly, the sky will not fall if the parent slips up occasionally, however, notice your pattern of behavior and check that it is sending the right message most of the time.

Record your goal. Write your long view for your child and yourself and put it somewhere that you will see it occasionally. It could be in your day planner, by your bed, or in your desk drawer, somewhere where you will see it and ask yourself, "How am I doing?"

Look for seeds of desired behavior and nurture them. When your daughter holds the door open for someone, you can say, "You held the door open for Mrs. Smith. That was kind." When your son gets most of his spelling words correct, you can comment, "You really studied this week. I can see your effort paid off."

Imagine your child as an adult with the values you value. If you value academic success, imagine your child as graduating from college. If you value caring, see him tutoring kids after work. If you value generosity, picture her creating a trust to help disadvantaged people.

Activity 3–14: Create a vision for your child

Describe what you want your child to be like as a grown-up.

Characteristic	**Description or explanation**
_____	_____
_____	_____
_____	_____
_____	_____
_____	_____

Review your long view yearly. Sometimes parents find that their values change over time. Other times the goals are still the same but parents need to change how they approach the values. You can review your values on New Year's Day, on your child's birthday, or at any other time you choose.

In this section, we have looked at creating a long view incorporating information about values, temperament, and developmental stage, and how you can use the long view. In the next section, we will look briefly at self-care and how it impacts your experience as a parent.

Self-care

Parenting is physically and emotionally draining. You will find dealing with children easier if you take care of your physical and emotional needs.

Physical well-being. There is no substitute for food, exercise, and sleep. When you feel tired, hungry, or stressed, children test you more often. You don't have the ability to think as clearly or the energy to follow through with rules. The children may become confused. You may get angry. This can be avoided if you are realistic about your needs. You may need to lower outside involvement or housekeeping standards to meet these needs.

Maria, mother of four, says: Sleep, sleep, sleep. Getting enough sleep is self-care that makes the biggest difference in my personality and my ability to parent effectively. I am calmer and have more mental energy to deal with things when I'm well rested. When I don't get enough sleep, I become cranky and demanding. When I get enough sleep, I can think about the situation, think of ideas, and act in a way that generally helps the situation.

Support system. Even when parents feel rested, parenting can be emotionally exhausting. You will need some ways to fill your emotional bank. If you do not, you will probably find yourself yelling at your children or escaping from them.

You can increase your well-being by developing a network of supportive friends, being realistic about what you can and can't do, and by taking a break when you need it.

If your family and friends are critical and demanding, find supportive friends. You can meet other parents at preschool, church groups, neighborhood centers, or in the park. Sometimes it works to start a babysitting co-op or play group. That way you get adult friends and occasional babysitting for your child.

Do something fun. Most parents find it easier to act effectively when they have something they enjoy doing. It can be a hobby like sewing, gardening, reading, carpentry, or sports. It can even be as simple as taking time to smell the roses or feel the rain on your face as you walk. The important thing is that the activities bring you a feeling of contentment or well-being. Do these things as a regular part of every day, not just as an occasional "self-indulgence."

Use positive self-talk and visualization. The language we use when we talk to ourselves affects how we interpret our children's behavior and how we respond to them. When you say, "I am a bad mom," or, "I can't control this child," you may create a self-fulfilling situation. The alternative is to program yourself for success. You can see this in Erin's story.

Before I open my eyes in the morning, I lie still for as long as I can (one to ten minutes), quietly coaching myself with positive self-talk. "I am a good mother. I love Chloe, 3, and Cody, 6." I remind myself what I like about each child.

I visualize myself being patient and attentive while we walk slowly to school and arrive on time, relaxed. I visualize smiling and speaking calmly, sincerely, and lovingly to my children throughout the day.

At night, especially when I stay up too late, I look in the mirror and remind myself, "I can be patient and kind even when I am tired. I am respectful with my kids. We love each other. I will remember to smile at them in the morning and tell them one or two reasons I am proud of them."

*What surprises me is that when I take the time to center myself before I get up, things **really do** go much better.*

Focus on growth. Another form of positive self-talk is to focus on your learning or improvement. Ruth reports her growth.

As a child, when my mom was angry at me, she would slap me so hard I would fall over. I am trying to learn how to guide my daughter in firm and gentle ways. At the beginning, any time I hurt Grace or yelled at her I felt very bad and told myself how bad a mom I was.

Over time I have learned to say to myself, "I am learning to parent better and better. I have tools that I can use and I am getting more skillful with them." And it's true. When I started STAR Parenting, I yelled at Grace at least once a day and spanked her a couple of times a week. It has been over a year since I spanked her and my yelling is way down too.

Take some time off. Everyone needs a break. Below are several ways parents have found personal time.

- **Request help.** *When my children were both less than 4 years old, it was surprising how frustrated I would get with them. I loved them and I enjoyed* *spending time with them. It was the relentlessness of caring for young children that got to me. My mother gave me a three-month membership to a yoga class for my birthday.*

I asked my husband if he would take care of our kids two mornings a week so I could go to class before he went to work. He agreed. I don't know if it was the regular exercise or the time off that helped, but I don't get as frustrated as before.

- **Join a babysitting co-op.** *When my kids were little, I used to get angry a lot. They really weren't doing anything wrong; I just could not stand the noise and movement all day long. My crabbiness extended into the evening when my husband was home, and to the next day if I wasn't careful.*

  I don't know how long this would have lasted if I had not taken an anger management class. We learned to look at the "seeds" of our anger. I discovered that I need time off. In my neighborhood there was a babysitting co-op which I joined. I found that four kids are not much more difficult than two, so providing time off to another mom was quite do-able. Then I could look forward to time off for myself in exchange.

- **Sell extra stuff on ebay for babysitting money.** *I had a very small house and relatives who loved to give my kids stuff. I asked them not to give my kids so much, but they continued. So, I informed the gift givers that, starting in three months, I would sell unused toys. This worked well. They felt free to give the gifts, and I was able to limit the number of toys in the house. I got extra money that I used to buy babysitting.*

- **Swap taking kids for a long walk.** *A neighbor and I were complaining about how ghastly the hour before dinner was. After joking about what we could do, we decided to trade taking kids out for a brisk, pre-dinner walk and see how it went. We also made a rule that during the first fifteen minutes of free time back in the house, Mom must do something she enjoyed before starting dinner.*

- **Trade one morning a week for a weekend every few months.** *I liked to hike, but that was not practical with two young children. A friend and I made a deal. I took her kids one morning a week so she could take a class. She took my kids one weekend a quarter. Hiking without kids every couple of months was enough time to really revive me.*

- **Do something enjoyable while kids nap.** *I used to use the time my twins napped to pick up the house, do the laundry, clean the bathroom, and do other chores. One day I was so frustrated after putting the girls down, that I sat down and started to read a book to calm myself. I read the whole time they slept. It felt so wonderfully decadent that I decided to lower house-keeping standards and involve them in what cleaning they were capable of. That way I could use their nap time as personal time.*

- **Schedule time off.** *My wife, Jackie, and I love to ski. Before we had kids, we skied almost every weekend. Although we love our kids, we both felt resentful that we couldn't ski any longer. After thinking about it for a while, we developed a schedule that really works for us. Jackie goes skiing the first weekend of the month, and I take care of the kids. Jackie takes care of the kids the second weekend while I go skiing. We pay for a babysitter for the third week so we can ski together. And we take the kids up on the fourth weekend. This way we each get to ski three weeks out of four. And, we only paid for babysitting once a month. Pretty neat solution!*

We have looked at support systems, positive self-talk, and finding personal time. However, important as taking care of yourself is, self-care alone won't improve your parenting unless you have appropriate parenting tools.

In the following STAR in Action Story and in the next five chapters, we will look at the tools on the five points of the star. Then we will take a couple of problems and run them through the whole STAR Parenting process.

Summary of
Consider Your Expectations

★ **Ask yourself,** "What do I want my child to be like as an adult?" List the characteristics or qualities that are most important to you. Keep them in your mind as you parent. You can modify them as your values shift in importance.

★ **Look at your child's behavior in terms of his or her age and developmental task.** Find ways for your child to meet his developmental tasks that are more acceptable to you. Accept that your child simply may not be ready for certain skills yet. Alter your expectations accordingly.

★ **Consider your child's temperament.** Identify which temperament traits may be difficult for the child and provide information and experiences to support his or her growth. Help your child learn to moderate extreme traits. Keep your expectations in line with his or her temperament.

★ **Create your vision.** Based on your values, decide what your long-term goals are. Who do you want your child to be as an adult?

★ **Self-care.** Parenting is easier when you are not running on empty. Monitor your personal physical and emotional energy. Refill your reserves before you run out.

STAR in Action Story[1]

Leave Daycare Gracefully

I am a working mother of two children, Reid, 2½ years old, and Rosie, 1½ years old. They both go to the same in-home daycare with four other children and really enjoy it. It is very comforting knowing that while I am at work, they are well cared for in a loving, safe, and nurturing environment.

When I drop them off, they say goodbye and wave to me. When I pick them up at the end of the day, leaving daycare has been uneventful until now. Now I am having a problem when picking up Reid, the 2½-year-old. He sees me, runs away, hides and screams because he is having so much fun he doesn't want to leave! He wants to stay! This was cute for a few days, but after two weeks it is no longer acceptable.

S—Stop and focus

I can't continue leaving daycare with a crying, screaming 2½-year-old and 1½-year-old in tow. It is exhausting and embarrassing. Trying to calm a screaming, flailing 2½-year-old so I can buckle him in a car seat, eat dinner, and unwind is impossible.

When I come to pick up my children after a long ten-hour work day, I want to be warmly greeted with a hello and/or hug and then leave calmly and respectfully. I want Reid, the older, to set a good example leaving for Rosie, the younger. In addition, because of their schedule, the children have only two hours to eat dinner, play, bathe, and go to bed. I want the treasured time we spend together to be relaxing and enjoyable.

T—Think of ideas

Reid was so adamant about staying that I knew it would take some thinking to figure out how to get him to come pleasantly. I went through all the points of the STAR.

Teach new skills

☆*Modeling:* I'll use a puppet to show him exactly what I want him to do.

☆*Re-do it right:* "Whoops, you forgot to leave gracefully. Let's start again."

☆*Shaping:* Begin by modeling what I want him to do, act out with puppets, and then role play the dialog.

Acknowledge feelings

☆*Active listening:* Saying, "Hmm," "I see," "Really?" when Reid is upset. Not appropriate for 2½-year-old.

☆*Active listening:* Reflect the feeling and problem. "You're sad that you have to leave daycare."

☆*Grant in fantasy:* Reid is too young to understand the difference between what is real and what is fantasy, so this tool is not useful.

Avoid problems

☆*Reduce stress:* Ask the daycare provider to give him a snack so he is not hungry.

☆*Change things:* Ask the daycare provider to put his shoes on before I come so it is one less thing to do.

☆*Two yeses:* "It is time to go. Do you want to walk or be carried?"

Respond to cooperation

☆*Attention:* Smile and stroke his arm when he is pleasant.

☆*Praise:* "I'm proud of you for choosing to leave gracefully."

☆*Reward:* "When you leave gracefully, you may choose dessert for dinner."

---

1 There is a STAR in Action Story at the end of each chapter. Each story is written by a parent in his or her own words and shows how that person adapted the STAR Parenting process to his or her own life.

These stories use tools from all points, so some may be unfamiliar until you have read the appropriate chapter. You can see how different parents, with different values or with kids of different temperaments, might make different choices.

Reasonable limits

☆*Clear rule:* Leave daycare pleasantly.

☆*Consequence:* "If you do not leave pleasantly, I will carry you to the car."

☆*A better way:* Not developmentally appropriate.

A—Act effectively

After reviewing all the points, I chose to focus on three points—teach new skills, acknowledge feelings, and avoid problems. Reid responds well to puppet shows, so I decided to have the puppet teach him to leave gracefully.

Preparation: *Teach new skills*

1. Every evening for five days, we had a puppet show, "Leaving daycare gracefully." I played the role of all the puppets, then we took turns being different puppets, and he was the "Reid" puppet.
2. I told stories before bedtime about "leaving daycare gracefully."
3. Finally we practiced acting out or role playing "Leaving daycare gracefully." (Mom: "Hello, Reid and Rosie, I am so glad to see you after a long day of work." Reid: "Hi Mom!" Mom: "Well, it's time to go home now." And so on.)

Preparation: *Acknowledge feelings*

The puppets told Reid, "You feel sad when you have to leave daycare because you are having so much fun with your friends and toys. It's okay to feel sad, and you can also look forward to coming back tomorrow. Do you want to give Nicki (the daycare provider) a hug or kiss goodbye?"

Reid mastered it and after a week it was time to put practice into reality.

Application: *Avoid problems*

I asked the daycare provider to be sure Reid has had a snack at the end of the day to avoid additional hunger issues and to put Reid's shoes on, one less hassle before leaving.

The first day I came to pick the children up, I envisioned us leaving gracefully. I took a few deep breaths and then said, "Let's leave gracefully." Another mother said, "That's never going to work." Reid had a meltdown, and he left screaming. That night, I thought about what happened and how I could do it differently.

The next day, I took a few deep breaths, then said, "How do you want to leave? Gracefully?" Reid had a meltdown and screamed, "NO graceful!" We humbly left daycare and one of the moms rolled her eyes at me. That night, I again thought about what happened and how I

could do it differently.

The third day, before walking inside the daycare, I envisioned myself in my self-calming spot—a beach with a lighthouse in Nantucket, Massachusetts. I took a few deep breaths, walked inside, then asked, "Reid, how do YOU want to leave?" and waited. After what seemed like a long while and was probably only a minute of complete silence, he thought about it and said, "I want to leave gracefully." And we put on his coat and walked out the door while I carried Rosie.

Respond to cooperation

In the car driving home, I told Reid how proud I was that he chose to leave gracefully. I told him how happy I was that he walked out of daycare like a big boy while I carried his little sister and how easy it was to buckle him into the car seat. I told him I was looking forward to eating dinner and reading stories together.

R—Review and revise

It took a total of four to five weeks of working on this situation before my son could consistently "leave gracefully." We practiced, practiced, practiced "leaving gracefully." I didn't let the other mothers' comments or glares discourage me. I did a lot of self-talk—this plan will work. It will take some time and practice. We will leave gracefully.

I learned that my son wants to retain some control, which is why the third time I asked him how he would like to leave daycare. He is in charge of his feelings. There was a day or two of regression and the phrase "leaving gracefully" seemed to snap him out of it. For the most part, we no longer had those awful, embarrassing meltdowns.

Two years later, we still use the phrase "leaving gracefully" and it has come in quite handy, leaving Auntie Ann's and Uncle Tom's, leaving playdates, even leaving preschool in the afternoon. We have avoided several embarrassing meltdowns.

Thank you, STAR Parenting!

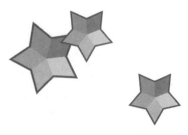

Part Two

STAR Parenting Points and Tools

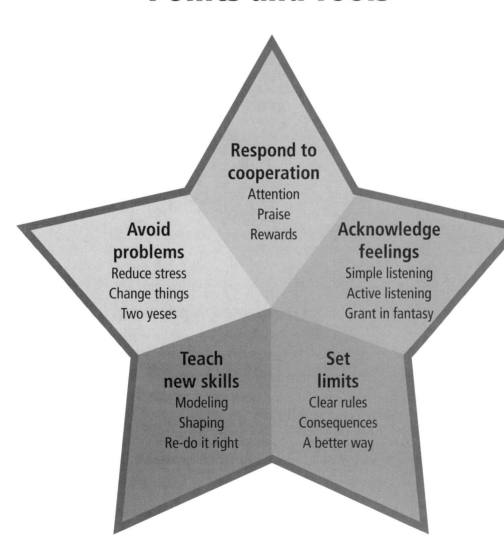

Respond to cooperation
Attention
Praise
Rewards

Avoid problems
Reduce stress
Change things
Two yeses

Acknowledge feelings
Simple listening
Active listening
Grant in fantasy

Teach new skills
Modeling
Shaping
Re-do it right

Set limits
Clear rules
Consequences
A better way

Chapter 4

Avoid Problems

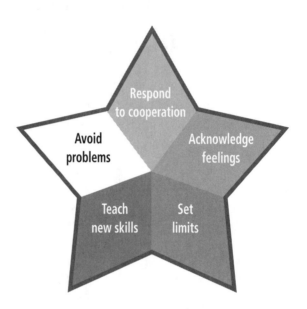

An ounce of prevention is worth a pound of cure

I like to start with ***Avoid problems*** as the first STAR Parenting point because it is often the easiest or quickest thing for a parent to do. Here are a few things to consider before we look at each of the three avoidance tools.

"An ounce of prevention is worth a pound of cure" is true for people working with kids of all ages and especially true for those with young children. Pour only as much milk as you are willing to wipe up. Move the plants up so the toddler won't pull the leaves off. Take a snack and some activities (toys or books) to your child's doctor's appointment that often runs late.

Whether you call it planning, prevention, or forethought, avoiding problems is a lot easier than dealing with the chaos kids create. Here is how Emily avoided an annoying problem.

When my daughter was 4, she loved to buy shoes. Every time she saw a shoe

**Tools to
*Avoid problems***

☆ *Change things*
☆ *Reduce stress*
☆ *Two yeses*

department she chanted, "Mommy, Mommy, Mommy, I need shoes." Explaining that she didn't need shoes had no impact. Eventually, I got very clever at avoiding shoe departments—we would walk down another aisle or I would hold an engaging discussion with her so she wouldn't notice the shoes.

In a parenting class once a man asked, "Aren't you avoiding the issue?"

"Yes!" I replied. "My kids are capable of creating as many 'issues' as seeds in a pomegranate. I want to spend my time and energy dealing with the issues that are important to me."

The first challenge of avoiding problems is anticipating them. The second is deciding how you can avoid them. And the third is deciding if it is appropriate to avoid them.

Identify potential problems

Understanding your child's temperament and developmental stage is a big help. It enables you to see a problem coming. Another way is to list the problems you have, consider which might be avoided, and choose an effective strategy to do so.

Development's impact on behavior. Certain challenges are predictable at certain ages. We looked at development in Part One; however, the following is a reminder of typical challenges at different stages.

Younger toddlers are only beginning to develop self-restraint, and they cannot be depended on to comply with any requests. They like to run away, touch forbidden items, and hit when upset.

Older toddlers (18–36 mo.) are still working on self-restraint and are beginning to understand and manage their feelings. They are prone to tantrums when they can't have what they want. Some of these tantrums you may wish to avoid, others you will face straight on. These toddlers say "No," are reluctant to share, and want to do things their own way.

Preschoolers (3–6 yrs.) are learning about power and identity. They are more able to do things. They assert their power with parents: "You're not my boss," and with their friends: "I won't invite you to my birthday party," or "I have more pretty ponies than you." Also, they are struggling to understand the difference between reality and fantasy.

School-age children (6–12 yrs.) are beginning to look beyond their family and immediate friends to find out how the world works. They like to make rules, want everything to be fair, and are prone to say things such as, "I like the cookies Josh's mom makes better than yours," or "Why do I have to make my bed every day? Josh doesn't have to make his bed."

Temperament's impact on problems. Remember, temperament is the character traits that your child is born with. Your child's temperament will dramatically affect the parenting challenges you face. Temperament can be mellow and easy going, or persistent, intense, and rigid. You can review temperament traits in Part One. Here, four parents describe how specific temperament traits played a significant part in their children's behavior.

- **Curiosity (high approach):** *I left the eggs from groceries I was putting away on a chair by the refrigerator and went to answer the phone. When I came back, my 30-month-old son was cracking the eggs on the floor. When I asked him what he was doing, he said, "Looking for baby chicks." Leaving the eggs on the chair was not one of my brighter ideas considering how curious Keiji is about everything.*

- **Persistence (high):** *Joel, 4, is a skillful problem solver, very persistent, and rarely gives up when he wants something. Today he wanted to play a board game I had put on the top shelf of the hall closet. I ignored his requests. Later I noticed him carrying a little chair from the kitchen and followed him. I saw him place the little chair on a dining room chair he had put in front of the open closet. He was planning to climb up and get the game. Given his persistence, I should have seen that coming. I had to remind myself that persistence is an excellent adult trait.*
- **Adaptability (low):** *Elisa, 3, is very attached to her lovey. We were going to a nursing home to celebrate her great aunt's 85th birthday. When we arrived, there were lots of people milling around, and everything was strange to Elisa. She wanted her lovey, but it was at home. She spent the whole time whimpering for it with her head pressed into my leg. I should have realized that things would be strange for her and remembered to bring her security blanket.*
- **Activity level (low):** *I often hear parents complain about how active their kids are. I have the opposite problem. I love to hike. My son, Willie, 7, loves to read. The only thing physical he likes to do is swim. For my birthday, I arranged for our family to hike into a lake where we could swim. I thought the idea of swimming in a lake would motivate Willie. WRONG. A trip that should have taken twenty to thirty minutes took over an hour with dawdling and complaints the whole way.*

How can you avoid predictable problems?

There are three tools on the ***Avoid problems*** point—☆*Change things,* ☆*Reduce stress,* and ☆*Two yeses.* We will consider each of these later in this chapter. First, we will see in the chart below how the parents could have avoided some of the hassles by adapting their approach to their child's age and temperament.

Table 4–1: Responding to age and temperament situations

Child	Challenging behavior	Avoided by
Keiji, 2½ High curiosity	Cracking eggs open	*Change things:* Put the eggs away or on the back of the counter before answering the phone. Keep a phone in the kitchen.
Joel, 3 High persistence	Stacking chairs to get a board game he wants	*Remove things:* Put the game in a place where he can't see it.
Elisa, 3 Low adaptability	Upset by lots of strange people	*Reduce stress:* Arrange to visit the great aunt without the crowd or bring lovey, or both.
Willie, 7 Low activity	Reluctant to walk very far	*Change expectation:* Expect to take breaks every five to seven minutes. *Foreshadow:* Talk about how long the hike will take. "It's as long as Sesame Street, and you'll have fun when you get there."

When is it appropriate to avoid problems?

Avoiding problems is a useful skill, and like many tools, can have a downside. Two questions to ask yourself when considering *Avoid problems* are:

1. Am I setting a precedent that may become difficult in the future?
2. Am I avoiding teaching some developmentally appropriate skills?

Let's see how these apply in two situations. First, let us return to the story starting the chapter, where Emily avoided shoe departments.

**Avoiding problems—
When healthy? When harmful?**

Two questions to consider:
1. Am I setting a precedent that may become difficult in the future?
2. Am I avoiding teaching some developmentally appropriate skills?

- *Did Emily set a difficult precedent?* No, the child was unaware of Mom's action. Second, the action creates no problems in the future.
- *Is Emily avoiding teaching the child something needed?* Probably not. There will be many other opportunities to help the child learn the difference between "needs" and "wants."

Now let's look at a second situation where Andrea faces a public tantrum.

Andrea took her two children, Isaac, 2, and Isabella, 4, to a toy store to get a birthday present for their cousin. The process took longer than Andrea expected, and Isabella needed to go to the bathroom. Isaac did not want to stop playing with a Brio train set that was on display. To prevent a major tantrum that was brewing, Andrea bought a train set for Isaac so she could take Isabella to the bathroom.

- *Did Andrea set a difficult precedent?* Yes. Buying a Brio train set to avoid a 2-year-old's tantrum is a dangerous precedent to set.
- *Is Andrea avoiding teaching the child something needed?* A task of 2-year-olds is to learn how to deal with their feelings. If Andrea's response is typical to a threatened tantrum, then she is probably avoiding teaching her son how to deal with his feelings.

All parents avoid facing situations that they should deal with from time to time because they are physically or emotionally exhausted. Children give their parents lots of challenges to deal with over time. If you deal with some and let others slide, that is typical and that is all right.

If you find yourself avoiding all conflicts or a particular type of conflict, then it may help to look a bit at your situation and find out what's going on. Do you need some time off, some new skills, or someone who can help your child learn his developmental business?

The purpose of avoiding problems is to reduce the number of hassles, so you can work on the important issues. You can avoid many problems by using these tools: ☆*Change things,* ☆*Reduce stress,* or ☆*Two yeses* (offering choices). We will look at each of these tools on the *Avoid problems* point in the sections that follow.

Avoid problems point:
☆*Change things* tool

Here are three ways of changing things. You can avoid some conflicts by changing the environment, the schedule (timing), or your expectations. There are two groups of problems this works easily for: problems that happen at a predictable time each day, like getting going in the morning or getting dinner ready, and problems that happen with specific items, like the television, a toy, or a favorite cup. Remember that the purpose of the *Avoid problems* tools is to reduce the number of hassles so you can work on what is important.

Change environment
You can change the environment by adding things, removing things, or rearranging where they are. If your toddler is fascinated with a glass figurine, you can move it so she can't reach it. If your 4-year-old is always losing his cap, you can buy a coat with a hood. If your 2-year-old is frustrated because he can't make the Lincoln Logs® work, you can put them away or replace them with Duplo® blocks. If your preschoolers are always squabbling over the marking pens, you can give them each a set. If your 10-year-old can't take his dirty clothes all the way to the bathroom hamper, you could give him a laundry basket in his closet to drop them in. Changing the environment doesn't mean you give your children duplicates of everything they quarrel over, simply a couple of things. So, add, remove, or rearrange things to avoid the problem.

Add to the environment. You can add things that make it easier for the child to comply or cooperate. Put childproof locks on the kitchen knife drawer. Buy shoes with Velcro® fasteners so independent toddlers can put on their shoes themselves. Use dark shades or curtains so children can get more sleep in the summer. Buy enough marking pens so children can draw freely without having to wait for the color they want. Give kids a healthy snack when they are hungry or when dinner will be late. Put a coat rack by the door for kids to hang their coats on.

Remove from the environment. This is something that many parents do automatically. For example, if a child bangs his drum relentlessly inside, parents may put it away until their ears recover. If your toddler is hitting you with his toy hammer, you take it away. Also, many parents turn the televison off when kids are doing homework to reduce the distractions.

You can also remove things proactively. For example, many parents find that their children play longer and more creatively when they have fewer toys. Yes, it does seem strange, but it really works for many kids. Some parents put away half to two-thirds of the children's toys and then rotate them every couple of weeks or months.

Rearrange things. Many good preschool teachers have mastered this technique. They watch children in their classroom and then rearrange the environment so problems disappear. This is what Casey did in her classroom.

Casey had a class of very active 2½- to 3½-year-olds. When outdoor play was over, they were supposed to walk inside for circle time. Instead they would run in and continue to race around the room. Requests to "Walk inside" were ignored.

So Casey posted an aide by the door (added to the environment) to remind kids to slow down. They slowed as they passed the aide and immediately began to run as soon as they were inside.

Then Casey moved a low four-foot-wide bookshelf near the door in the path the children took as they came in. The presence of the bookshelf slowed the kids down and forced them to turn either right or left like at a "T" traffic intersection. By moving the bookshelf (rearranging things), she was able to eliminate the frustrating behavior of running in the classroom.

How do you find ideas? Part experience and part magic-and-pretend. Experience comes from trial and error. For example, Juana's daughters fought over the marking pens. So Juana bought another package and put all the pens in a basket for the girls to use. Again they fought over the markers, "I don't want that one—the point is smushed." Juana tried again. This time she bought two sets of marking pens and some stickers. She gave her older daughter one set of pens and the kitten stickers; she gave her younger daughter a set of pens and the bunny stickers. Each girl decorated her own pens, so it was clear who the pens belonged to.

When you are having trouble thinking of ideas, magic-and-pretend may help, as it did when Casey was having trouble getting the kids to slow down after outdoor time. She thought, "If I were a magician, what would I do to slow the kids down?" The first thought that popped into her head was to "create a mountain" the kids had to walk around. She thought for a moment and decided that a bookshelf would do as well.

Change the schedule

You can do this by doing things earlier, later, or sometimes not at all. For example, if you have trouble getting your boys to bed after they have wrestled with Dad, you could change the routine. Dad could wrestle before supper and then read to them for a quiet time before bed.

If you find you are always running late getting kids up, fed, and dressed in the morning, you could set your alarm for twenty or thirty minutes earlier. Or, do some tasks, like fixing lunches, the evening before so you don't have as many things to do in the morning.

If your school-aged kids have trouble settling down to do homework as soon as they are home, you could try encouraging them to run off some energy outside for twenty or thirty minutes before starting homework and see if that helps.

Sometimes people have trouble getting things done because they are trying to do too many things. A wise woman once said, "You can do anything, you just can't do everything." I had been a Girl Scout leader for several years before and after my son was born. However, I gave up the troop when my daughter was born because I knew I could not do everything with the responsibility for a new baby. I reminded myself that I could get back into Scouting when my daughter was in school if I wished.

You can do anything; you just can't do everything.

Change expectations

Sometimes the simplest way to handle a situation is to change your expectations. You can rethink expectations for your children or expectations for yourself. It often helps to consider your values, and take your child's developmental stage and temperament into consideration.

Rethink expectations of children. Parents often get frustrated when children aren't fast enough. Parents get upset when kids dress slowly, eat slowly, get up slowly, and—

- dawdle or resist brushing teeth
- amble to the car looking at everything along the way
- play with toys rather than putting them away promptly
- stall going to bed
- refuse to do their chores
- resist getting into their car seat
- fight diaper change
- stare into space instead of doing homework
- stay on the phone too long
- balk at practicing the piano
- delay leaving a friend's house
- linger in the bathtub, even when the hot water is gone

Children are slow; plan for it.

This slowness is part developmental, part temperament, and perhaps partly a bid for attention (see chapter five). Children, particularly young children, are slow—except when running away in the parking lot. Parents often think that because they can dress in three minutes, their kids can dress themselves that fast too. Sometimes they expect their child to dress quickly because he, she, or a neighbor's child dressed in five minutes once.

Developmental stage impacts a child's "speed" several ways. First, young children simply take longer than adults to do anything. Second, there is a difference between being able to do something once and doing it routinely. At every developmental stage, mastery takes repetition, and progress is in a forward–backward fashion. For example, a child may be able to do a puzzle one day and not the next, or he might be able recite math facts perfectly one evening and not the next. Also, speed takes a back seat to developmental tasks. If the child's internal priority at the moment is learning independence, doing it on his own is more important than doing it quickly.

Temperament also influences the probability that children will slow us down. If a child has low adaptability or high persistence, it will be hard for him to shift from his plans to yours. If a child is highly distractable, she will stop what she is doing and get diverted from your wishes before she is finished. Look again at chapter three for more information on temperament.

One way to deal with unreasonable expectations is let go of them. If your child is slow, you could decide that you need to change your expectation for speed and learn to "stop and smell the roses," letting your child be your guide. If your child is easily distractable, you could plan to teach him skills to stay focused. To do that you could use tools from the **Teach new skills** point of the star. Note that changing developmental behavior or temperament traits takes both time and effort.

Consider expectations of yourself. We have expectations of ourselves, and others may have expectations of us as well. Some are reasonable, some are not.

It is a challenge to decide what is most important. This goes back to values that we discussed in chapter three. Often parents need to let something slide. It could be fancy meals, house cleaning, working long hours, remodeling the house, playing on a sports team, or singing in a choir. Think about what brings you the most pleasure or is central to your values and keep those. Let some other things go.

Liz loved the winter holidays and wanted to create the perfect Christmas for her children—with an elegant tree they cut themselves, perfect gifts beautifully wrapped, stockings stuffed, lots of beautiful Christmas cookies, caroling, wreath and decorations out front, lovely Christmas cards. . . .

The burden of the perfect Christmas fell on her shoulders. Each year she got madder and madder because she felt she did not get the support she needed from her husband and children. Finally, she acknowledged that her dream of the perfect Christmas was not shared by her family. She looked at what elements were most important to her and scaled back her holiday expectation dramatically.

She decided to switch the focus from a perfect preformance to pleasant participation. The family picked a homely tree from the local lot to decorate, baked Christmas cookies, and sang carols. She scaled way back on gift giving and chose not to send Christmas cards. Although it was hard to give up The Perfect Christmas, Liz found that more modest plans were actually much more enjoyable. She was not as stressed, and the whole tone of the holiday changed to fun and anticipation rather than anger and resentment.

We have looked at several ways you can avoid problems. You can practice generating ideas in the activity below.

Activity 4–1: Change things to avoid the problems

Directions: Read the behavior on the left and suggest one or two ways you could change things to eliminate the problem.

1. Toddler runs away at the mall.	• •
2. Preschooler is attracted to matches.	• •
3. Eight-year-old plays with the shovel and leaves it in the rain.	• •
4. Ten-year-old drops her stuff all over when she comes home.	• •
5. Kids are reluctant to help with dinner.	• •
6. Kids leave toys all over the house.	• •

Possible answers: **1.** *Add:* Put her in a stroller. *Remove:* Go without her. *Change:* Hold toddler's hand or use a kid harness at the mall. **2.** *Remove:* Put matches out of sight and reach. *Remove:* Put matches in a locked drawer or cabinet. **3.** *Remove:* Lock the shed so he can't get out the tools. *Add:* Buy him a small shovel. **4.** *Add:* Make a landing place by the door with a coat rack, stool, boot tray, book bag hooks. *Change:* Lock the front door so she comes to the side door near her room. **5.** *Change schedule:* Establish rotating responsibility for meal preparation. *Add:* Play music the kids like while working in the kitchen. **6.** *Remove:* Toys left out "disappear" for a week. *Change:* Create a library of toy containers to be checked out one or two at a time, which must be returned before checking out other toys.

The first tool we looked at on the *Avoid problems* point was ☆*Change things*. We saw how you can change your environment, your schedule, or your expectations. The next tool we will look at is ☆*Reduce stress*. Children, like adults, are more difficult when they feel hungry, tired, ignored, or fearful of change. You can reduce a number of problems you face by keeping children fed, rested, and exercised.

Avoid problems point:
☆*Reduce stress* tool

Another way to avoid problems is to ☆*Reduce stress*. When people, both children and adults, are stressed, they have fewer resources to deal with the events that come their way. Tempers often flare and things deteriorate from there. In Taylor's story below you can see the part stress played.

Taylor, the lead teacher for the New Horizons Preschool, was a compassionate person. She was drawn to 4-year-old Nicole in spite of the girl's sullen and volatile behavior.

Gradually, Taylor connected with Nicole and found that she lived with her single mom, Lisa, who was trying her best to create a life for herself and her daughter. Lisa spent long hours at work and at school. The care she arranged for her daughter while she worked and went to school meant that Nicole ended up going to six different places each day!

Nicole stayed with a neighbor until the van picked her up and took her to before-school care. Then she went to New Horizon's Preschool for the morning, after which she went to lunch at one place and afternoon childcare at still another, and after that she stayed at a home daycare near afternoon care until her mom could pick her up.

Taylor thought, no wonder this little girl is so grumpy. Every day she has six sets of adults to adjust to, six sets of children to interact with, and six sets of rules to remember. It would be difficult for most of us to cope with all that. With considerable creativity, Taylor was able to arrange childcare for Nicole so she had only two settings to deal with. Nicole blossomed into a charming little girl once the stress of dealing with all the transitions and changing rules was decreased.

Stress can come from many places—unreasonable expectations, life events, even a person's own imaginings. Some people find it easier to identify stress using the "HITS Principle" described below.

Notice stress

Problems can arise from adult stress, children's stress, or a combination.

One mom shared her "HITS Principle." When she feels like yelling or hitting one of her kids, she checks to see if anyone is hungry, ignored, tired, or stressed. If so, she deals with that before she reacts to the situations.

Sometimes parents feel toddlers and preschoolers are too young to feel stressed. That is not true. Children feel stressed when they need to adapt to changes. Tran-

HITS Principle: Kids have trouble when they feel hungry, ignored, tired, or stressed.

sitioning from one setting to the next, the arrival or departure of a sibling or parent, and moving are some of the times a child will commonly experience stress. Children also feel stressed trying to figure out what people want from them. This is particularly true for active, intense, or slow to adapt children, who are still learning language and developing personal skills. Transitions between activities and going to and from places are hard for many children. Children who are slow to adapt find any change of routine stressful, even events they want.

The biggest stressor for children is parental stress. Children pick up stress from their parents. This is unfortunate. Just when we most need them to be cooperative, they are often needy and demanding.

Make time for exercise

You can help children deal with stress by being sure they get lots of physical exercise, even in cold and wet weather. Children need to make big, free movements—to run, swim, dance, and climb. Although gymnastic classes and the like are helpful, they usually require all the children to do the same thing and involve a lot of waiting, and so they may increase stress.

Exercise is a wonderful way to reduce stress for both parents and children. Here are ways parents have found to work in physical activity for their kids.

- *Every day, rain or shine, we bundle up and walk around the block. I had to buy rain gear to use, but it was well worth it. Sometimes we hunt for things, like signs of spring. Other times the kids run. I like to do this late in the afternoon when tempers begin to get short.*
- *My daughter loves jumping and has since she was about 2 years old. We bought a trampoline and put it in the corner of the living room. She uses it almost every day. When we are out or she doesn't think of it, the evening and bedtime routines are much harder.*
- *When Dad gets home, he takes the kids outside and they play kick ball. It is a sort of wild time when they run around and kick madly. Bob doesn't try to teach the kids soccer. He just wants them to have fun and be active.*
- *We have dance time. I put on a record and we dance around any way we want. Sometimes I get out scarves or dress-ups, but usually we just march or move around.*
- *Because I don't like being out in the rain, we either go to a community center that has a gym or to the mall. I walk briskly while Brian runs or marches nearby. Remarkably, I find the trips reduce my stress too.*

Clarify expectations

Small children see the world from a dramatically different perspective than adults. Much of the difference arises because of children's literal nature and limited experience.

Differentiate between questions and polite commands. When you say, "Your coat's on. Shall we go to the car?" or, "Would you like to leave now?" you confuse kids. Most children will take your questions literally and will probably answer, "No!" If you are offering a choice, then ask a question. If you want action, make a statement.

Parents also give away control by tacking "Okay?" onto the end of a request. When you say, "It's time to leave the park, okay?" that "okay" changes the sentence

The biggest stressor for children? Parent stress!

"Okay?" often gives away control.

from a request into a question. That choice permits the child to say, "No. I'm not done." If you intend a choice it is fine. If you want them to come now, the "okay?" confuses the issue.

Distinguish between free choice vs. limited choice. When you give kids a free choice, they can come up with anything they like. When you offer them a limited choice, you restrict their options. For example, if you ask your child what she wants for breakfast, you have given her a free choice and she will answer with what she really wants, perhaps ice cream or pizza.

Guided choices. Sometimes when you offer a child a limited choice, he may refuse both alternatives. When that happens you can rephrase the question as a guided choice. For example, if you ask your little girl, "Do you want to put on your pink jammies or your purple jammies?" and she says, "No," you can change the question. Say, "It's time to put your jammies on. Do you want to choose which pair to wear or do you want me to?" If she again replies, "No," then you can say, "I see you want me to decide tonight."

Similarly, at bedtime you can say to your son, "It's bedtime. Do you want to walk to bed or be carried to bed?" If he says, "No!" you can reply, "I see you want to be carried to bed."

Expect cooperation. Parents sometimes signal a child that they expect him or her to resist by saying, "If you . . . then . . . " For example, "*If* you get your room cleaned up, *then* you can go next door and play." The child may decide that cleaning his room is too much trouble, so he will forgo the treat. You can increase the odds of getting what you want with Grandma's Rule. Grandma's Rule expects cooperation. It signals this by saying "When . . . then . . . " "*When* you get your room clean, *then* you can play next door."

Make eye contact and speak simply. When you speak to a child, get down on his or her level and speak in simple sentences. That often means getting on the floor. If you have ever sat on the floor and held a conversation with an adult standing above, you can probably remember how uncomfortable looking up was.

When clarifying expectations vary your sentence length with the child's age. With toddlers use one or two word sentences: "Come," "Sit here," "Touch gently." With preschoolers use longer sentences and limit parts to two: "When you sit . . . I'll put your shoes on." Or, "Wash your hands . . . so you can eat lunch." With older preschoolers you can use three-part commands: "Go to the living room. Get my purse. Bring it to me." Use the simplified language strategy when you want to make your expectations clear. At other times, use more elaborate vocabulary and sentences to increase children's language skills.

Clarify understanding. You need to clarify expectations with older children too. Sometimes you zip through a room, speaking as you go. "Clean up your toys and wash your hands before supper." The child answers, "Uh huh," however, real communication may not have occurred.

The child may hear his mom only as a background noise, and she heard his response without clarifying that they were on the same page. For example, did Mom want him to stop right now and put things away or put them away before supper? If later is okay, how will he know when he needs to clean up? Further, does he pick up just his toys, all the ones only he has used, or all the ones that are out? Remember that children are literal and hear what you said, not what you meant to say. The need to clarify is apparent in Dave's story.

Dave's 4-year-old daughter, Kari, wanted to eat in the playroom. The family had a rule that you had to get a parent's permission first and stay on the eating blanket till you were done. Kari asked her dad if she could eat in the playroom. He said, "Yes, as long as you stay on the blanket while you eat." She said, "Okay."

Before Kari moved away, Dave remembered to verify her understanding. He squatted down and asked, "What if you have toast in your hand and go to the TV?" When she didn't know, Dave answered, "I'll take away the toast and fold up the blanket." Again he asked, "What will happen if you have toast in your hand and go look out the window?" Again she didn't know, and Dave replied, "I'll take away the toast and fold up the blanket."

A third time Dave asked, "What happens if you have toast in your hand and you go to the bookshelf?" This time Kari answered, "You will take away the toast and fold up the eating blanket." "Right," Dave replied.

As Dave reflected on their interchange, he was surprised that Kari did not know what would happen. She had made requests for permission for almost two years, but apparently she really didn't know what it meant. Rote asking was simply the magic key to getting what she wanted.

Dave discovered that a child may not really understand expectations even though she appeared to. Let's see how it might look if Mom clarified her expectation about getting ready for supper. Mom could kneel on the floor beside her son and say his name to get his attention and explain what she wanted. She might say, "Dinner is almost ready. The timer will ring in five minutes. When it rings, put away all the toys and wash your hands for supper. Is that clear?" If he said, "Yes," then she could check understanding with, " Fine. What will you do when the timer rings?" He might reply, "Put away the toys and wash my hands."

Activity 4–2: Clarify expectations

Directions: Read the statement and write a new correct statement.

1. [The crayons are all over the floor.] "Maggie, the crayons belong on the table. Would you like to pick them up?"

   _____

2. Mom holds coat out and says, "Jacob, we are going to leave soon. Put your coat on, okay?"

   _____

3. "Emma, why don't you let me help you put your shoes on?"

   _____

4. "Michael, it's time to go to the doctor. Okay?"

   _____

5. "If you get your homework done, we can play ball."

   _____

6. "Matthew, do you want to put away your toys before we go to the park?"

   _____

7. "William, the trash basket is full. Why don't you take it out now?"

_____

8. "It's time to get dressed. What do you want to wear today?"

_____

9. "This is a beautiful morning. What would you like for breakfast?"

_____

Possible revision: **1.** *"Maggie, please pick up the crayons so they won't get broken."* **2.** Mom holds coat out and says, "We are about to leave. Time to put your coat on." **3.** *"Emma, do you want me to help you put your shoes on or do you want me to put them on you?"* **4.** *"Michael, it's time to leave."* **5.** *"When you get your homework done, we can play ball."* **6.** *"Matthew, put away your toys before we go to the park."* **7.** *"William, take the trash out now, please."* **8.** *"Do you want to wear your red shirt or your blue one?"* **9.** *"What a beautiful day. Would you prefer eggs or waffles this morning?"*

Foreshadow events

Some of children's obnoxious behavior happens because they don't know what to expect or what they may do if they are unhappy. You can foreshadow new experiences, like going to the doctor, or a birthday party, or visiting Great Aunt Sally, and with common events, like going to the grocery store or visiting Grandma.

Foreshadowing *explains the event, clarifies expectations* (what the child will be expected or permitted to do), *describes feelings* (what she may feel like), and *offers coping strategies* (how she can cope with those feelings).

Let's see what this would look like for a check-up at the doctor's office. ***Explain the event:*** First, we'll enter a waiting room. The waiting room will have chairs, magazines, and a few toys. The waiting area may have lots of people or just a few. ***Clarify expectations:*** We will sit quietly and wait for our turn to see the doctor. You may walk around the room if you want. You may play with the doctor's toys if no one else is, or you can play with what we brought. ***Describe feelings:*** You may feel bored or restless while you wait. ***Offer coping strategies:*** If you feel bored or restless, tell me and I will help you find something okay to do.

Repeat for the treatment room. ***Explain the event:*** When it's our turn, a nurse will lead us to the treatment room. She may take your temperature and blood pressure. When the doctor comes, she may look in your ears, listen to your heart, and thump your knees. She may also poke you and squeeze you in different places. When the doctor is done, a nurse may give you a shot to keep you from getting certain diseases. ***Clarify expectations:*** You will need to sit still on the examining table while the doctor and nurse examine you. ***Describe feelings:*** You may feel uncomfortable, worried, or scared when the doctor and nurse prod you. Most people do when someone is poking their body. ***Offer coping strategies:*** If you do feel uncomfortable, you can take deep breaths to calm yourself or ask me to hold your hand.

If the event is several days away, you can expand foreshadowing by reading books and acting out the different scenarios that might happen and how the child can cope if they do.

Foreshadowing is useful to prepare for new experiences and particularly helpful for kids who are slow to adapt or uncomfortable in new situations.

Activity 4–3: Foreshadowing

Directions: Read the situations. Write what you could say to explain the event, clarify your expectation and describe possible feelings and coping strategies.

Situation 1. You and Isabella, 3½, are going to go shopping to buy her a new pair of dress shoes.

Explain the event	Clarify expectations	Possible feelings and coping strategies
	• • •	• • •

Situation 2. You and Jacob, 6, are going to pick strawberries at Aunt Eleanor's farm.

Explain the event	Clarify expectations	Possible feelings and coping strategies
	• • •	• • •

Possible answers:

Shopping. We are going to buy you a new pair of dress shoes. A sales clerk will measure your feet. You will try different shoes on. The clerk will check how they fit. We will purchase one pair.	• Use an inside voice. • Try on several different shoes. • Walk on carpeted area. • Tell me how the shoes feel.	• Bored/restless—take wiggle break outside. • Timid—hold my hand, take deep breaths, or hold your doll, Molly. • Confused—if you can't decide which shoes you like, toss a coin to decide.
Strawberry picking. We will pick strawberries. Most will go in a box. You may eat a few. Wear your hat as the sun will be strong. Take your water bottle so you can drink when you get thirsty.	• Walk in the garden. • Stay on the paths (don't bruise the plants). • Pick all the ripe berries on a plant. • Pick ten berries for each one you eat.	• Excited—breathe deeply. • Tired—leave the garden and sit down in the shade. • Bored—imagine how good the shortcake will taste. Listen to music on a portable music player. Alternate hands picking strawberries.

Avoid problems point:
☆*Two yeses* tool

☆*Two yeses*

Make effective choices
by changing the:

- time,
- place,
- thing, or
- activity

This is one of the most powerful tools for children of all ages. Many conflicts and tantrums can be avoided by giving children positive choices. Tell your child where or how he may do what he wants, rather than only saying "No!" For example, "No jumping on the sofa," can become, "You may jump on the floor or sit on the sofa." The choices tell the child what he or she may do.

Some parents would like to offer choices, but don't know how to get ideas. If parents with their experience have trouble thinking of alternatives, then it must be even harder for the child.

Finding choices

You can find ideas by changing the place, time, thing, or activity. Ask yourself when or where this activity is okay, or what else the child could do in its place.

You may not play the drum in the hall when your sister is sleeping. You may—

- Read a book in the hall (Change activity)
- Play your drum in the basement (Change place)
- Play your drum here when she wakes up (Change time)

You may not throw blocks inside. You may—

- Throw the foam ball (Change thing)
- Throw the blocks outside (Change place)
- Build a tall tower (Change activity)

You may not pour your water on the floor. You may—

- Pour water in the kitchen sink (Change place)
- Drink your water (Change activity)
- Pour it on the floor when I wash the floor (Change time)

This tool works for older kids and teens too, as Annika discovered.

Annika was getting ready to go out one evening when her teenaged son Bjorn noticed Annika's attire and blurted out, "Mom, you can't take the car tonight!"

Annika replied, "I don't remember seeing the car reserved by you on the calendar." "I know," Bjorn said. "I forgot to write it down. But I still need the car tonight. I want to go to the ball game."

Annika thought a moment. She could enforce the rule by saying, "Your name is not on the calendar and mine is, so I get the car." However, she decided to try offering him options. "You can't have the car the whole evening. You may drop me off and I'll get a ride home. Or, you can take the bus." Bjorn gave her a quizzical look and said, "Hold on a moment, I'll get my coat and drop you off."

A couple of things happen when you offer your children positive choices. First, they feel understood—as though they are important. And, second, you direct their thinking in constructive ways. Also, you teach that many things are negotiable.

You can exercise your creativity in the following activity and find ☆*Two yeses* for each situation. When you're done, you can look at the chart and see how to use the different tools to avoid problems.

Activity 4–4: Develop ★ *Two yeses*

Directions: Read the situation and think of two or more different ideas for a ☆*Two yeses* statement.

Situation	Choices
1. Jessie wants to jump on the living room sofa.	• time: • place: • thing: • activity:
2. Tony wants to eat ice cream for breakfast.	• time: • place: • thing: • activity:
3. Will and Matt, 8 and 10, want to throw a football back and forth in the living room.	• time: • place: • thing: • activity:
4. Hannah was trying to balance on her unicycle and ride to the corner but kept getting distracted by what was going on around her.	• time: • place: • thing: • activity:

Possible answers: **1.** Jessie wants to jump on the living room sofa.• *time:* Jumping on the sofa is not okay anytime. • *place:* Jump on the old sofa in the basement. • *thing:* Jump on a mattress on the floor. • *activity:* Turn on music and do a silly dance.

2. Tony wants to eat ice cream for breakfast. • *time:* Eat ice cream after lunch. • *place:* No place where ice cream is okay for breakfast. • *thing:* Eat yogurt with granola. • *activity:* Make and eat eggs. Then eat ice cream.

3. Will and Matt, 8 and 10, want to throw a football back and forth in the living room. • *time:* No time is appropriate in the living room • *place:* Play football outside. • *thing:* Toss a foam football. • *activity:* Read a book about football.

4. Hannah was trying to balance on her unicycle and ride to the corner but kept getting distracted by what was going on around her. • *time:* Practice later when no one is around. • *place:* Pick a shorter distance, OR go somewhere calmer to practice. • *thing:* Ride a bike and practice ignoring the activity. • *activity:* Stop riding and watch the hullabaloo.

Fine tuning choices

☆*Two yeses* is a powerful tool: not only can it reduce the current hassle, it can also teach children that there are several ways to get their needs met. Over time children can begin to look for alternatives themselves. For this tool to work, however, the choices presented need to work for the child. Here are some questions you can ask yourself.

Are both of the "yeses" under the child's control? Occasionally, parents will offer a choice that is not possible for the child. The choice may be impossible because the child is not developmentally ready, he does not have the resources, or the situation is in another person's control.

Dependent choice: Asha wants to go outside and see birds. She can read a book about birds (depends on reading ability or having a book) or play with the bird puppet when her sister finds it (depends on the sister's cooperation).

☆*Two yeses:* She can look at a book about birds or make a "bird dance." (Both possible for the child.)

Do the ideas meet different parts of the child's need? Sometimes it is hard to know what part of a child's request is most important.

Olivia came into the kitchen and asked, "Juice in the red glass, please." The red glass was in the dishwasher and Mom, assuming that Olivia wanted juice, asked her, "Do you want juice in the blue glass or the yellow glass?" Olivia burst into tears and said, "Juice in the red glass!"

Mom took a deep breath, and asked herself, What are the elements at work here: juice, red glass, timing? She thought a moment and then rephrased her choice, "Olivia, the red glass is in the dishwasher. Do you want juice in the blue glass now, or juice in the red glass when the dishwasher is done?"

Now it was Olivia's turn to think. Did she want juice now more or juice in the red glass more? She decided, "Juice in the blue glass."

By clarifying the elements of the decision and offering different choices, Mom was able to help Olivia make an acceptable choice. Positive choices defused the conflict.

Are both choices positive? Offering choices differs from consequences that clarify what will happen if the child chooses by not complying. Consequences are choices between something pleasant and something unpleasant. ☆*Two yeses* is a choice between something pleasant and something else acceptable.

Positive choices often defuse conflict.

Mom wants Charlie to clean up his toys before he goes to a puppet show with his friend, Brian. Charlie is looking forward to the puppet show. She reminds Charlie that he needs to put his toys away, but he ignores her.

Consequence: *You must tidy up before you leave. If your toys are not picked up by 2:00 when Brian is expected, you will have to stay home.*

☆**Two yeses:** *Charlie, you may continue to play with your toys, or you can clean up and go to the puppet show.*

The beauty of ☆*Two yeses* is that over time, it teaches children there are many ways to get their needs met and, if one approach doesn't work, to try another.

☆*Two yeses* has been used successfully with teens, spouses, and disgruntled customers. The major challenge is to just slow down and focus on the other person to determine what he or she wants.

STAR Parenting offers three ways to avoid problems—☆*Change things,* ☆*Reduce stress,* and ☆*Two yeses.* When you have a problem that happens over and over the same way, imagine how you could apply each of the three tools to that problem. The chart below illustrates using all three tools for three different situations.

Table 4–2: Avoid problems with all three tools			
Situation	*Change things*	*Reduce stress*	*Two yeses*
Toddler wants to play with the TV remote.	Put a sheet over the TV and remote (change environment).	Be sure he gets enough food and sleep.	Say, "You can play with the buttons on the old radio or you can change the channel for us when we turn the TV on."
4-year-old wants to help chop carrots for dinner.	Prepare dinner while he is at daycare (change time).	Feed him a small snack so he won't get so frustrated.	Say, "You can peel the carrots or cut the banana." (One choice focuses on carrots, the other on cutting.)
10-year-old is so exhausted from school and activities that all she wants to do is watch TV.	Move televison to a closet out of sight so she isn't reminded of it (change things).	Reduce the number of activities she is involved with so she is not so tired.	Say, "You can watch TV when your homework is done or help me make cookies."

Although avoiding problems is an important skill for people working with children, you need to use it wisely. When you avoid problems that need to be addressed, like dealing with a temper tantrum, you can prevent the child from learning the skills he needs, thereby creating frustration for yourself and your child in the future.

In chapter five following the STAR in Action Story, we will look at the STAR Parenting point, **Respond to cooperation**. This point looks at why it is important to focus on the behavior you want, plus three tools to encourage cooperation.

Summary of
Avoid Problems

★ **List things your child does that bother you.**
Look and see which ones happen at predictable times or with predictable items.

★ **Look for ways to change things.**
Can I move something, add something, or change something that will help? Can I change the schedule to reduce the problem?

★ **Offer two yeses.**
How can I change the time, activity, thing, or location so the child's activity is okay with me?

★ **Reduce stress.**
Could the child feel hungry, ignored, tired, or stressed? Would it help to make time for exercise, clarify expectations, or foreshadow events? If so, how can I avoid the problem?

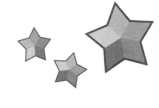

STAR in Action Story[1]

Christina Returns

Christina, 5, and Caitlin, 2½, are very close. When Christina (Tina) started school this fall, Caitlin (Cait) felt abandoned. When Tina comes home, the first thing she usually wants is a little mommy time. This infuriated Caitlin and she tried to hit Tina. I tried to prevent it, but when Cait did manage to hit her, Tina screamed, "Cait hit me. Do something."

At first, I thought that Cait liked having my undivided attention and hit Tina because she didn't want to share me with her. However, that does not seem to be the case because the few times Tina has played with Cait as soon as Tina got home, everything went well.

I have done the usual "Touch gently" and explained that her sister will not want to play with her if she hits her, but nothing has worked. So-o-o-o I have decided I must do something different. I have pulled out the STAR Chart and I'm going to use the whole STAR process step-by-step.

S—Stop and focus

The first step of the process is to focus on myself, my expectation, and the child. Cait is a self-possessed child who is very direct about her needs. I am glad she is clear about what she wants, and frustrated that she hits her sister. I remind myself that at 2½, she is still working on finding appropriate ways to deal with her feelings. However, difficult or not, she must learn to express them appropriately.

Long view: I want both my girls to have a good relationship as adults.

Development: Tina's developmental task is power and identity. Cait's task is to learn to manage her feelings and think clearly.

Temperament: Tina is generally a mellow kid. Cait is intense and persistent.

Desired behavior: I want Cait to express her feelings with words rather than hitting, and also to find appropriate ways to meet her needs.

T—Think of ideas

Since I was out of ideas, I decided to sit down and deliberately generate ways to use every tool.

Avoid problems

☆*Reduce stress* ① Make sure I spend some time each day with Cait when Tina is at school so her "love bank" is full. ② Make sure Cait gets some physical activity while Tina is at school to work off any extra energy. ③ Ask Cait what she and Tina could do for one minute when Tina gets home that might help. Then arrange with Tina to try that.

☆*Change things* ④ Change the routine—Pick Tina up at school and go to a park. ⑤ Change activity—Get a compelling activity that Cait can do only when Tina comes home, so Tina can have a few minutes to herself. ⑥ Create a new ritual—As soon as Tina comes home, the three of us have a group "welcome home" hug. I hope this will meet both Cait and Tina's immediate need. ⑦ Ask Cait to give Tina four minutes of mommy time when she comes home. Give Cait a timer to set for four minutes when Tina comes home. Ask Tina to play with Cait as soon as the timer rings.

☆*Two yeses* ⑧ Tell Cait she can have one minute with Tina when Tina walks in or ten minutes later when Tina is settled.

Reward cooperation

☆*Attention* ⑨ Let her sit on my lap near Tina as long as she is pleasant while Tina talks to me. ⑩ I could gently stroke Cait's arm as she waits for her turn to play with Tina.

☆*Praise* ⑪ When she wants to get Tina's attention and touches gently, say, "Cait, you remembered to touch gently when you were trying to get Tina's attention." ⑫ If Cait takes a deep breath or uses another self-

---

1 There is a STAR in Action Story at the end of each chapter. Each story is written by a parent in his or her own words and shows how that person adapted the STAR Parenting process to his or her own life.

These stories use tools from all points, so some may be unfamiliar until you have read the appropriate chapter. You can see how different parents, with different values or kids with different temperaments, might make different choices.

calming tool, I can praise her behavior by saying, "Wow, you were frustrated and remembered to take a deep breath."

☆*Reward* ⑬ Ask Cait to wait three minutes when Tina comes home before asking to play. Help her set a timer so she will know when the time is up. Tell Cait, "When you wait till the timer rings to ask Tina to play, then I will let you wear my charm bracelet until dinner." (Cait loves my bracelet.) ⑭ Teach Cait a new self-calming tool. Then tell her, "Each time you try to use the tool when you are upset, you may have a bright new piece of construction paper (or something else she wants)."

Acknowledge feedings

☆*Simple listening* ⑮ Let Cait know I am listening by making noncommital comments like: "I see." "Oh." "Really?" (A reminder to self: this does not usually work for kids less that 3 years old.)

☆*Active listening* ⑯ Say, "You feel hurt that Tina left you all morning." ⑰ Say, "Looks like you're angry Tina wants to talk to Momma before she talks to you."

☆*Grant in fantasy* ⑱ Say, "Wouldn't it be fun if you were a little bird and Tina could take you everywhere she went? You'd go visit her school, ride on the school bus, and play with her at home. Tina could feed you parts of her snack."

Set limits

☆*Clear rule* ⑲ Touch gently. ⑳ Tell people how you feel.

☆*Consequence* ㉑ Do a kindness when you hurt someone to put good energy back into the relationship. Since Tina does not want a hug from the sister who just hit her, perhaps Cait could "draw" a picture for Tina. ㉒ Spend time by yourself and think of a better way to handle the situation.

☆*A better way* ㉓ My way is you touch people gently. You want to let Tina know how mad you are. What is something you can do that will work for both of us? *Note:* This tool does not usually work for children less than 3 years old.

Teach new skills

☆*Modeling* ㉔ Show her how to think about what I want. For example, say, "I'm feeling restless this morning. I wonder what is bothering me. I wonder if it is ____, or ____. Oh, I know, I'll bet it is ____." ㉕ Ask for what I want. For example, "Cait, would you please bring me my purse?"

☆*Shaping* ㉖ Teach Cait to deal with disappointment. (1) Choose a self-calming tool like taking belly breaths and teach the action when she is calm. (2) When she can belly breathe, remark on how the deep breathing helps calm the feelings. (3) When she can notice a calmer feeling, ask her to use the tool in pretend. For example, to help a character in a story. (4) When she can use belly breathing in pretend, invite her to rehearse using it when Tina leaves in the morning. (5) Then when she first starts to get upset, remind her that she can change her feeling.

☆*Re-do it right* ㉗ When she hits, say in a pleasant voice, "Oops, Cait, you forgot to touch gently. Let's re-do it right."

A—Act effectively

I considered the various options and decided to use a three-pronged approach. First, I would avoid, or at least reduce, the problem by offering Cait a strategy to give Tina a little bit of time. Second, I would establish a consequence if Cait hit Tina. And third, I would take this opportunity to teach Cait how to deal with feelings of disappointment.

A strategy. It is often hard for kids to wait, so I decided to get a timer for Cait to use. We would set it for three minutes together and as soon as Tina got home Cait would start it. The timer would give Cait something to do with her hands and hopefully she could wait while she saw the numbers change. I decided not to reward Cait for using the timer, hoping that success would be reward enough.

A consequence. I decided that if Cait hit Tina, Cait would have to do a kindness for Tina. The problem was that Cait wanted to hug Tina and Tina didn't want to be near a person who hit her.

Teach a calming tool. I decided to teach Cait to use belly breathing, using the shaping procedure I outlined above. I plan to practice one a day while Tina is at school.

R—Review and revise

I decided to review the plan after one day and one week.

First day. Well, the first day was a disaster. Cait set the timer. Tina refused to play with her, so Cait hit her. Unfortunately, I had not coached Tina to be ready to play with Cait when the timer rang.

At first, Tina didn't want to be governed by the timer, particularly when it meant playing with Cait. So I decided to reward her for cooperation. We decided that she could stay up fifteen minutes later in the evening and have special time. After that, the timer worked fairly well. It is surprising how much you can do in three minutes.

Since Cait hit Tina, Cait had to do a kindness for her.

Since Tina didn't want a hug, we decided that Cait could draw a picture for Tina. Granted, the picture was not much, but Tina accepted it in the spirt it was intended.

A week later. Tina and Cait have both settled into the timer routine. We might be able to do without it, but I'm not willing to try that yet.

Teaching a new skill is coming along, but slower than I expected. We are still in step two, the "notice the calm" feeling phase. I struggle with finding a good time to practice—one where she is a little annoyed so that breathing can help, but not so upset that she doesn't want to cooperate. We are moving, just slowly. At this rate, it will probably take two more weeks. So I will check back in two weeks.

Comment—This has been an interesting exercise. Two things have happened: one, the situation has improved; and, two, I don't feel as helpless anymore.

Chapter 5

Respond to Cooperation

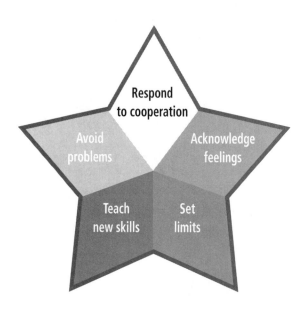

What you notice is what you get

The need for recognition is more powerful than the need for reward. Training yourself to see and comment on appropriate behavior is critical if you wish to change children's behavior. When you focus on unwanted behavior, you get more of it. When you focus on desired behavior, you get more of that too. Look at Jeni's heartwarming story.

I had been trying for years to get my boys, 4 and 8, to play pleasantly. I consistently enforced the rule by saying, "Be gentle with your brother," but it made little difference. While taking a STAR Parenting class, I decided to practice what I was learning and comment on any little kindness I saw. After a couple of days, there was a noticeable improvement. What really floored me was when about a week later my older son commented, "Mom, you really do like it when we are nice, don't you?"

All the times Jeni told her boys to play nicely had less influence than a week of noticing and commenting on it when they were nice. The notice can take the form of ☆Attention, ☆Praise, or ☆Rewards. Before we look at these tools, let's consider the human need for connection or attention.

Tools to Respond to cooperation

☆ Attention
☆ Praise
☆ Rewards

The need to connect is basic. It is what binds children to parents, even to those who are abusive. It is what drives teens who feel unwanted into gangs. It is what drives adults to seek new jobs even at lower pay. Children will do what they must in order to connect with their parents. Watch how it plays out in this cartoon.

The strip situation goes on—"If you don't stop bothering the dog right now, you'll be sorry. On the count of three I will take you to your room." What did the child learn in this exchange? Did Dad pay attention when the boy asked nicely for a

From *Magic Tools for Raising Kids* by E. Crary. Used with permission

story? No, Dad paid attention only when he pulled the dog's tail. Next time Sonny wants attention, do you think he will ask for a story or pull the dog's tail?

One reality of parenting is that you have control over how your child gets attention, not whether he or she gets your attention. If your child wants your attention badly enough, he knows exactly how to get through to you. This is wonderful, because it means the child's basic needs are met. It is also frustrating, because it may mean you end up reinforcing behavior you don't like.

How do you want your child to interrupt you when you wish to be left alone? In my STAR Parenting classes, I often ask parents to share what they would like their child to do.

I remember one class where a mom shared that she wanted her kids to say, "Excuse me" and then continue with what they wanted. Her husband, who spoke next, said he wanted them to come to him, tug on his shirt cuff, and then wait to be recognized. His wife shuddered and remarked, "So that's why they do that to me."

You will save both yourself and your children considerable frustration if you decide how you want to be interrupted, tell your children, and then honor their requests.

What you comment on is what you get. When you come into a room with two children playing together in a huge mess, your response tells the children what is

What's your preference?

How do you want your child to interrupt you when you wish to be left alone?

Write your preference and share it with your partner or a friend.

important to you. You could say, "Look at this mess. Can't you kids ever play neatly?" Or, you could say "Wow, it looks like you kids are having a lot of fun playing cooperatively together." Your children decide what is important to you by what you comment on. So if you wish to change your child's behavior, hunt for good behavior and comment on it.

How do you find "good" behavior?

We often miss good behavior because we are busy with our own activities or we really don't know what we are looking for. There are several ways you can find good behavior: plan time to look for it, ask others for examples, look for the behavior in other kids, visualize your child with the ability, or look for the seeds of what you want.

Plan time to look for desired behavior. Often our schedules keep us hopping from one thing to another. Set aside time to look for good behavior: choose a day, an hour, or half an hour to set aside to look for good behavior. Make a list of the qualities or behaviors you are looking for. For example, if possible, position yourself close enough so you can tell what your child is doing, without being so close as to change his behavior.

Ask a teacher, friend, or relative to give you examples of when the child has behaved appropriately. Sometimes, our interactions with a child are so colored with negative emotions that it is hard to see anything positive. Other times, the child may behave well outside the house but be obnoxious at home. In both cases, it is helpful for other people to look for examples of the behavior you want and report back to you.

Look for the behavior in other kids. Sometimes it is easier to see desirable behavior in someone else's child. Go to the park alone, visit a classroom, or watch children when you're at the mall. Look for the behaviors you want and the context they appear in. Then you will know where to begin looking with your own child.

Visualize what you want. If you know what you want, great; if not, let this technique help you. Use as many details and senses as you can. Julia tried visualization when her daughter, Torrey, was struggling with arithmetic.

> *I was frustrated because Torrey would sit at the table with her homework, but she didn't do* **anything**. *I decided to visualize Torrey as competent. I imagined how I would feel when she brought home a math paper with a ninety percent on it. I pictured her face beaming. Mentally, I reviewed the nights she and I spent practicing and practicing. I saw how my presence with her at the table helped her focus. I pictured myself helping her chart her correct answers each evening so she could see she was improving even though it was slow and hard for her. I visualized teaching her positive self-talk to increase her confidence. What was interesting to me was that by visualizing her as successful, and how she would have achieved success, I created a road map I could use to help her.*

Look for the seeds of what you want. Sometimes we cannot find the behavior because it does not yet exist. If that is the case, look for the seeds of the behavior you want. For example, if you want your son to keep his floor clean and he just doesn't do it, look for something he does take care of, like his baseball card collection or his favorite music CD. Then you can build on the successful behavior to create a new one.

We have looked at why it is important to respond to cooperation, and how

You can control how your child gets attention, not whether he gets it.

you can notice desired behavior. When you find the behavior, respond with simple ☆*Attention*, verbal ☆*Praise*, or traditional ☆*Rewards*. You may ask, "Why should I reward my child for doing what he should do?" The simple answer is—it works.

Respond to cooperation point: ☆*Attention* tool

☆*Attention* is the first tool on the **Respond to cooperation** point of STAR Parenting. When you give attention, the child feels connected. Attention, used as a STAR Parenting tool, is non-verbal, which distinguishes it from praise. Giving attention can be as simple as watching or listening to your child, or as complex as creating an elaborate hello or goodbye ritual.

Types of attention

When you wish to give attention, stop what you are doing and look at your child. Three classic ways to give nonverbal attention are being near (proximity), making eye contact, and giving loving touches. In addition, you can use gestures or rituals to convey your approval of your child's behavior.

Closeness. Young children particularly like to have their parents around. You can sit beside them or they can sit in your lap. When your children are playing pleasantly, try sitting nearby.

The flip side of this closeness is separation. If you have been holding your child on your lap as you talk on the phone and she begins to talk loudly, stand up and turn away. If your child is sitting on your lap listening to a story and starts poking you, put him off to the side. This separation (physical distance) conveys the idea that the behavior is unacceptable.

Eye contact. When the toddler is pleasant, face him and look into his eyes. As children grow, you will wish to make eye contact and smile to let your children know you appreciate their behavior.

Again, when a child is misbehaving, the flip side is to remove eye contact and shake your head with a serious or subdued expression. If the child does not quit the behavior, then step away.

Touch. Stroking a cheek, ruffling hair, and holding hands all convey loving attention. Brushing or braiding hair can be attention if the child wants it. A high five, bear hug, or companionable punch in the shoulder are often appreciated by energetic children.

Gestures. Gestures can be used to signal to your child you like what she did. An okay sign, peace, or victory sign, wave, or thumbs up gesture all convey approval of the action that preceded it. You can even create a private family gesture that means "Well done."

Rituals. You can develop a family ritual that means the child did well. One family uses a special red dinner plate to celebrate that the person did something noteworthy.

Another family has a cardboard crown with the word "kind" written on it in fancy letters and a smiley face. When Mom notices a child doing something kind, she puts the crown on that child's head. She encourages the children to notice when someone does something kind to them and to put the crown on that person's head.

Withdrawing attention

Attention is helpful when it encourages desired behavior. However, parents can inadvertently encourage unwanted behavior by giving attention to it. When this happens, you can correct it by deliberately withdrawing attention to discourage unwanted behavior, as Margaret did.

When Riley was about 28 months old she would hit Dan and me. We would tell her "No" and explain that hitting hurt, or take her for a time-out, but it seemed to make things worse. She was deliberately hitting us several times a day, and I found myself shrinking from her when she approached. So I asked my parenting class teacher for help. She suggested we withdraw all contact, physical, verbal, and visual, when Riley hit us, then give her lots of attention as soon as she was appropriate.

I started immediately just turning my back on Riley when she hit me, or turning her away from me if I was holding her. It was a little harder for Dan to change his response since he wasn't with her as much.

Riley's a smart kid and it took her only a few times to understand the new approach. She didn't like it one bit, and I have to admit that the results have been dramatic. After a few days, Riley rarely hit me or Dan anymore, and when she did, it was a small hit as if to test our reaction.

Riley used hitting to engage with her parents—not desirable from her parents' perspective, but very reliable from the child's perspective. When hitting no longer worked, she stopped the behavior.

You can use ☆*Attention* to encourage specific behaviors or you can use it preventively to meet a child's need for attention before he has to be difficult to get it. Sometimes this proactive approach is called quality time.

Activity 5–1: Identify attention

Directions: Read the situation on the left and decide what the attention is and what behavior is encouraged.

Situation	Attention and behavior encouraged
1. Isabelle, 24 months, is sitting on the floor struggling to put on her pants. Dad sits down near Isabelle and watches her as she struggles.	Attention: Behavior encouraged:
2. Gabe, 3½, pulled his sister's hair and then ran away. Mom caught him and said, "That wasn't nice. You need to take a time-out." He wouldn't go. As she dragged him to the time-out chair he pleaded, "I'll be good."	Attention: Behavior encouraged:

3. Rosalita, 6, was running in the park. She tripped on a root, was startled, fell down in the soft dirt, and started to cry. Mother ran over and hugged her and asked if she was okay.	Attention: _____ _____ Behavior encouraged: _____
4. Practicing the piano was hard for Akio, 8. He found it difficult to focus for twenty minutes a day. Mom would sit near him on the sofa and knit.	Attention: _____ _____ Behavior encouraged: _____
5. Math was hard for Madison, 10. As she worked on math problems, Mom sat at the table beside her, paying bills and balancing her checkbook. Occasionally, she would smile at her.	Attention: _____ _____ Behavior encouraged: _____

Possible answers: 1. *Attention:* Dad's presence near Isabelle. *Behavior encouraged.* Persistence putting on her pants. **2.** *Attention:* Dragging him to time-out. *Behavior encouraged:* Hurting his sister. **3.** *Attention:* Hugging Rosalita and talking to her. *Behavior encouraged:* Crying when she falls. **4.** *Attention:* Sitting near Akio. *Behavior encouraged:* Practicing the piano. **5.** *Attention:* Smiling and sitting nearby. *Behavior encouraged:* Practicing math facts.

Quality time

Research has found that fifteen to twenty minutes of quality time a day dramatically reduces obnoxious behavior in children. In order to be perceived as quality time, it must be child-directed, one-on-one, and predictable.

Child-directed means you focus on what the child is interested in and follow his lead. If he wants to play with cars, you watch or join as requested. If your toddler wants to build a Duplo® tower, watch or hand her blocks if she is willing. Quality time is not the time to teach letters, or colors, or anything else—your job is simply to follow the child's lead.

One-on-one means, as you guessed, one parent with one child. It is a special time when the child does not need to share the parent with the phone, the computer, a sibling, or anyone else. With the busy lives that many people live, it can be challenging to find such time. However, many people find that it reduces stress and often saves time because the child is not as demanding.

Predictable means that your child can count on getting special time every day. Ideally, the quality time should be at the same hour each day, and may lose its effectiveness if it is not. When the child knows she will have fun time with the parent at ten o'clock in the morning or when her sibling takes a nap, she can hold herself together until the time comes. But if it sometimes happens and sometimes doesn't, she may worry about whether she will have time today and become more stressed and demanding. It is like the experience of the mom whose husband takes the bus and comes home at 6:15 every evening. As long as she knows he is coming, she can keep her cool with the kids, but if he misses the bus or phones that he has to work late, then things often fall apart.

Scheduling. Finding quality time sometimes takes creativity and persistence. You need to review your priorities and take a new look at how you do things. Certainly if nothing changes there will be no time for quality time. Some approaches people have used are:

- Letting one child stay up twenty minutes later for special time
- Scheduling it during the other child's nap time
- Hiring a mother's helper to occupy the other child
- Using the time your partner puts the sibling to bed
- Trading time with a neighbor or nearby friend
- Lowering housekeeping standards to make more time
- Reducing your work schedule or stopping work
- Decreasing your outside commitments, again to make more time available

Quiet acknowledgment. Attention might be preferred when you want to be subtle. For example, imagine you have several families over and the parents are talking on one side of the room and the children are playing on the other side. Suppose you notice your daughter let another child hold her favorite doll. You might praise her but that would interrupt the adult conversation. So you could make eye contact with her and give her the okay sign to let her know that you both noticed and appreciated her generosity.

Another time when attention might be most appropriate is with a shy child who doesn't want to be singled out or a teen who is embarrassed by praise. You could smile and give them a thumbs up and few people would notice.

We have looked at ☆*Attention* tools you can use to encourage desired behavior and as a preventive measure. Next, we will look at the STAR Parenting tool, ☆*Praise.*

Respond to cooperation point:
☆*Praise* tool

☆*Praise,* the second tool on this point, offers verbal encouragement to children. There are several types of praise, and some forms are more effective than others. Some forms of praise may also have unwanted long-term results.

Effort factor

Kids need praise for effort as well as success.

Kids need praise for effort as well as success: To the toddler trying to get her pants on, "Boy, you gave those pants a workout this morning. You kept at it for five whole minutes," or, to the third grader, "I'm impressed with the way you keep studying your math facts. They are hard, and you keep working at it. Each day you get a little better."

When you praise primarily success, children often conclude that things should come easily to them. When things are hard, they may be reluctant to try. You can read a bit more about this phenomenon in the side box on "Research on the Effort Effect."

Types of praise

There are five types of praise: descriptive, appreciative, reflective, evaluative, and exaggerated. The first three are constructive and the last two are usually not helpful.

Descriptive praise states what the child did that you liked. "You closed the door gently when you came in." "You asked your sister for a turn with the markers." Use descriptions as a sports announcer might. When you notice and comment, children are more likely to repeat the behavior.

Research on the Effort Effect

Carol Dweck, a Stanford University professor, believes that our own theories about ourselves and our aptitudes actually shape our character and actions. In particular, she focuses on whether students believe that intelligence is innate and fixed or is the result of effort and can change. Below is a description of some of her research.

Dweck had hundreds of preteens take a test. The problems were from a standard IQ test, and most of the kids scored okay on the test. But when Dweck praised the kids' performance, she didn't praise them all in the same way. She praised some for their natural talent (*What a great score! You're so smart!*), while others were praised for their effort (*What a great score! You must have worked very hard!*).

This may seem like a subtle difference, but to the developing mind the two messages are as different as night and day. The former conveys the belief that people's abilities and traits are fixed, written in concrete, while the latter underscores the potential for growth and the value of old-fashioned effort. The results were immediate and unambiguous: The kids who were told they were smart immediately became cautious, shying away from any further testing that might expose weaknesses. The kids who were praised for their effort, by contrast, became hungry for new challenges. What's more, when the kids were subsequently required to solve very difficult problems, on which they all did poorly, the "smart kids" took the failure as a blow to their self-worth; where they had been smart, they were now dumb, irrevocably. The effortful kids just dug in more and worked harder.

But here's the kicker. As a final part of the experiment, Dweck had all the kids write out their thoughts about the test, ostensibly for other kids who would be taking it in the future. There was also a space for them to write in their scores. Nearly forty percent of the kids who had earlier been praised for their raw talent lied about how well they had done on the test. They inflated their scores. They were in effect using lying as a way to deny their imperfections, which had become shameful to them.

Appreciative praise clarifies what the child did and expresses your appreciation for his effort. "Thank you for closing the door when you came in." "I notice you asked your sister if you could use some markers. I appreciate your remembering to use your words." Appreciative praise is useful when a child succeeds in something she has been struggling with or has done something that you particularly like.

Reflective praise describes the behavior you like and asks the child how he feels about it. "You asked your sister for a turn. How did it feel to remember?" "I notice you got a ninety percent on your math test. How do you feel about that?" Reflective praise is useful as children grow older. It can help them think about their behavior and develop their own standards.

Evaluative praise passes judgment on the person, their actions, or their achievements and pronounces it good. When brief, like "Well done," or "Good job," it does not describe which behavior was acceptable. Although intending to be encouraging, it often leaves the child in doubt and wondering if he or she will be good enough next time. In some cases, if the child believes he does not deserve the praise, he creates a situation to show his parents how bad he feels he really is. Yolanda shared this story.

> *Our family was celebrating 3-year-old Gloria's first dance recital with a fancy dinner. All the talk and attention was focused on Gloria. Dad realized that 5-year-old Miguel was totally left out, and turned to him to compliment his pleasantness and said, "Good boy."*
>
> *Suddenly Miguel, who it later turned out had been thinking of all the awful things he could do to his obnoxious sister, knocked over the milk pitcher and threw his salad bowl across the table. We sat in stunned silence for a moment. Miguel looked like he was trying to prove that he was not a good boy.*

In this case, if Dad had offered descriptive praise ("I notice that you have been sitting quietly while we talk to Gloria") or appreciative praise ("I appreciate how you have let Gloria take center stage this evening. That shows a lot of restraint"), then Miguel would have been less likely to erupt.

Evaluative praise is not always bad. It can be helpful when used with descriptive praise to establish a standard. For example, "Your bed is made, your clothes are put away, and your toys and books are on the shelves. Good job." In this way, the parent establishes the elements of a good job of room cleaning.

Exaggerated praise overstates the value or importance of a behavior. "Your term paper is brilliant [when only average]" "The picture is great. You're a little Picasso." "You ride your bike like Lance Armstrong."

Parents sometimes exaggerate praise, intending to make the child feel good about what she did. However, this form of praise has a couple of potential problems. It may:

- *Reduce children's motivation.* "Well, if I am doing so great, maybe I don't need to work so hard."
- *Decrease parental credibility* for children who have a realistic sense of their achievements. "If she thinks this is good, boy is she stupid. I wonder what else I could get away with?"
- *Encourage an unrealistic image of their ability,* or create a sense of entitlement, "If I'm that good, other people should treat me special." Or, "Maybe I don't have to do what others say."

Characteristics of effective praise

Effective praise is specific, immediate, and sincere

Specific praise is more effective than general praise. It would be clearer to say, "Thank you for hanging up your coat" than "Good boy," so that the child knows what he did that you liked.

From studies, we have learned that very general praise, unrelated to effort or achievement, is viewed by children with suspicion. They need evidence of why they are good, capable, smart, etc. Otherwise, they may think you are easily fooled, or maybe even that they are devious for fooling you! You can create specific praise by describing exactly what it was the child did that you like.

Immediate praise works better than delayed praise. Children live in the present moment. When you delay the praise, they may have difficulty remembering exactly what they did to get it, as in "Thank you for holding still this morning when I put your shoes on." When you are helping the child with his shoes, it would be clearer, and consequently more effective, if you were to say at the time, "Wow. You held your foot still. Thank you. That was very helpful."

Sincere praise helps your child feel competent. Children usually know when praise is sincere and when it is not. If you want to praise and the whole job is not adequate, praise a part that you like. For example, if the room was still messy, you could say, "You did a nice job putting away your toys and books." When the praise is delayed, it feels more manipulative than appreciative. Watch what happens when Ellen changed her tune.

I used to be the classic nagging mom. Always nagging. Always telling them what to do. "Put your socks on." "Get your shoes on now." "Put your coat on immediately." "Why can't you ever do things without reminding?" It seemed like the more I nagged, the slower they went.

Finally, I decided to try commenting on what was happening instead. "I see a girl with her shirt and pants on." "Shirt, pants and one sock. That's an improvement." "Look at that, now she has two socks on." It sounds kind of silly to me but it works. I am amazed how much things have improved. Not only is she dressing quicker, but she is more pleasant in general.

> *Effective praise is specific, immediate, and sincere.*

Activity 5–2: Identify effective praise

Directions: Read the statement and decide if the praise is effective or flawed. Write an **E** for effective or an **F** for flawed in the space before the number. If it is flawed, rewrite it as effective praise.

___ 1. "I'm glad you remembered to bring some toys to Aunt Judy's house. That was good thinking."

___ 2. "I'm glad you remembered to take your homework to school today. I hope you won't forget tomorrow."

___ 3. "The room looks really nice. You put your blocks away, and the puzzle, and the books."

___ 4. "For such a little girl, you did very well."

___ 5. [To a small child trying to get his pants on] "Boy, you sure gave those pants a workout. Putting your clothes on is hard work."

___ 6. "It was so nice when you played quietly before lunch. Could you play quietly now?"

___ 7. "I see you are sharing your trucks with Trey. That's nice. I'll bet he is enjoying playing with them."

___ 8. [To a child who has brought in a long slimy worm that disgusts his parent] "Yes, Sam, it is a pretty worm."

___ 9. "Thanks for holding the door. That was helpful."

___ 10. [To a child practicing soccer] "Wow. You are the best runner in the world."

Possible answers: **1.** Effective. Encourage thoughtful thinking **2.** Flawed—When you say "hope" it implies the child will forget. Change: "I'm glad you remembered to take your homework to school today." **3.** Effective. Tells the child specifically what he did well. **4.** Flawed—If you have to add "for a little girl" it wasn't good. Change: "You did well," or comment on a part she did well. **5.** Effective. Praised effort. **6.** Flawed—The comment was delayed. Change: Use praise before lunch. **7.** Effective. Tells the child specifically what he did well. **8.** Flawed—Insincere. Change: "You're pleased with the worm you found." **9.** Effective. Tells the child specifically what you appreciated. **10.** Flawed—Exaggerated. Change: "You enjoy running" or "Wow, you are fast."

Some kids don't like praise. For whatever reason, some children do not want a parent's praise. Look at the type of praise you give. If the praise is judgmental or exaggerated, she may not want it. In this case, you need to change the type of praise you give and use the three forms that are more effective. As alternatives, you can use nonverbal praise, indirect praise, and reported praise.

Nonverbal praise is essentially attention that we have discussed previously. Try giving a high five, a smile, or a back rub.

Reported praise passes on a compliment that someone else said. For example, you could say, "Mr. Green next door wanted me to thank you for helping him bring in his garbage cans this afternoon," or, "Debbie mentioned how well you danced."

Indirect praise involves saying kind things about your child to someone else within the child's hearing. For example, you could tell your partner how helpful your son was in bringing in the groceries today.

Next, we will look at using the STAR Parenting tool, ☆*Rewards,* another way to encourage desirable behavior.

Respond to cooperation point:
☆*Rewards* tool

☆*Rewards* is the third STAR Parenting tool you can use to encourage desirable behavior. A reward increases the behavior that immediately precedes it. A reward is something a child wants or needs—something he wants enough to change his behavior.

Nature of effective rewards

Effective rewards can be intrinsic or external, big or small, and real or symbolic.

External or intrinsic. Intrinsic rewards are present or inherent in a situation. External rewards are not present in the situation; they are brought in or added to the situation.

When people think of rewards, they usually think of external rewards—money, stars, stickers, candy, or toys that you promise in the future. Intrinsic rewards involve using elements already in the situation. Let's contrast the two types of rewards.

Suppose Mom wants her toddler to stop running around and drink from a sippy cup he has asked for. If she were to say, "Here is your sippy cup. Stop running around and drink your juice. I will read you a story when you are done," the story would be an external reward as it was not in the situation. It is quite probable that her son would take the cup and continue to run around. On the other hand, if she said, "Here is your sippy cup [showing it to him]. You may have it as soon as you are seated," the sippy cup has become the intrinsic reward. In order to get the drink, he must sit down, so he gets rewarded for cooperation.

Big or little items. Rewards can be physical like stars, toys, or stickers. They can also be intangible, like time or a privilege. Below are some examples of both.

stars	making cookies	sugarless gum
stickers	play money	time with you
file cards	small cars	dinosaur erasers
doll clothes	staying up late	building a birdhouse
pennies	extra story	skipping a chore
crackers	back rub	tickets for a concert
computer time	trip to the mall	use of the family car
music CD	inviting a friend	sleepover at friend's

Activity 5–3: Types of rewards

Read the list of rewards above and decide if the reward is a thing or is intangible. Put a ✓ in front of items that are intangible, such as privileges.

Activity 5–4: Rewards for different ages

Read the list of rewards above. Put a **P** in front of items of interest to toddlers and preschoolers, an **S** for school-aged kids, and a **T** for things teens might like. Put multiple letters if you think it interests multiple ages.

Activity 5–5: Make a list of rewards for different ages

Directions: Notice what children at different ages are interested in.

List things you think might motivate children at each age (4, 8, 12) to change their behavior. Be specific! Instead of saying "money," suggest how much money (5¢, 25¢, $1, etc.). Instead of just saying "toys," include one or two examples.

Rewards a 4-year-old might like.	Rewards an 8-year-old might like.	Rewards a 12-year-old might like.
• • • • • •	• • • • • •	• • • • • •
Money: pennies, dimes, quarters *Food:* M&Ms®, gum, a few pretzels *Things:* coloring book, leap frog, action figures *Activity:* read a story, play with Legos®, get toenails polished *Privilege:* extra half hour of TV	*Money:* quarters, $1, $5 *Food:* gum, ice cream, special dessert *Things:* video, art supplies, a Barbie *Activity:* bake cookies, watch a CD, or go to the zoo *Privilege:* stay up late, rent a movie, or have a friend over	*Money:* $2–3, $5, $10. *Food:* special dinner *Things:* Basketball and hoop, PSP, make-up *Activity:* trip to mall, aquarium, or baseball game *Privilege:* more screen time, a friend over-night, or being a part of a special after-hours school function

Real or symbolic. When you give a reward, it can be of real interest itself, or it can be symbolic of something the child wants. For example, if you are having trouble getting your 4-year-old to bed, you could give him a star each night he is in bed on time. Then when he has collected five stars he could stay up thirty minutes late on a Friday night. The stars are symbolic and can be converted into the real reward when he gets five.

There are many types of symbolic rewards—tokens that can be traded in for something else. A CD cover can be cut into a sixteen-piece puzzle, so the child needs to collect all sixteen pieces before he gets the CD. Marbles can be dropped into a jar for cooperation; when the jar is full, the family has a fun family activity.

Points for privileges. One family wanted to encourage cooperation. Particularly, they wanted their kids to understand that if you help me, I will be more likely to help you in return. They established a point system for chores and learning new behaviors. They also extended the point system to include privileges or services the child wanted from the parent—being driven to school, a trip to the mall, staying up late one night, watching TV, or using the computer. The family worked together to develop the point system and posted it on the refrigerator.

When 12-year-old Colin practices the piano for half an hour a day, five days a week, for one month, he earns enough points to have a friend spend the night.

When 6-year-old Timothy is on time for school each weekday, he can earn a Saturday trip to the swimming pool.

Characteristics of effective rewards

A reward is something the child wants enough to change his behavior. Below are characteristics of effective rewards.

Clear goal or expectation. "Be nice to your brother" is not clear enough. What does "be nice" mean? That he should refrain from hitting and teasing, or something proactive like sharing his toys or helping when asked? The criteria need to be clear enough that someone else could give the reward for the behavior you want.

Immediate delivery. A reward reinforces the behavior that immediately preceded it. So, the reward should be given as close to the behavior as possible. For example, whether you are giving tokens or foods or coins for cooperation, carry some in your pocket so you can give one as soon as you see the behavior.

Proportional to effort. Some parents get in the habit of always giving the same thing to motivate their children. However, it is more effective in the long run to vary the reward with the effort you request of your child. For example, if you want your child to take the trash out, you can give him a nickle each time he takes the trash out when asked, and a dime when he takes it out before being asked. This way there is an added incentive to think of it himself.

Appropriate reinforcement schedule. When and how often you give a reward influences what your child learns. You can give the reward every time the behavior happens, at scheduled intervals, or randomly. If you give the reward every time the child does what you want, learning is fastest. However, when you stop rewarding, forgetting is also fastest. On the other hand, if you give the rewards every couple of times the child performs as you wish, learning is slower and forgetting is also slower. With intermittent reinforcement, learning is slowest and forgetting is also slowest.

Fortunately, you can combine the approaches by reinforcing every time when the child is learning a new habit, then switch to decreasing the frequency of rewards, and finally reinforcing the behavior only occasionally.

The dark side of the reinforcement schedule is that when your child begs for a cookie before supper and you say "No" several times and then give in and give him a cookie, you are rewarding begging, making the behavior almost permanent through intermittent reinforcement.

Troubleshooting problems

Rewards sometimes fail because the first step required of the child is too big a step, or the child is not interested in the reward.

Too big a step. Some parents want to make the child "work" for the rewards, so they require a big change for the reward. The large step often discourages the child, and he or she doesn't try very hard. It is more effective to make the first step what the child can comfortably do, and then gradually increase the requirement for the same reward. Here's what Linda did.

Music is important in our family, and Melody wanted to learn to play the piano. I explained that if we were going to invest in lessons, she would need to practice thirty minutes a day, five days a week. That was fine with her—for about three days, then she began to get distracted or "forget." I guess she didn't realize how long it would take her to learn. I was nagging her constantly, but the most she would practice was ten minutes. So I thought I should do something proactive.

I decided I would reward her with tokens. When she got twenty tokens, she could turn them in to purchase a new music CD. The first week I gave her a token each time she practiced for eight minutes. She practiced sixteen minutes on four days, so she had earned eight tokens. It wasn't the thirty minutes a day that I wanted, but it was better than the five to ten minutes she had been doing. Life was pleasant again.

The next week she needed to practice ten minutes to get a token. The following week she needed twelve minutes. By the middle of the week she had enough tokens for a CD, so we went out and purchased one. Gradually, I increased the length of time required to get a token. Eventually, Melody was practicing thirty minutes on a regular basis, so I began to taper off giving her tokens.

At first, she didn't notice that I stopped giving tokens. Then she asked why I wasn't giving her tokens anymore. I said that she had developed the habit of practice and could now be in charge of her music. If she wanted, she could find ways to reward herself. She started to leave and then turned back and asked, "Mom, could we use rewards to help me learn math facts? They're awful hard."

The ability to motivate or reward oneself is a great skill to teach a child—ultimately that is where you want a child to end up. In this case, Mom could help Melody develop a procedure for practicing math facts, and then gradually reduce the amount of help she offers, so Melody can learn to motivate herself.

Reward is not attractive to the child. Sometimes parents are stumped for a reward. The thing the child wants may be too expensive or conflict with family values. When it is too expensive, parents can use an intermediate reward as Linda did with her daughter in the story above, or the reward can be exchanged for a privilege as Victoria did with her son, Finn, below.

Finn was enrolled in a preschool where the children had to put their hat, coats, mittens, scarf, and boots in their cubbies when they came in from playing outside. To encourage putting things away, the school decided to give kids stars. Well, my son was not interested in stars, so he chose to leave his clothes on the hall floor.

When the teacher told me he did not hang up his clothes, I wondered what I could do. I decided to tell Finn that if he hung up his clothes and brought home the star he could trade it for an extra half hour of televison. Suddenly, the star had value to Finn. He hung his clothes up, brought home his star, and had an extra half hour of screen time.

Activity 5–6: Identify errors with rewards

Directions: Read the situation below. Then read each statement, identify the error, and indicate how the error could be avoided.

Situation: Linda's niece, Sally, 3, was coming to stay for five days while her mother was on a business trip. Linda was afraid her son, Josh, 5½, would take toys away from Sally as he sometimes did with younger kids in the park. Mom decided to reward the behavior she wanted.

1. Josh, Sally is going to visit us for several days. If you are kind to her, I will give you a treat each day right after supper.

   Error: _____ Change: _____

   _____

2. Josh, I know you were kind to Sally today, but I don't have time to get you a treat until tomorrow.

   Error: _____ Change: _____

   _____

3. If you are kind to Sally today, we can go out for dinner when her mom comes next weekend.

   Error: _____ Change: _____

   _____

4. If you let Sally win at board games, share your toys and art supplies, and speak to her in a pleasant voice, we can go to the bookstore and get a book when she leaves.

   Error: _____ Change: _____

   _____

Possible answers: **1.** *Unclear goal.* Mom might add, "Kind means to speak pleasantly, touch gently, and share your toys with her. **2.** *Delayed reward.* Mom broke her agreement. She might have put a treat on a high shelf so she didn't need to hunt. **3.** *Reward is too far* away. Rewards need to be near the behavior you are encouraging. If Linda wants to offer dinner in a week, she can give him a certificate good for the dinner, so he has a tangible acknowledgment of his effort. **4.** *Too big a step required.* That is a lot to require if Josh is not comfortable with them all. Better to give a point for each morning, afternoon, and evening that he succeeds, then convert the points to dollars for a book.

How to get started with a reward

Using rewards effectively involves thought and planning. Let's look at the process and see the steps Linda might have used to encourage her daughter to practice the piano.

1. *Collect information.* Before you establish a goal for your child, as usual, remember to collect data on how often the child does the behavior you desire, or the one you wish to stop. It is also helpful to consider what is reasonable for the child's developmental stage, temperament, and experience.

   Linda logged Melody's practice each day for a week and found it varied from five to ten minutes, with an average of a little over eight minutes. She also realized that the sound of the televison in another room distracted Melody.

2. *Make a specific, measurable goal.* If Linda had said, "I want Melody to practice more," Melody and her mother would have trouble agreeing on

whether Melody had earned the token. To be effective the goal needs to be clear, measurable, and include a time frame.

Linda decided that to earn a token, Melody needed to practice the agreed length of time before supper. The length of time needed for a token would gradually increase over time. Mom wanted her daughter to practice five days a week, however, Melody could decide which days to practice.

3. **Decide on a reward and reinforcement schedule.** The reward must be something the child needs or wants enough to change her behavior, not something that the parent wants to give the child. It is nice, but not necessary, for the reward to be linked to the desired behavior. Also, plan how long you will give the reward and how you will taper off.

Linda chose to reward practice with a musical CD since Melody liked to listen to music. Melody would receive one CD for each twenty tokens. In the beginning Melody could earn two tokens a day by practicing the agreed time twice in the day. Mom decided that she would continue to give rewards as long as Melody continued to practice longer at each sitting, each week, or until thirty minutes a day was reached. When thirty minutes was reached, Linda would continue the reward for one more month so Melody could solidify the habit and receive one more CD (four weeks with five tokens each).

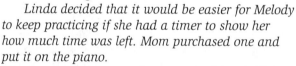

Plan how long you will give the reward and how you will taper off.

4. **List what the child needs** to be able to perform the behavior. It can be skills, items, information, or attitude. If you want your son to pee in the toilet, he may need a stool to stand on. If you want your daughter to calm herself, she may need to be taught specific strategies. If you want your son to write a report, he may need information on how to do it, or he may need a quiet place at a desk or table, writing materials, and reference sources.

Linda decided that it would be easier for Melody to keep practicing if she had a timer to show her how much time was left. Mom purchased one and put it on the piano.

5. **Develop a system to track progress.** If the child does the work but you do not give the reward promptly, your child will not learn the behavior and you will lose credibility.

The first week, Linda planned to sit in the living room and set the timer on her watch so she could reward Melody as soon as her eight minutes was up. After the first week, Linda planned to set her watch to remind her to stop what she was doing and give Melody a token if she practiced without getting distracted. Linda also decided to record the time Melody practiced each day on a chart and post it on the refrigerator.

6. **Explain the plan.** Introduce your plan to the child, clarify what she needs to do to get the reward, and what will happen if the child does not make the needed effort.

After dinner one evening, Linda observed that Melody seemed to be having trouble practicing thirty minutes a day. She had an idea that might help, if Melody was interested. Melody said she was interested. Mom explained that the goal was for Melody to practice thirty minutes a day, but they would start out slowly and increase the time. Mom added that each time Melody practiced the agreed time for that week, she would get a token.

Twenty tokens could be turned in for a CD. Mom proposed they start at eight minutes a day the first week. However, if Melody wished, she could practice two eight-minute stretches for each of five days and she would earn ten tokens, half way to a CD. Mom then asked if Melody would like to do that, which she did.

Linda continued by saying she would keep giving the rewards as long as Melody kept practicing longer and longer each week. Then Mom asked, "What do you think will happen if you stop practicing as agreed?"

"Umm. You will stop giving me tokens?" Melody questioned.

"Right," Mom said, then added, "What do you think will happen when you can practice steadily for thirty minutes a day?"

"I don't know," Melody replied.

"After two months I'll stop giving you tokens," Mom explained.

"But that is not fair," Melody objected.

Mom replied, "The tokens are to help you learn a new habit. When you have learned, it will be your job to reward yourself if you want to."

7. ***Implement the plan and acknowledge your effort.*** Implementing the plan involves doing what you have agreed to do. If your plan is dependent upon certain items, then get them. If your child needs skills, then arrange to teach him. Sometimes that means getting support for yourself, so you can remain firm when you need to be. Also, it is helpful to reward yourself for your effort.

Once Linda explained "The Plan," she asked her daughter when she would like to start. Melody said tonight, then amended herself to "Tomorrow, 'cause it's after supper now." Mom then ordered the timer to put on the piano. She also arranged to call a friend once a week and report how things were going. When Melody was practicing thirty minutes a day, she planned to get together with her friend for a special lunch to celebrate.

Note: Remember to turn the job over to the child so she is in charge of her behavior. When Melody achieved the thirty-minute level, Mom told her that she would continue to give the reward for two months. In that time, Melody could decide how she would eventually reward herself.

Common concerns about rewards

Sometimes parents are reluctant to try rewards because they are afraid of what might happen. That's a little like saying, "I don't want to drive a car because I might get hit." Yes, you might have an accident driving a car, but you can dramatically reduce the chance with careful driving. Several common concerns about rewards are addressed below.

I don't want to bribe my child. Rewards and bribes appear similar, but are very different. You can think of bribes as the dark side of rewards. Rewards are earned and are given after good behavior. Bribes are given to stop bad behavior before good behavior has begun. That means if a child wants another reward, he has to continue to behave well. If he wants a bribe, he will misbehave.

I'm afraid I will have to reward her forever. Most of the time, this is not as much of a problem as you might think. As children are learning a new habit or skill, they may need external rewards to keep them motivated. When the skill becomes more solid, children usually forget rewards as the success becomes an internal reward.

Rewards are given after good behavior; bribes are given to stop bad behavior.

If you think your child will expect a reward to continue, you can structure the reward so it doesn't. You can either set up the reward for a specific period, being clear that it will end at the agreed upon time or you can gradually increase what the child must do to get the reward. Cathy did this, as you see in the following story.

My son, Timmy, 4, is cautious and slow to adapt. I wanted him to learn to swim, and he was reluctant to try lessons. He very much likes to go to a park with a twisty slide. I used his fondness for the slide to encourage him to take swim lessons. Each week I increased the achievement required to get the same reward.

- *Week 1: We stop at the park on the way home if he sits quietly and watches the kids during the swim lesson.*

- *Week 2: He sit and dabbles his feet in the water as he watches.*

- *Week 3: He gets in the pool for five minutes.*

- *Week 4: He stays in the water for half the lesson.*

- *Week 5: He stays in the water the whole lesson.*

If you wanted to encourage your daughter to use the potty, you might first give her a sticker for sitting on the potty with clothes on. Then up the requirement. Give her a sticker when she sits on the potty with a bare bottom, and eventually only when she pees in the potty. Later, she might get a sticker for going all by herself.

For some children, the sticker may be enough. For other children, the sticker may be symbolic of a privilege or treat to come, as it was at Rachel's house.

Bedtime was a battle zone in our house. Every night it was a three-hour battle with our son, Elliot. We tried several approaches, but he didn't want to go to bed, period. Anywhere. This had been going on for weeks. The anger and frustration were so bad they were tearing us apart.

I decided to try to reward Elliot for going to sleep. I knew something he would really, really like, but I was reluctant to use it. So I set the system up for one week.

I told Elliot that we all needed sleep. I told him that I knew it was hard for him to go to sleep, so I would reward him for his effort. He could have a donut each morning after he stayed in bed quietly the night before. I explained that if he screamed going to bed or got into our bed at night, he would not get a donut. If he stayed quietly in his bed, he would. We put the donut in a bag where he could see it.

It was wonderful. He went to bed without a fuss and stayed in his room the whole night. He was proud and excited in the morning when he earned the donut. The same thing happened for two more nights. The fourth night he decided to sleep with us after an hour in his bed. We said, "That's fine if you want to. And remember, if you sleep with us, you may not have the donut in the morning." After thinking a bit, he decided he would rather have the donut and went back to his own bed.

The second week I offered smaller donuts. At first he objected. I reminded him that if he wanted, he could sleep in our room, but he would not receive a donut. He again chose the donut. This week I am offering him a small donut hole, but he is already losing interest in the donut hole. I feel pretty good about that, so if rewarding him with a donut hole goes on for a while, I don't mind. What is one donut hole in the morning compared with a three-hour bedtime battle at night?

I'm concerned about giving my child food as a reward because of increasing childhood obesity and diabetes. If you can find another effective reward, then by all means use it. Remember that it must be something a child wants or needs enough to change her behavior. A week or two of food as a reward once a day is not going to make a child obese. However, if food becomes your primary way of modifying your child's behavior, you may well have a problem; similarly, if sweets become very important. Factors that encourage childhood obesity are: drinking pop (sweetened *and* low calorie types) and excessive snacking, poor food choices (high calories, fast foods), and little exercise. See Resources for help on this topic.

I don't want my child to be mercenary. Giving children rewards will not make them mercenary, any more than giving them markers will make them great artists. However, if the rewards you offer are "things" and the only strategy you use is rewards, you may develop a problem. Instead of only using material things, try privileges and attention as rewards, and use a variety of parenting tools which includes things besides rewards.

Suppose your child demands, "What will you give me?" You could respond lightly with, "Two hugs, a pat, and a sprinkle of pixie dust." Then ask, "How would you like to reward yourself for doing it?" The purpose of rewards is help the children get started. You can teach them to reward themselves.

Kids should do what's right without rewards. Yes, they should, but for whatever reason they do not. There should not be crime, war, or natural disasters either, but there are. Would you go to work without the reward of a paycheck? Don't get stuck in the "should" or you may never get anywhere. One mom put it this way.

I was "shoulded" to death as a child. I was made to feel ashamed and guilty if I didn't do what was asked. I thought I was a bad person. It took me seven years of therapy to undo all that. I won't do that to my kids.

You can teach kids to reward themselves.

Most parents find it is usually easier to start where their child is and go on from there.

I don't want to build a dependancy on praise or rewards. One benefit of using rewards is that it can teach your children to motivate themselves. Certainly if you continue to structure and reward your child through preschool and grade school as you did when he was a toddler, you may create dependence. However, if you gradually turn the process of motivation over to children, they can learn to motivate themselves.

For example, in the beginning you can structure the reward yourself. Then you can involve your child a bit by asking him for more and more input about how to structure it. Finally, you can turn the process over to the child and ask him how he will reward himself.

How do I taper off rewards? You have a couple of choices. You can require more effort for the same rewards, wait for your child to ask for the reward and say, "This is the last week," or ask the child what she would like to work on now. Let's see how each of these might work.

Require more effort for same rewards. Melody's mother used this when setting up her piano practicing plan. Each week Melody practiced longer for the same token.

Wait for the child to ask for the reward. Often, as children learn a skill, they lose interest in the reward. If you expected your son to hang his coat up when he came in from playing in the snow, you could reward him with a cup of hot cocoa when he hung his coat up. At first, you could give him the cocoa, then you could wait for him to ask you for it. Once the novelty wears off, many kids forget to ask.

Say, "This is the last week." When you think your child has learned the desired behavior, tell him that this is the last week to receive the reward. Ask him what he would like to do to celebrate his ability to do the new skill. Then celebrate his success and turn responsibility for it over to him.

When you run out of rewards, you're done. Start with a limited number of rewards and when they are gone, don't get any more. One woman did this when potty training her son. He liked cars, so she bought car stickers for when he tried to use the toilet and little tiny cars for when he was successful. With luck, shortly after he has learned to use the potty, she will run out of stickers and cars.

Ask the child what he or she would like to work on next. If you think the child has mastered the behavior but she would still like to earn the reward, ask her what new skill she would like to learn and start a new plan.

In this chapter we have considered how to **Respond to cooperation,** beginning with how important it is to find good behavior. Then we looked at how to encourage cooperation by using the tools ☆*Attention,* ☆*Praise,* and ☆*Rewards.* In chapter six, we will look at the STAR Parenting point, **Acknowledge feelings.**

Summary of
Respond to Cooperation

★ **Decide what behavior you want and look for it.** Encourage the behavior by giving attention, praise, or rewards.

★ **Decide how you want your child to get your attention when you wish he would leave you alone.** Remember that if your child wants your attention badly enough, she will resort to bad behavior to get it. Respond quickly when your child asks for attention appropriately.

★ **Use effective praise.** Praise immediately, specifically, and sincerely.

★ **Use rewards wisely.** Define the behavior you want and explain it to your child. Pick something the child wants as a reinforcer. Look for the behavior, reward it, and plan how to turn responsibility for rewarding herself over to your child.

STAR in Action Story[1]

Don't Hurt the Baby

Daniel was 3½ years old and had a 5-month-old baby sister, Emma. He squeezed Emma's foot until she cried. I reminded him that it hurt her and gave him a time-out. The time-outs were getting longer and longer. I had to drag him to the chair and hold him in. Time-outs were not working, since I had to give him more and more.

Yesterday, when I nursed Emma, Daniel cried and screamed. I ended up giving him eighteen time-outs! I just didn't know what to do. After putting him to bed, I decided to call my Aunt Beth. She came over and helped me work through the STAR Parenting process.

S—Stop and focus

I asked Aunt Beth for a good consequence to make Daniel stop hurting Baby Emma. She told me to slow down, that we would get to ideas later. First, we needed to figure out what was going on.

I explained that Daniel had always needed a lot of time, but now that Emma was here, it was worse. She asked if every day was the same or if some days were better than others. After thinking a bit, I realized that some days were good and some were bad. The difference was that on the good days, the three of us went to the park. On the bad days, one of my sisters, a friend, or someone else came to visit. She asked me questions about Daniel's temperament and what I wanted. My answers are below.

Long view: I want Daniel to be a caring, resourceful, and intelligent adult.

Temperament: Daniel is very persistent and not easily distracted. He keeps after things he wants for a long, long time.

Development: The task of a 3- to 6-year-old is to explore how to get what he wants. Daniel may be using physical power (hurting Emma) to interact with me.

Child's goal: Daniel may hurt Emma to get my attention.
Parent's goal: I want Daniel to touch Emma gently. And I want him to ask for my attention when he wants it.

T—Think of ideas

Once I figured out the specifics I wanted, we began to generate ideas. Aunt Beth suggested that we consider all points and tools. At first, we wrote down all the ideas we could think of. Next, we decided which point of the STAR the ideas belonged on. Then, Aunt Beth wanted us to fill all the gaps so we had ideas for all points and tools.

Avoid problems

☆*Change things* ① Keep the children separate unless I am present. ② Take the baby with me when I leave the room. ③ Put the baby in a playpen to put her out of Daniel's reach. ④ Hire a mother's helper to watch Emma in the afternoon to give Daniel some alone time with me. ⑤ Have some special toys, such as a train set, play dough, or a special book, that he can use only when I am nursing or tending Emma.

☆*Reduce stress* ⑥ Put on music and dance to it. ⑦ Go out running with Daniel each day to de-stress. ⑧ Spend quality time with Daniel to reduce his stress (see box on page 110).

☆*Two yeses* ⑨ "You may make a funny face for Emma or sing her a song." ⑩ "You can pick out Emma's clothes or give her a toy."

Teach new skills

• Touch gently

☆*Modeling* ⑪ Stroke the baby's foot gently.

☆*Shaping* ⑫ 1. Daniel can learn how a gentle touch feels. 2. He can demonstrate gentle and firm touch on someone else. (Praise him when he's gentle.) 3. He can touch the baby's foot under supervision.

---

1 There is a STAR in Action Story at the end of each chapter. Each story is written by a parent in his or her own words and shows how that person adapted the STAR Parenting process to his or her own life.

These stories use tools from all points, so some may be unfamiliar until you have read the appropriate chapter. You can see how different parents, with different values or kids with different temperaments, might make different choices.

☆*Re-do it right* ⑬ Say, "Hey, buddy, you forgot to touch gently. Let's re-do it right."

• How to ask for attention

☆*Shaping* ⑭ 1. Read *What About Me?* by Eileen Kennedy-Moore to Daniel. 2. Act out the ideas in the book with him. 3. Ask Daniel which idea he would like to act out, and then practice it. 4. Read a story and ask what the character can do when he feels left out. 5. Recall a recent situation where Daniel felt lonely and act out the situation with the chosen strategy.

☆*Modeling* ⑮ Think about what to do. For example, I can model saying, "I want Daddy to give me a hug, and Daddy is changing Emma's diaper. What can I do? I could hug Dad's back right now, or I could look at a book until he is done."

☆*Re-do it right* ⑯ If Daniel hurts Emma say, "Oops, you forgot to ask for attention. Re-do it right."

• How to play with baby—Aunt Beth reminded me that I would probably need to teach Daniel how to play at each stage of Emma's development. (See Table 5–1: How babies learn to play on page 112.)

☆*Modeling* ⑰ Show Emma a picture. Comment to Daniel on how long it takes for her to focus.

☆*Re-do it right* ⑱ If Daniel holds the picture too far from Emma, say, "Whoops, she can't see it. Let's move it in closer."

☆*Shaping* ⑲ 1. Explain that "Babies need to be able to coordinate their eyes and hands to play with others. Learning this happens gradually over six months." 2. Show Daniel how to hold a picture close to Emma's face. 3. Allow him to hold the picture, and comment on how Emma wiggles or quiets when she notices it. 4. Help him find a suitable picture to show her. 5. Watch as he shows Emma the picture. 6. Repeat teaching for each stage of development.

Respond to cooperation

☆*Attention* ⑳ Sit near Daniel and watch as he plays gently with Emma. ㉑ Stroke his back gently as he touches her gently. ㉒ Give him fifteen minutes of quality time each day.

☆*Praise* ㉓ When Daniel touches gently, say, "You touched gently." Or, ㉔ "You remembered to touch gently." Or, ㉕ "That touch was a very gentle touch." When he asks for a hug, say, ㉖ "Thank you for asking. " Or, ㉗ "I'm glad you asked for

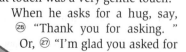

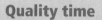

Quality time

Research has found that fifteen to twenty minutes of quality time each day dramatically reduces unwanted behavior. To be effective the time must be:

• **Predictable**—similar time each day (like when the baby naps or when Daddy comes home) so the child knows it will happen.

• **One-on-one**—with no distractions. Focus on the child (not planning shopping list, daydreaming, reading a book, or watching another child).

• **Child directed**—activity chosen by the child. Parent does what the child wants (within reason).

a hug. I like giving you hugs." ㉘ When he shows Emma a picture, say, "Emma enjoyed looking at the picture of Grandpa. That was thoughtful of you."

☆*Reward* ㉙ Give Daniel a hug (or attention) immediately when he asks for it. ㉚ Give him a sticker each time he touches Emma gently. ㉛ Give him a token (poker chip) each time he touches Emma gently. When he earns five tokens, read him a story or play trains with him. ㉜ Get a coloring book. Each morning or afternoon that he does not cause Emma to cry, he may choose a page to color.

Set limits

☆*Rule* ㉝ Touch gently. ㉞ Ask for attention when you want it. (Note: I must respond immediately at first or Daniel will not try again.)

☆*Consequence* ㉟ "When you hurt the baby, you must do a kindness for her." For example, draw a picture of the baby or make the baby laugh.

☆*A better way* ㊱ "When you are feeling lonely (ignored), my way is for you to ask me for a hug, your way is to hurt the baby. What is a better way?"

Acknowledge feelings

☆*Active listening* ㊲ "You feel lonely because you want to play with Mommy right now and I'm busy." ㊳ "You're frustrated that Mommy has to change Emma's diaper." ㊴ "Mommy's nursing Emma, and you're angry because you want me to play trains with you."

☆*Simple listening* ㊵ When Daniel talks, listen and respond with neutral statements like "Uh huh," "Oh," "I see," and "Really?"

☆*Grant in fantasy* ㊶ Say, "Wouldn't it be fun if we had three mommies? One for you, one for Emma, and one to take care of the house."

~~~~~~

A—Act effectively

I was amazed at how many ideas we came up with. With forty-one ideas I was sure I could solve the problem. The challenge now was deciding what to do.

Making a rule and consequence still appealed to me somewhat, but Aunt Beth pointed out that no matter what consequence I tried, Daniel would probably break the rule if that was the only way to get attention.

A lot of the ideas had potential. I liked the idea of teaching him to ask for attention, but that would take time *and* I had to be willing to stop what I was doing and attend to him.

Quality time seemed like it might work, but it seemed like a lot of time to commit, until Aunt Beth asked how much time I spent giving him time-outs. That was a shocker! It took at least five minutes, dragging him to the chair and holding him there. That was one and a half hours a day! Maybe fifteen to twenty minutes was not so bad—if it worked. Eventually, I decided to take one idea for each point.

Avoid the problem—First, I would give Daniel twenty minutes of quality time when Emma went down for her morning nap. I would start tomorrow.

Teach new skills—I could model thinking out loud about getting what you want. For example, I could say, "I want a hug, and Don (my husband) is changing Emma's diaper. What can I do? Well, I could see if I could get a hug from someone else. Who else could give me a hug?" That verbal thinking would start tomorrow evening when Don was home.

Respond to cooperation—When Daniel touched Emma gently, I would praise him and say, "That was a gentle hug. Emma liked it."

Set limits—Rule: Touch gently. Consequence: If Daniel hurts Emma, I will pick her up and take her to my room without saying a word to Daniel. Our house is childproof, so I could do that for a couple of minutes.

Acknowledge feelings—If he seems upset that I'm caring for Emma, I will acknowledge his feelings. "You're frustrated that Mommy has to change Emma's diaper." Or, "Mommy's nursing Emma and you're angry she can't play with you right now."

This is Tuesday. I will try this plan for five days. I'll count the number of times Daniel hurts Emma, and mark them on the calendar so I can tell if things are getting better. Sunday evening I will call Aunt Beth and tell her how things are going. If I keep my plan of quality time each morning, I will buy a new plant for my African violet collection.

~~~~~~

R—Review and revise

Daniel's behavior was so much improved and so quickly that I called Aunt Beth Friday evening to let her know Daniel hurt Emma only twice on Thursday and not at all on Friday. It is amazing how much difference giving him attention when he is pleasant (quality time) and giving no attention when he hurts Emma makes.

Table 5–1: How babies learn to play

Before babies can play with others, they need to be able to coordinate their eyes and hands. This happens gradually over six months. When Emma can control her eyes, she will begin to learn to control her hands and reach towards something interesting.

Newborn	**Emma is learning to focus.** A newborn's vision is fuzzy, like an out-of-focus photograph. Faces interest her most. She sees things best when they are held at about eight to twelve inches from her face. ***Activity:*** *You can put your face close or hold a picture so she can focus on it. (Find pictures in magazines.)*
8 weeks	**She is learning to move her eyes** where she wants them to go. It is hard for her to follow your movement when you are fast. ***Activity:*** *Hold a toy up for her to look at and move it slowly. Watch her eyes to see if they move in the same direction. If not, stop so her eyes can find the toy, then move it more slowly. She may even turn her head to keep the toy in sight.*
10 weeks	**Baby's hands are usually open** and she is ready for you to put something into one. ***Activity:*** *If you put a rattle in her hand, she will wave it, hear the sound, look at the rattle, and see her hand.*
3 months	**Baby's eyes judge the distance.** She will look back and forth between the rattle and her hand as she moves her hand to touch it. When she grasps an item, she will bring it to her mouth to explore. ***Activity:*** *Hold an item still and watch as she gradually moves her hand toward it. Wait patiently so she can succeed in getting it herself.*
6 months	**Baby can reach directly** for things and will immediately put them in her mouth. ***Activity:*** *Offer a variety of interesting toys to practice reaching for.*

Chapter 6

Acknowledge Feelings

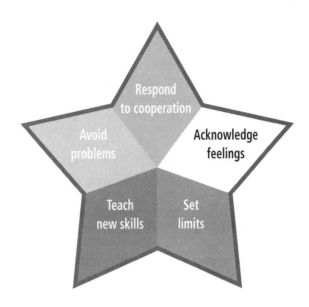

When a person feels understood, not judged, he can change

Aaron was having a tough time at preschool. His mom was helping at school, and he didn't what to share her with other kids. He wanted to go home.

The teacher hovered around him, trying to interest him in some activity. "I'll read you a story." "Do you want to play at the sand table?" "We have a new puzzle I bet you'll like." He whimpered, "No. I want to go home," as he nibbled his thumb.

When his mom noticed what was happening, she went over and asked what was the matter. Aaron replied, "I want to go home. I want to go now!"

She responded, "You're disappointed you have to share me with all these people. You want to go home and have me all to yourself." Aaron looked up, smiled and said, "Uh huh."

And that was the end of the problem. He was able to let go of his disappointment and join the group.

> **Tools to**
> ***Acknowledge***
> ***feelings***
>
> ☆ Simple listening
> ☆ Active listening
> ☆ Grant in fantasy

Feelings are neither good nor bad.

Mom understood how Aaron felt and acknowledged his feelings. She didn't try to change them. She didn't explain that this was her day to work at school. She didn't try to solve his problem. She simply acknowledged his feelings.

When you acknowledge feelings, you are accepting them, not judging or agreeing with them. It is helpful to remember that feelings are neither right nor wrong. They simply exist. When you acknowledge children's feelings, they have the space they need to grow and change. I wish I could guarantee that doing so would eliminate the problem every time. I can't, but it happens often enough to make acknowledging feelings a worthwhile approach.

Three tools you can use to acknowledge feelings are: ☆*Simple listening,* ☆*Active listening,* and ☆*Grant in fantasy.* However, before we look at the tools, we will look a bit at the nature of feelings and four ways parents discount children's feelings.

Nature of feelings

Our emotions are neither good nor bad. They are different from actions. They can be expressed in different ways.

Feelings are neither good nor bad. They just are. Feelings are the body's response to life events. You can read more about this in the box on "How the Brain Processes Information," page 117.

Some people think love is good and anger bad, but both are feelings, and both can be expressed in healthy and unhealthy ways. Wanda Holloway's actions (Texas 1991) are a dramatic example of love gone astray. Wanda plotted to kill Verna Heath, a prospective cheerleader's mother, to clear a place for her own daughter on the cheerleading team. This was love, but unhealthy love.

Love, however, can go awry in less dramatic ways. For example, when a parent always fixes things whenever her child is upset, that expression of her love is unhealthy because it prevents the child from learning the skills he needs to manage his feelings and his life.

Similarly, anger can be both healthy and unhealthy. It is healthy when it is expressed in a way that encourages growth. For example, a heartbroken mother channeled her anger at her 13-year-old daughter's death by a drunk driver into something positive. With several friends, she started MADD (Mothers Against Drunk Driving) to help victims and to create the public conviction that drunk driving is unacceptable and criminal.

Feelings are different from actions. It is okay to be mad, and it is not okay to hurt people. It is helpful to teach children that feelings are on the inside and actions are on the outside. Feelings give us clues about what is happening or what we are thinking about. The challenge is to identify the feelings and think about how you will respond. For example, a child might feel bored and go pick a fight with his sister. Feeling bored is fine, and picking a fight with his sister is not. There are other ways to deal with boredom. Again, all feelings are okay, but all actions are not okay.

Feelings can be healthy or unhealthy

Healthy anger	*Unhealthy anger*
Clears the air	Hurts emotionally
Motivates change	Injures people or
Increases	things
communication	

Healthy love	*Unhealthy love*
Is supportive	Is overprotective
Is caring	Inhibits growth
Is unconditional	Is conditional

Feelings can be expressed in different ways. If a child gets frustrated, you can teach her self-calming tools like taking a deep breath, using positive self-talk, or shaking out irritation. The book, *Dealing with Disappointment: Helping Kids Cope When Things Don't Go Their Way,* gives twenty-four calming techniques and talks about how to teach self-calming skills.

For example, if a child is bored, he can read a book, ask his sibling to play, offer to help her with what she is doing, create a fort, make a surprise for someone, or ask a parent for ideas. In fact, boredom can encourage creativity by forcing children to think of something interesting to do. You can help kids know that feelings can be expressed in different ways by clarifying your thoughts and actions. When you are upset, you could say, "I am so mad! I want to yell and scream, but I'm not going to. I'm going to take three deep breaths and then decide what to do next."

Roadblocks to feelings

There are four ways adults block children's feelings: deny them, reduce them, discount them, and solve the problem. We will look at each briefly.

Deny. Tells kids that they are not feeling what they think they are feeling. "Stop crying. You're not really hurt. You'll be fine in just a minute" or, "You don't hate Billy. He's your friend."

Reduce. Tells the child he is overreacting. There may be a problem, but it's not as serious as the child thinks. "It's not that bad. You'll feel better in a minute." Or, "You're making a mountain out of a molehill." Or, "Don't be so upset. I'm sure Billy didn't mean to break your plane."

Discount. Tells the child that she has no right to feel that way—she created the problem. "Stop crying. You wouldn't have fallen if you had looked where you were going." Or, "Be quiet. If you had put your plane away, Billy would not have broken it."

> **Ways adults block kids' feelings**
>
> Deny—"You don't feel that way."
> Reduce—"Oh, it's not really that bad."
> Discount—"You have no right to feel that way."
> Solve it—"I'll 'fix' your feelings."

Solve it. Fixes the problem so the child won't have the strong feelings anymore. Over time, this may make the child feel that feelings are not okay, and he comes to rely on adults to "take care of the situation." The parent might say, "Come and I'll put a band-aid on the cut." Or, "Give me the plane. I will glue the wing back on." The trouble with this response is that it takes responsibility for feeling away from the child.

Alternatives to roadblocks. There are four alternatives to the roadblocks: simple listening, active listening, active listening with limits, and active listening with an offer to fix.

☆*Simple listening* supports the child's concern without making any judgment. ☆*Active listening* reflects the child's feelings and the situation. These are both tools on this STAR Parenting point, ***Acknowledge feelings,*** and we will discuss them in more detail.

Active listening with limits acknowledges the child's feeling and sets a limit. "You're upset that your sister went into your room, and we touch people gently, even when we are mad. It is not okay to hit her."

Active listening and offering help or support acknowledges the child's feelings and lets her remain in charge of her feelings and the situation. She can decide if she wants your help or if she wants to solve things her own way.

Table 6–1: Examples of roadblocks and alternatives

Situation: Ethan can't quite get the hang of riding his new two-wheeled bike. After trying for half an hour, he angrily throws his bike down and shouts, "I hate this bike!"

Deny—"No, you don't. You love your new bike. Remember how excited you were when you got it yesterday?"	**Simple listening**—"Humm," "Oh," "I see."
Reduce—"Relax. Don't make such a big deal out of it. It takes everyone a while to get the hang of riding a two-wheeler."	**Active listening**—"You're frustrated you can't ride your new bike yet."
Discount—"Quit crying. If you would just do as I say, you wouldn't have a problem."	**Listening with limits**—"It's okay to be angry, and you still need to treat your bike gently."
Solve it—"Here, I'll put the helper wheels on 'till you get accustomed to the bike."	**Listening with an offer to fix**—"Sounds like you're upset that you can't ride your bike. Would you like me to put the training wheels on to give you a chance to get used to the bike a bit?"

Now that we have looked at the nature of feelings and roadblocks to feelings, we will look at ☆*Simple listening,* the first tool on the ***Acknowledge feelings*** point of the star.

Acknowledge feelings point
☆*Simple listening* tool

The purpose of ☆*Simple listening,* or simple acknowledgment, is to support the child while he or she works through whatever is upsetting. This tool is effective with school-aged children and teens. It is not usually effective with toddlers and young preschoolers.

☆*Simple listening* leaves control of conversation with the child. It asks no questions. It gives no advice. ☆*Simple listening* gives children and teens room to vent their feelings, then think about the problem and find a solution. This process is made easier if the parent connects emotionally to the child or teen and leaves control of the issue with him.

How to simply listen. ☆*Simple listening* involves stopping what you are doing and focusing on your child. If you're reading a book, put it down. If you are at the computer, turn away. Let your child know you are listening with nonjudgmental comments, such as these:

Oh	*I see*	*No kidding*
Ummmm	*Really?*	*How about that*
Yeah	*Gosh*	*Tell me more*

How the Brain Processes Information
by Susie Leonard Weller[1]

The brain consists of three parts: the survival brain, the emotional brain, and the neocortex.

Your survival brain is wired for fast reflexes. The oldest layer of your brain operates on instinct to quickly protect and defend. If you've ever said or done something in the heat of the moment that you regretted afterwards, you were reacting from your survival brain.

The emotional brain is the middle layer. It serves as a gatekeeper between the survival and the higher-thinking, creative brain. If you notice your children "pushing your buttons," they've typically triggered a long-term memory of frustration or pain stored in your emotional layer. When the brain becomes flooded with stress chemicals, emotions take over. These chemicals can "hijack" your ability to choose appropriate responses.

In the neocortex, or most sophisticated layer of the brain, you're able to make choices, not just react. It supports your ability to calm down, switch gears, and explore other options. Once it's been flooded with adrenaline or intense emotions, it typically takes the body twenty minutes to physically calm down for the higher-thinking brain to regain full function. This is why it's important for parents to stop and calm down before acting. Otherwise, the survival and emotional layers of their brain are over-functioning and their creative brain is under-functioning.

Children's brains are only twenty-five percent developed at birth. By the time they are 3 years old, about eighty percent is developed, and by age 5, ninety percent. Experience shapes their brain. Babies have mirror neurons which encourage them to learn by imitating whatever behavior they see in their environment. An infant's brain is like wet concrete. The earliest impressions—both positive and negative—have the deepest impact.

Parents need to develop realistic expectations about young children's behavior. Sometimes, they expect toddlers to know how to correctly behave after giving a few instructions. Adults become frustrated when children don't comply and seem to be misbehaving "on purpose."

Repeated experiences become hardwired in the brain as established pathways for future behavior. Parents need to become patient teachers. Hardwiring the brain to fully function takes time and repeated practice.

[1] Author of *Why Don't You Understand? Improve Family Communication with the 4 Thinking Styles*

These are the same sounds people often make when they are listening to a friend on the phone. The comments let the other person know that you are paying attention.

So how do you insert these into a conversation? Easy, check the dialog below and see how Dad responded to his son Aidan.

Friend troubles

Aidan comes in from playing with a friend next door.

Aidan	Dad
I hate Bobby.	*Oh?*
Bobby's mean.	*Gosh.*
Yeah, he won't let me play with his new car.	*Really?*
He says it's breakable, and I can't touch it.	*Ummm.*
But I won't break it. I'll be real careful.	*I see.*
Maybe if I take my glass pig over for him to look at, he'll let me touch his special car.	*Uh huh.*
Bye, Dad.	*Bye.*

Contrast simple listening to parent controls. How do you think the conversation would have gone if Dad had begun by saying "You don't hate Bobby. He's your best friend." Or reminded Aidan that he broke Bobby's model airplane when he threw it in the air to see if it could really fly? Or if he suggested that Aidan take something over to share? Aidan would probably have ended up justifying himself or storming out of the room. Instead, Dad gave Aidan enough time and support to think of something himself.

☆*Simple listening* works well with older children and teens. You can see this as Carlos vents his feelings below.

Teacher troubles

Mom is balancing the checkbook at the kitchen table. Carlos comes in from school grumpily.

Carlos	Mom
[Stomps into the room.]	*Hi, Carlos.*
[Slams books on counter.]	*Sounds like you had a tough day.*
[Says nothing.]	*I'll be here if you want to talk about it.*

[Fixes a snack and mutters to himself.] He is stupid. Stupid. **Stupid. STUPID!**   *[Says nothing.]*

[Turns to Mom.] Teachers are stupid!	*Really?*
Yeah. Mr. Brown is so stupid he couldn't find his way out of a paper bag.	*Goodness.*
He doesn't know his left hand from his right hand.	*Umm.*
He doesn't like me helping José in study hall.	*I see.*
José has trouble with math, and I was explaining it to him. We weren't disturbing anyone.	*Oh.*
Yeah! But Mister Big Shot insisted we were too noisy.	*Ummm.*
Uh huh. I guess we can meet after school. But it is stupid not to use the time in study hall. That's what it's for—studying.	*Yeah.*
Maybe it would work if we told him what we were doing and ask where we could work.	*Maybe.*
Bye, Mom.	*Bye*

Mom wisely refrained from taking control of the situation or trying to bridge the gap when Carlos ignored her. It is almost as though he was testing her, "Is she going to let me deal with this myself or is she going to butt in?" By waiting for Carlos to turn to her and speak, Mom conveyed her willingness to let him work things out himself.

Why does simple listening work? ☆*Simple listening* works because adults give kids the support and separation they need to find their own solutions to problems. One benefit of this approach is that it develops skills that the child can use on his own. When you move in, however kindly intended, and ask questions or give advice, you take control of the situation and are encouraging dependence on your wisdom. In the example below, you can see how the tool allows Jacek to think independently. Jacek's aunt recounted the event.

We took my sister, her husband, and their two teenaged kids out to dinner at a very nice restaurant to celebrate her daughter Samantha's graduation from high school. The grown-ups and Samantha were all dressed nicely as befitted the occasion. Jacek, Samantha's younger brother, couldn't be bothered to change his clothes, so he wore an old T-shirt and jeans with holes.

Shortly after we arrived at the restaurant, Jacek said in a shocked tone, "I look like crap." He had just noticed that he was underdressed for the occasion. I replied, "Well, only your clothes. And people usually feel embarrassed when they are underdressed. Fortunately, no one is hurt and the food will still taste very good."

Later, on the way home, I commented to Jacek that I thought he handled the situation very well. "You were pleasant, spoke quietly, and participated in the general conversation." Then I added, "I'm wondering how you could prevent being so underdressed from happening again."

Jacek thought a bit and said, "Easy. I can look around and see what other people are wearing before we go, and, I can check with the restaurant to find out what they suggest."

Thinking about the incident later, I suspect Jacek's parents were wise to let him wear what he did even though he was embarrassed. If they had pressured him into wearing appropriate clothes, he might have spent the whole evening justifying his resentment by pointing out everyone who was underdressed rather than looking to see what was appropriate to wear.

Activity 6–1 helps you identify ☆*Simple listening.*

Activity: 6–1: Identify ☆*Simple listening*

Directions: Read the dialog below. If Mom's response is simple listening write "okay" in the status column. If Mom's response contains an error (a judgment, advice, or question) mark an **X** and list the error.

Christy:	Mom:	Status
[Comes in and lets the door slam.]	Hi. How was practice?	1.
I hate Stacy.	That's not nice.	2.
And I'm never going to eat ice cream again.	Really?	3.
After practice we got ice cream and went to the park. My ice cream fell off the cone onto my lap. See?	Oh, you should get that right into the washer.	4.
I jumped up to knock the ice cream off and it slid into my shoe.	Gosh.	5.
When I shook my foot to get rid of the ice cream, my shoe came off.	Why didn't you use a tissue?	6.
I hopped over to get it, and a dog picked it up and ran away.	I see.	7.
Stacy laughed at me.	Ignore her and see how she likes it.	8.
Then everyone started laughing at me.	How embarrassing.	9.
I thought Stacy was my best friend.	What are you going to do?	10.
But she did chase the dog and get my shoe.	Really?	11.
Yes. And it was kinda funny with me hopping around.	I don't see anything funny.	12.
At least it would have been if it was someone else.	Oh.	13.
Well, maybe I should phone Stacy and thank her for getting my shoe.	Forget her and find a new friend.	14.
Bye, Mom.	Bye.	15.

Answers: Odd numbers are simple listening. **2.** Judgment, **4.** Advice, **6.** Question, **8.** Advice, **10.** Question, **12.** Judgment, **14.** Advice

How to stay separate. Sometimes parents may be afraid that if they don't take control, their child will really botch things up. That may be true, or it may not. You won't know unless you let the child try. There are five things you can do to ease the challenge of remaining separate.

Use positive self-talk. When your child is having trouble, you can tell yourself, "He will ask for help when he wants it." Or, "I will give him time to figure this out himself."

Visualize success. Imagine him successfully dealing with the ups and downs of life. Feel how pleased you are. Notice what skills he is using to cope or what he might use. Whenever you feel scared for him, replace those feelings with the picture of success and pleasant feelings.

Make a plan. When you have a plan, it is easier to stay separate and wait. For example, you can say, "If he ____ [*behavior:* stomps into the kitchen when he gets home from school] for ____ [*length of time:* a week] I will ____ [*your action:* find a gentle way of asking him what is going on]. This way you can remain separate and give him a chance to respond without abandoning him.

Remember the proverb. It is helpful to remember that the learning process is full of bumps. There is a proverb that applies here—"Wisdom comes from experience. Experience comes from bad judgment."

Get help for yourself. If you have a lot of trouble remaining separate from your child, try counseling to discover why it is difficult for you to remain separate and to develop specific skills you need in order to change.

We have looked at the tool of ☆*Simple listening* from the **Acknowledge feelings** STAR Parenting point. As you have noticed, a theme for this tool is: "Leave the child in charge of his feelings." We will now look at the tool, ☆*Active listening.*

> *Wisdom comes from experience, experience comes from bad judgment.*

Acknowledge feelings point
☆*Active listening* tool

☆*Active listening* reflects both the feeling and the situation that has upset the child. No judgment. No questions. No solutions. ☆*Active listening* gives children a feelings vocabulary and helps them separate feelings from actions.

Think back to the beginning of the chapter where Aaron was upset in preschool. When Aaron's mom said, "You're disappointed you have to share me with all these people," she was using ☆*Active listening.* The idea is to name the feeling and the situation that bothers the child. You can see how this works in the table below.

Feeling	Situation
You're angry . . .	*. . . you need to come in now.*
You feel frustrated . . .	*. . . you can't balance the block way up on top.*
You're mad . . .	*. . . it's time to go to bed.*
You feel disappointed . . .	*. . . you can't go to the party with your brother.*
You feel bored . . .	*. . . practicing the math facts over and over again.*
You feel sad . . .	*. . . you weren't invited to your friend's party.*

It is helpful to reflect positive, happy feelings too. For example:

You're proud . . .	*. . . you dressed yourself this morning.*
You feel excited . . .	*. . . your grandma and grandpa are coming to visit.*
You look contented . . .	*. . . curled up in that blanket, reading a book.*
You're pleased . . .	*. . . you got an A on your math facts.*

How to use ☆*Active listening*

To use ☆*Active listening,* name the feelings, describe the situation that precipitated the feelings, and ignore the temptation to insert your feelings.

Use a variety of feeling words. When you label feelings, reflect a variety of feelings. Often parents use the same couple of words over and over—sad, mad, or frustrated. This shortcut sometimes masks the child's true feeling and makes it harder for her to identify it. Many psychologists and counselors believe that anger is a secondary feeling and masks another feeling, like fear or jealousy. As you experiment with active listening, you can gradually try different feeling words.

Avoid pseudo-feelings. For example, "You wish you didn't have to go to bed now" is not ☆*Active listening.* It does not reflect a feeling. *Hope, want,* and *wish* are not feeling words; they are pseudo-feelings, words that sound like feelings but are not. A simple test is to put the word in the sentence "I feel . . . " and see if it makes sense. For example, "I feel *happy*" makes sense, and "I feel *wish*" does not. To say "You wish you didn't have to go to bed now" is fine, it just isn't ☆*Active listening.*

Describe the precipitating problem succinctly. It is helpful to state why you think the child is happy, mad, or frustrated. Sometimes young children are unaware that their feelings are linked to anything. They may think the feeling springs into existence without reason. When they notice the same feelings in similar situations, they can begin to learn different strategies to handle the situation.

Avoid inserting your feelings. For example, when you say, "I'm sorry your balloon broke," you are talking about your feelings, not your child's. Even if you say, "I'm sorry you're upset that your balloon broke," your feelings are still dominant. It is better to simply say, "You're upset that your balloon broke." Then there is no confusion, and you allow the child to take full ownership of her feelings.

Avoid using thinking words when describing feelings. Some thinking words are: "I know," "I believe," "I understand." When you insert a thinking word, it again focuses the action on you, rather than on your child's feelings. For example, "I know you're sad that Forrest can't come over today" focuses on what the adult knows. "You're disappointed that Forrest can't come over" focuses on the child's feelings.

Comfortable and uncomfortable words

Happy	Angry
Curious	Annoyed
Dreamy	Depressed
Excited	Disappointed
Ambivalent	Embarrassed
Joyful	Furious
Pleased	Sad
Proud	Scared
Silly	Terrified
Welcome	Worried

Activity: 6–2: Practice ☆*Active listening*

Directions: Read the situation, and then guess the child's probable feeling and describe the reason as if you're talking to the child.

Situation	Probable feeling	Reason
Example: It is time to leave a friend's house, and your daughter announces she "Won't go."	You feel . . . *frustrated/ disappointed*	because . . . *you still want to play.*

1. 16-month-old son Adam does not want to get in his high chair. You are in a hurry and put him in anyway. He cries.	You feel . . .	because . . .
2. You are at a park and a big dog goes bounding over to your daughter, 4, who freezes.	You feel . . .	because . . .
3. Your 6-year-old son and 3-year-old daughter just finished building a tower using all the blocks. They are jumping up and down.	You feel . . .	because . . .
4. Your daughter is moping around because she was not chosen to be the princess in the class play.	You feel . . .	because . . .
5. Your son, 11, comes in bouncing up and down and tells you about the point he scored in the soccer game.	You feel . . .	because . ..

Possible answers: **1.** You feel *angry* because *you want to be on the floor.* **2.** You are *scared* because *the dog is so big.* **3.** You are *excited* because *the tower is so tall.* **4.** You're *disappointed* that you *didn't get the part you wanted.* **5.** Looks like you're *proud* that *you made the winning point.*

Common errors

There are several errors that people make when they intend to reflect the feeling with ☆*Active listening,* as you can see below.

Table 6–2: Examples of common ☆*Active listening* errors

Situation: Carla and her daughter, Heidi, were going for a walk. Suddenly, a dog started barking furiously and came running at them. He crashed into the fence that separated them. Carla and Heidi both jumped and Heidi began to cry. Quickly Carla took Heidi a safe distance from the fence and knelt beside her and said—

Error	Example of error	Cure
No feeling word	"You wish the dog didn't bark so loud."	*Insert feeling word.* "You're scared of the noisy dog."
Missing situation	"You're really scared. I can tell by how stiff your body is."	*Add the situation.* "The dog barking really scared you. Your body is stiff."
Parent's feelings	"I'm so sorry the dog scared you."	*Omit parent's feeling.* "The dog scared you."
Asking question	"Why are you crying? He's loud, but there's no need to be scared."	*Omit question. Reflect feeling and situation.* "You're scared of the noisy dog."

Solving the problem	"You're scared of the dog. I will hold you so you feel safe."	*Ask if child wishes help.* "You're scared of the dog. Would you like me to hold you so you feel safe?"
Giving advice	"Cover your ears, The dog won't seem so loud."	*Ask if an idea is wanted.* "Would you like an idea of how to reduce the noise?"

Common concerns

The following are some of the questions and concerns people have about acknowledging feelings.

I'm afraid I might not guess the right feeling. You don't need to worry about guessing the right feeling. In the beginning, children need to know that feelings have names and that they are different from actions. Young children are just beginning to develop a feelings vocabulary. When children begin to have a sense of their feelings, they will correct you if you are wrong (and sometimes even if you are right).

Should I acknowledge the feelings or the situation first? Either option is fine. "You're frustrated you can't tie your shoe," works as well as "You're having trouble tying your shoe and that's frustrating." Do whichever feels and sounds most natural to you.

Sometimes my kids object when I use active listening. Some teens and school-aged children don't like their parents to use active listening. The child or teen may snarl, "Don't say that," "No, I'm not," or look bored and roll her eyes. Three common reasons why this happens are the parent talks too much, particularly about feelings, the child feels that the adult is prying, and your response sounds strange.

Too much feeling talk. Some parents deliberately try to make feelings a "discussable" topic. It is important to acknowledge children's feelings; and like all the other tools, it can be overdone. You can counteract that tendency by monitoring how many times you talk about your feelings or theirs, and then cut the number in half or possibly a third.

Getting personal. When children are little, it is helpful to label their feelings, "You're upset Daddy has to go to work." However, as they grow older, they may feel patronized when you state what you think they are feeling. You can use distancing phrases like, "It seems to me," "It looks like," "I was wondering if," or "Some kids your age. . . . " If these strategies don't work then try ☆*Simple listening* or ☆*Grant in fantasy.*

Response may sound insincere. Sometimes when you try a new approach or learn a new skill you may sound awkward, phoney, or manipulative. This annoys some kids more than others, so it is helpful to acknowledge feelings with as much sincerity as you can muster. Also, if you feel very awkward, you can explain you are practicing a new skill and ask the children to be patient with you as you learn.

We have finished looking at ☆*Active listening* on the **Acknowledge feelings** STAR Parenting point. You can practice identifying errors in Activity 6–3. Then we will look at the tool of ☆*Grant in fantasy.*

Activity: 6–3: Correct ☆*Active listening* errors

Directions: Read each sentence below in which the parent is responding to Amy, who is upset.
Circle the feeling word,
Cross out any thinking words, and
Double **X** any adult thoughts or feelings.
If there were any errors, rewrite the statement in the space below.

Situation: Amy wants to play with the dump truck Megan is using. Amy asked to use it and Megan said, "No."

1. "I know you're disappointed Megan has the truck."

2. "You're frustrated you can't have the truck now."

3. "You wish Megan gave you the truck when you asked."

4. "I'm sorry you're upset."

5. "You really want that truck right now."

Possible answers: 1. I ~~know~~ you're (disappointed) Megan has the truck. *Know is a thinking word.* **2.** You're (frustrated) you can't have the truck now. *Okay.* **3.** You ~~wish~~ Megan gave you the truck when you asked. *Wish is not a feeling.* **4.** I'm so**XX**rry you're (upset). **5.** You really *want* that truck right now. *Want is not a feeling.*

Acknowledge feelings point
☆*Grant in fantasy* tool

☆*Grant in fantasy* is the third tool on the **Acknowledge feelings** point. It gives children in pretend what you cannot give them in reality. To do this, you need to tune in to the child's feelings and imagine how you might grant his wish. Jessica shares her experience with ☆*Grant in fantasy.*

We were driving to Grandma's. It was a three-hour drive, and we didn't have time to stop and cater to the kids' wishes. Ellie saw an ice cream store and wanted a cone. Instead of being "logical" and explaining yet again that we couldn't stop, I turned to pretend.

"Ellie," I said, "you want an ice cream cone? What if we could turn our car into an ice cream-making machine and ice cream shop? If we could, I would like a single scoop of pralines and cream on a sugar cone. What would you like? . . . What kind of cone? . . . How many scoops? . . . Do you want sprinkles on top? . . . Where would you like to eat it—a seat by the window or one by the ice cream machine?"

Soon her older brother piped in with his requests. We spent quite a bit of time making the "perfect ice cream cone" and planning how our car could be a tiny ice cream parlor. I was surprised that pretending satisfied the kids.

☆**Grant in fantasy can calm people down where logic may stir resentment.** When you tell children why they can't have what they want, they often feel as though they have been dismissed or discounted. When you offer them what they want in pretend, they feel heard. You have shared their feelings. You can see how easily Ryder was calmed.

My wife, Laura, worked an early evening shift at a nearby hospital, and I put the boys to bed each night. This particular evening, Ryder, 3½, wanted his mother.

I explained that Mom was working. She would kiss him good night when she got home and talk to him in the morning. The more I explained, the more agitated and emphatic he got. He wanted her now!

In desperation, I decided to try ☆Grant in fantasy, a tool I had learned the previous week in a STAR Parenting class. I didn't see how it could help, but I didn't think things could get any worse.

I made a large circle with my arms representing a crystal ball. Then I said, "Wouldn't it be fun if we had a big crystal ball and could watch Mommy at work?" I peered into the crystal ball and added, "Then when she was all alone I could stick my hand in and bring her home." I made the motion of putting my hand in the crystal ball and bringing Mom home as I spoke.

Much to my amazement Ryder gave a sigh and agreed, "Yes, I'd like that." Ten minutes of logic and coaxing did no good. Two minutes of pretend calmed him down.

Sometimes ☆*Grant in fantasy* can be wild and exaggerated in nature, as Marie's story demonstrates.

I was trying to give my boys a bath. Allen was upset because he wanted another action figure. I explained that this was bath time and he had enough action figures, but he only got madder. So I tried ☆Grant in fantasy.

"Allen, I wish I could give you the action figure you want. I wish I had five new action figures to give you. I wish I had ten action figures to give you. I wish I could drive a dump truck of action figures up and dump them in the tub with you. I wish I could take the roof off and fill the whole house with action figures for you!" By then, Allen was laughing and the bath continued pleasantly.

☆**Grant in fantasy**

Gives in pretend what you can't give in reality
• Affirms child's wishes
• Is clearly pretend
• Avoids power struggles

When you use ☆*Grant in fantasy,* you need to listen to the child and grant what the child wants, rather than what you might want in the same situation or what you think he should want. The grant can be as simple as an ice cream cone or as exaggerated as a spaceship full of action figures.

Use caution when making a ☆Grant in fantasy. Be sure the grant is clearly a fantasy. If you are driving down the street and your child sees an ice cream shop, and you say, "Wouldn't it be fun to have an ice cream cone? What flavor would you like?" your child is likely to think you have just agreed to buy an ice cream cone—because it is possible. However, if you say "Wouldn't it be fun if our car was an ice cream maker? And we had to eat really fast so we could see out the window?" that is clearly fantasy.

☆*Grant in fantasy* is a fun tool to try when kids are upset and you have no idea what to do. Just remember to make sure it is clearly fantasy and not taken as a put-down.

There are many benefits of acknowledging feelings. It lightens the mood. It increases a child's self-esteem by being listened to and not judged. It helps children develop a feelings vocabulary. It helps them separate feelings and behavior. It encourages them to respect their own feelings and others'. Finally, it lets children solve the situation themselves.

Activity: 6–4: Find errors in ☆*Grant in fantasy*

Directions: In each situation, decide whether there are any errors in the ☆*Grant in fantasy.* If so, describe the error.

1. Our son Griffin whined at meals all the time. It was so annoying I decided to respond differently and try ☆*Grant in fantasy.* When he whined, I said, "Wouldn't it be great if everyone whined all the time?"

☐ correct, ☐ error	What is wrong?

2. Natalie was jumping on the sofa. I asked her to please stop and she got very angry with me. I sat her down and said, "Hey, wouldn't it be fun if the entire living room was filled with couches—all sizes and colors, and we could jump and bounce from one to another all night? And if one broke we could keep on jumping because it would magically replace itself in a new color and shape?"

☐ correct, ☐ error	What is wrong?

3. Daniel remembered a toy he wanted. When I suggested that he put it on his birthday list, he got angry. I tried to respond with a ☆*Grant in fantasy:* "Wouldn't it be fun if we could go to the toy store and buy anything we wanted?"

☐ correct, ☐ error	What is wrong?

***Possible answers:* 1.** Error: Does not meet the child's need. It is unlikely that Griffin wanted to hear whining. **2.** Correct. It acknowledges the jumping and the magical fixing is clearly fantasy. **3.** Error: Not clearly fantasy. Many children believe their parents can buy anything they want.

Acknowledge feelings and set limits

Acknowledging feelings does not mean letting kids do anything they want. Feelings are okay, but sometimes how children express those feelings is not. If a child is angry and hurting people or things, the behavior needs to stop. Acknowledge the feeling and restate the limit. Use any of the phrases below:

Acknowledge feeling	Set limits
It's okay to be mad . . .	*. . . and you may not hit your sister. Find another way to tell her how mad you are.*
You feel really scared . . .	*. . . and you still have to go to the doctor.*
It's all right to be frustrated . . .	*. . . and not to disturb all of us. Find another way to be miserable.*

When you acknowledge feelings thinking can begin.

A note on "but" and "and." It is important to use "and" rather than "but." The word "but" erases or discounts the previous phrase, while "and" connects them and says they are *both* important. Say these two sentences to yourself and notice how different they feel.

"I love you, *but* you can't go."

"I love you, *and* you can't go."

In the first sentence, the dominant message is "You can't go." It is as though "I love you" were not there at all. In the second sentence both "the love" and "the limit" come through. A child may feel left behind, but not abandoned.

In this chapter, we have looked at three tools to *Acknowledge feelings:* ☆*Simple listening*, ☆*Active listening*, and ☆*Grant in fantasy*. When their feelings are acknowledged children can let go of the tension or move on and solve the problem. In the next chapter, the *Set reasonable limits* point, we will look at three tools to set boundaries and how to go about setting limits.

Summary of *Acknowledge Feelings*

★ **Ask yourself, "Who owns this problem?** Did I create the situation? Will the outcome affect me directly?" If your child owns the problem, give him or her support rather than judgment or advice.

★ **Separate your feelings from your child.** Remind yourself, "If I try to make my child happy, I will prevent him from developing the skills to make himself happy."

★ **Acknowledge the child's feelings.** Use ☆*Simple listening*, ☆*Active listening*, or ☆*Grant in fantasy*.

★ **Establish limits for unacceptable behavior.** Acknowledge feelings and follow with a clear limit. For example, "It's okay to be mad, and you may not draw on the wall."

Diana's "New" Clothes

Diana, 4½, recently received a large bag of "new" clothes for her to wear from Margie, a friend who is a little older than she. Most of the clothes in the bag consisted of shorts, tank tops, and little short-sleeved T-shirts.

The other night she had her Judo class. The Judo studio is extremely chilly these days with it being so cold outside in December. We are the only ones using the building at night, and we enter a very old and unheated building.

As we are getting ready to leave for her Judo class, Diana comes out with one of her new outfits, looking great if we were heading to the beach on a summer day, but way too underdressed for going out into the cold.

I told her she was going to be way too chilly in what she was wearing and that she would need to go back and find something warmer. She whined and began to cry and marched off with, "That's no fair—Margie gave me those clothes and now you won't let me wear them!"

S—Stop and focus

I took a deep breath and thought about how excited Diana was to get and wear these new clothes. However, I also wanted her to understand that the weather dictates what we can and cannot wear. I want her to be sensible and warm. She was more concerned about being fashionable. I had to come up with some good ideas fast!

T—Think of ideas

I decided to think of an idea for each point of the star.

Avoid problems

I started out thinking I could have avoided the problem by sorting through the clothes earlier and putting the ones away that were for summer.

Acknowledge feelings

I could try, "You're disappointed because you want to wear Margie's clothes."

Teach new skills

I could have taught her a new skill by sending her out into the backyard to stay for one minute in what she was wearing so she would see for herself that she was not dressed appropriately.

Respond to cooperation

I could praise her cooperation if she changed her clothes, "You are now dressed for December. Thank you for cooperating so quickly."

Set limits

I could try ☆*A better way*. For example, "My way is that you wear something that keeps you warm because it is cold outside and it will be cold at Judo. Your way is to wear the summery outfit. What is a better way that will make both of us happy?"

A—Act effectively

I was unsure what would work so I decided to acknowledge her feelings and then set a negotiable limit.

First I acknowledged her feelings by ☆*Active listening*, "You are disappointed because you want to wear Margie's clothes." She quieted a bit, but declined to change her clothes. However, at least Diana was listening now.

Then I tried ☆*A better way*. "My way is that you wear something that keeps you warm because it is cold outside and it will be cold at Judo. Your way is to wear the summery outfit. What is a better way that will make both of us happy?" Without saying anything, she stomped upstairs.

She came down with some jeans and a long sleeved shirt. I rewarded her cooperation by telling her I was really

---

1 There is a STAR in Action Story at the end of each chapter. Each story is written by a parent in his or her own words and shows how that person adapted the STAR Parenting process to his or her own life.

These stories use tools from all points, so some may be unfamiliar until you have read the appropriate chapter. You can see how different parents, with different values or kids with different temperaments, might make different choices.

proud of her for making a wise choice (☆*Praise*). I then let her pick out her snack to eat on the way to Judo.

~~~~~~

R—Review and revise

The problem was solved with a minimum of hassle—she dressed appropriately. Acknowledging her feelings set the stage so she could respond to ☆*A better way*. I wish she had gone upstairs pleasantly to change or responded pleasantly to begin with. I guess that is work for another day. But I am really, really glad we resolved the situation without a major confrontation.

Chapter 7

Set Reasonable Limits

*Clear, reasonable boundaries keep
kids safe and increase self-esteem*

There are three tools on the **Set reasonable limits** point of STAR Parenting—
☆*Clear rules,* ☆*Consequences,* and ☆*A better way.* These describe how to set
reasonable limits, but first lets's discuss the nature of rules and the reason to
have them.

*Three-year-old Evan was enjoying playing on the sofa of his friend Anders's
house. Evan ignored his mother's hints that it was time to go. Trying to get him to
leave, his mother said, "It's time to go. I'm leaving. Do you want to come with me,
or do you want to stay here?" Evan continued to play.*

*Anders's dad went over to Evan and said, "Evan, that's not your choice. Your
choice is, 'Do you want to walk to the car, or do you want me to carry you?'"*

*Evan looked up at Anders's dad, as though he were judging the likelihood that
he would really carry him out. After a moment, he pronounced, "Walk."*

Some rules are clear and helpful. Others are vague or demoralizing. Effective limits are clear, immediate, a true choice, and dependable. In the story above, Evan had learned to discount his mom's rules because she did not follow through with action.

Why have rules and limits, anyway?

Rules and limits provide a stabilizing force in any group. Some people are afraid that rules will limit their child's creativity or damage their psyche. The opposite seems to be the case. Several reasons are listed below.

Rules keep kids safe. Some familiar safety rules are: "Don't run in the street." "Don't stick things in the electrical sockets." "Don't go with strangers." The rules are a mental shortcut. If the child has to stop and evaluate every single action he might take, he won't have time for much else.

Rules help kids feel secure. When kids have an open area to play in, they stay away from the edges. When there are boundaries such as a fence or bushes, kids use the whole defined area.

One way I explain this to parents in Seattle is to ask them to think of our floating bridge. It is 1.4 miles long with two lanes each way and a fence on each side. People barrel across the bride at 60 mph. Next, I ask parents to imagine that the bridge is exactly the same, except that there is no fence on either side. People usually shudder. When I ask,"Do you feel safe?" the answer is always "No." So knowing that the boundaries are there makes people feel safe, even though they may never test their effectiveness. Similarly, your child feels safer when he or she knows you are in charge and will consistently provide the "fence."

When I ask parents how they would feel if the bridge's fence were six inches or a foot from the side of the car, they frown and say it would feel oppressive or threatening, and hard to move. So reasonable rules (limits that are present, but not rigid) help children feel safe. Unreasonable or too strict rules stifle them.

Rules model how to say "No." As children grow, they have many opportunities to do mean, stupid, or dangerous things. When you set boundaries, you model how they can say "No" to their peers when asked to shoplift, do drugs, engage in sex, or steal. Kids do not spank or ground their friends, so when you set respectful limits, it shows them how to set boundaries for others.

Rules clarify society's expectations. "Don't take things that belong to someone else; don't steal; don't borrow without permission." "Don't enter homes (or yards) without permission." "Don't touch people without permission." "Drive on the right side of the road." "Wear clothes in public." There are many subtle rules on how to conduct yourself around others. There is a story I want to share to illustrate society's expectations.

Carol was raising her grandson. He had lived unsupervised in a drug house for three years before he came to live with her. One day, they were walking in a hilly park. Tyler, her 3½-year-old grandson, saw a family eating a picnic, complete with watermelon, on the side of the hill a little above him. He broke away from Carol, ran up the hill to the family, grabbed a piece of watermelon, and tore back down the hill to Grandma. Tyler's behavior made sense in the setting where he had lived—the only way to get anything was to take it. However, he now needs to learn that in the rest of society, wanting something does not justify taking it.

Healthy and unhealthy limits

We mentioned that reasonable limits help children feel secure and too strict limits suppress them. Kids need reasonable limits, but not all limits are healthy. The clearest way I know to explain the difference is with the "Limit Line" developed by Jean Illsley Clarke. The limit line is a continuum describing six types of rules—four unhealthy and two healthy.

Limit Line					
Rigid	*Critical*	*Non-negotiable*	*Negotiable*	*Indulgent*	*Absent*

Rigid rules do not change. They are cast in concrete. They do not adapt with new information or changing circumstances. The adult believes that following the rules is more important than anything else.

The message children may get is "You are unimportant," "Don't think," or "If you make a mistake, I will abandon you."

Critical rules label a person as bad, rather than setting a clear standard of behavior. Adults create rules that belittle, negate a child, or exaggerate the child's faults. They tell the child how to fail.

Children may hear "You are bad," "Don't be capable or successful," or "You are not lovable."

Non-negotiable rules clearly state requirements on behavior and must be adhered to. Children know there are rewards when they follow the rules and consequences when they don't. However, even though the rules are non-negotiable, they can be revised when circumstances change, particularly when the welfare of family members depends on it.

The message children may hear is "Your safety and welfare are important to me. I am willing and able to be in charge."

Negotiable rules are negotiated and then consistently enforced. They teach children to think clearly and solve problems. They also state requirements clearly and must be adhered to.

Children may think, initiate ideas, and negotiate. Children may get the message that "Your needs are important and other people's needs are important too."

Indulgent rules grant freedom without requiring responsibility. These marshmallowing rules may sound sweet to the child, but have no substance. They sound kind, but imply that the child cannot, or does not need to comply.

Children may hear "Don't be responsible," "I expect you to fail," "You can have your way, be obnoxious, and still get along okay," or "I need to continue taking care of you. My needs are more important than your need to grow."

Absent rules are no rules. The adult is not available to the child for rules, protection, or contact. The adult may be gone, ill, on drugs, too busy, or mentally and emotionally absent.

Children may conclude the parent is not willing to care for them. Their needs are not important to the parent. They may conclude that if they are to survive, they must do everything for themselves as Carol's grandson, Tyler, concluded.

Practice identifying the six types of rules in Activity 7–1.

Activity 7–1: Sequence the limit line

Directions: Unscramble the responses for the candy consumption limit line below. Place the letter of the statement that best illustrates each step in the correct box below the limit line.

Rigid	Critical	Non-negotiable	Negotiable	Indulgent	Absent
A. Candy is always available. No rules.	**B.** Grandma usually brings sweets when she comes. You may have one piece after each meal.	**C.** Why, you little sneak! You know you're not supposed to have candy. I'll bet you stole it.	**D.** You sure like candy. I guess there is no point trying to restrict your sweets.	**E.** No candy. It is bad for you. End of discussion.	**F.** You love candy. I don't want you to eat candy. What's something that works for both of us?

Answers: **A**—Absent, **B**—Non-negotiable, **C**—Critical, **D**—Indulgent, **E**— Rigid, and **F**—Negotiable. Correct order:

Rigid	Critical	Non-negotiable	Negotiable	Indulgent	Absent
E	C	B	F	D	A
No candy. It is bad for you. End of discussion.	Why, you little sneak! You know you're not supposed to have candy. I'll bet you stole it.	Grandma usually brings sweets when she comes. You may have one piece after each meal.	You love candy. I don't want you to eat candy. What's something that works for both of us?	You sure like candy. I guess there is no point in trying to restrict your sweets.	Candy always available. No rules.

As you have no doubt determined, the healthy rules are non-negotiable and negotiable rules. The unhealthy rules are rigid, critical, indulgent, and absent. The healthy rules encourage kids to feel lovable and capable. The unhealthy rules encourage incompetence, dependence, and a sense of being unlovable.

Table 7–1: Healthy and unhealthy limits—"Limit Line"

Rigid	Critical	Non-negotiable	Negotiable	Indulgent	Absent
Once made, rigid rules do not change. They do not adapt with new information or changing circumstances.	The rules label the child as bad, rather than setting a clear standard for behavior. They tell the child how to fail.	Rules clearly state requirements for behavior and must be adhered to. Non-negotiable rules can be rewritten when circumstances change.	These rules are negotiated, clearly stated, and then consistently enforced. They teach children to think clearly and solve problems.	Indulgent rules grant freedom without requiring responsibility. They sound nice but imply that the child does not need to comply.	Absent has no rules. The adult is not available to the child for rules, protection, or contact.

The message children may get is—					
You are unimportant. Don't think. If you make a mistake, I will abandon you.	You are bad. Don't be capable or successful. You are not lovable.	Your safety and welfare are important to me. I am willing and able to be in charge.	You may initiate ideas and negotiate. Your needs are important and other people's needs are important too.	I expect you to fail. You can have your way and be obnoxious. I need to take care of you. My needs are more important than yours.	I'm not willing to care for you. Your needs are not important to me. If you are to survive, you must do everything for yourself.

Table 7–2: Examples of six types of rules

Rigid	Critical	Non-negotiable	Negotiable	Indulgent	Absent
Drugs: If you use drugs again, don't bother coming home.	You are always doing something stupid. Now you're using drugs. Just like my brother. You know what a failure he is.	You may not use drugs until you are of legal age and responsible for your own decisions. If you do, the consequence will be . . .	You may find yourself where other kids use drugs. If you do, find different activities so you don't spend your free time with them.	Drugs aren't good for you, but all kids use drugs sometimes. I guess it is unreasonable to expect you to decline.	I don't want to talk about it.
Homework: You must do your homework immediately after school. If you goof off once, I'll send you to the farm. Uncle Nick will teach you discipline.	You should do your homework. But you are too stupid to know what to do. You're just like Aunt Martha.	Schoolwork is important. You must finish your homework before you do anything else.	Schoolwork is important. You must complete it each day. If you don't want to do it immediately after school, we can make a plan for how to get it done.	You should be doing your homework right now, but I guess it is too much to expect.	Do what you want. I don't care.
Toilet training: You must poop in the potty every day. If you don't, I'll give you a medicine to make you poop.	You're such a baby. You're not smart enough to poop in the potty. You'll graduate from school wearing a diaper.	Poop belongs in the potty. You can poop in the potty, or poop in your diaper and then empty it into the toilet.	Poop belongs in the potty. Tell me how I can help you and I will.	Poop belongs in the potty, but I guess you are too young for me to expect that.	I don't care where you go. Just leave me alone.

The Limit Line helps you look at the messages or conclusions children may draw from your rules. How you phrase your rules will influence how seriously children take them. This is explained in the language of limits.

Language of limits

Sometimes parents sabotage themselves by how they tell the child what they expect.

It is helpful to distinguish between requests, rules, questions, and commands.

Rules vs. wishes (requests). Sometimes we tell kids things that we wish them to do, but are not willing to stop what we are doing to enforce. If parents don't put in the energy to encourage compliance, it is unreasonable to expect kids to put in the energy to cooperate. Wishing for compliance is understandable, but you are unlikely to get it unless you work for it.

Questions vs. non-questions. "It's time to go the doctor. Do you want to put your coat on?" Most grown-ups recognize this as a polite way of saying, "Put your coat on," however, young children are literal, and they assume you are asking for their opinion. If the child says, "No" and the parent says, "We are going, so put it on anyway," then the child learns that his opinion doesn't matter. If you wish to teach your child to make good decisions, then you need to respect his choice if you ask for it.

Ask a question only when you are willing to take "No" as an answer. I remember learning this when my kids were little. When my son said, "No," I would reply with, "Then we will go in a minute." Gradually, I learned to think before I spoke, and only ask "yes" or "no" questions if I was willing to accept either answer.

Commands vs. requests. "Take the trash out." Is that a request as in, "Please, take the trash out," or a command as in, "Take the trash out NOW," or somewhere in between? If you have a child who is a natural pleaser, you are usually home free. She will hear a request and willingly comply. However, with other children you need to signal to them what your expectations are. If you want them to have a choice, then accept their decision without trying to change it. Don't say, "Are you sure you want to . . . ? You will miss . . . if you do." If you want compliance, then state what you want clearly.

Commands vs. rules. Commands tend to be one time "do it now" statements: "Take off your shoes. They are muddy." Rules are principles that govern ongoing behavior. "Take your shoes off," becomes the rule "We leave our shoes by the front door in our house."

Sometimes several commands or small rules can lead to a principle rule. For example, hold my hand in a parking lot, look both ways before crossing the street, point knives and sharp items away from you, leave rocks on the ground (not in your mouth), stand back from the oven when it is hot—all these can be grouped into a principle rule such as "Act safely" or "Act wisely."

How do you distinguish between rules, requests, and wishes? Parents I work with agree that there is a difference between things children must do (rules), things they want children to do but do not enforce regularly (requests), and things they would like their children to do but don't enforce at all (wishes). The challenge becomes clarifying how to distinguish among them.

> *Ask a question only when you are willing to take "No" as an answer.*

Table 7–3: Rules, requests, and wishes

Rule	Request	Wish
Expects compliance	Implies a choice	Is a vague desire
Very important, really matters	Kind of important, sort of matters	Unclear whether or not it matters

Adult *works* to assure the child's compliance	Adult *hopes* for the child to cooperate	Adult *dreams* about possible cooperation
Tells the child to . . . , and assists the young child to comply or gives older kids a consequence for failure to comply	Asks the child to . . . , but does not always require compliance (sometimes lacks follow-through)	Occasionally asks the child to . . . , but rarely, if ever, expects compliance
Firm or strong tone (not mean, angry)	Polite or casual tone	Uncertain, vague or disconnected tone
Stop what you are doing, go to the child, get on their level, make eye contact*, speak clearly	May speak from across the room as passing through or while doing something else	Statements rarely directed toward child
Uses direct statement. • *It is time to put your coat on.* • *Put your coat on now.* If the child doesn't comply, the adult assists him. For example, "Do you want to do it yourself or do you want me to help you?" Helps the child if he doesn't put the coat on.	Uses "please," questions, preferences, "Okay?" • *Put your coat on, please.* • *Do you want to put your coat on?* • *Put your coat on, okay?* • *I would like it if you put your coat on.*	Uses "hope," or vague statements. • *I sure hope you will put your coat on.* • *It would be nice if you put your coat on soon.* • *I wish you would put your coat on before it gets real late.*

*Some children have trouble looking at someone and listening to them. For others, eye contact is not culturally appropriate.

How kids learn limits

Children learn limits the way they learn many things—first from the outside (parent supplies the action), then from internal control (child initiates the action or restraint). This is how they learn language, to walk, or to bounce a ball. When children are little, they have neither an understanding of what the rule means, nor the self-restraint to do what is required. With practice and assistance, they develop the self-control.

"Assisted compliance" fosters self-restraint. In the beginning, children have neither understanding of what the rule means nor any self-restraint. For example, if you make a rule, "Hold a grown-up's hand in a parking lot," the child must identify that this is a parking lot and wait for a hand to hold. If the child moves away without a hand, then take his hand and remind him that we hold hands in the parking lot.

Consistency speeds learning. The closer together two events happen, the easier it is for kids to notice the connection between them and learn what you want them to do. This is why most children quickly learn to be wary of a hot stove once they have touched it—the feedback is instantaneous. It is easy for children to connect the two events. The longer the gap between the action and the response (consequence), the harder it is for kids to connect them. If the consequence happens sometimes and not other times, it is also difficult for the child to know when he may do as he wishes and when he must comply.

Repetition solidifies learning. The number of times an adult has to repeat a statement or action depends on the child's temperament and experience. If a child is a pleaser, one statement may be enough. However, for most children parents need to pair words and action fifty to five hundred times. Inconsistency increases the number of repetitions needed, as does a child's persistent temperament. The need for consistent repetition is illustrated by Anwen's story below.

My son, Crandell, was (and is still) very persistent. When he was a toddler, he liked cars and he liked to bang them. He would bang his car on the table, the floor, the walls, the bookshelf. We had the rule, "Cars drive on the floor," however, he continued to explore the rule. He would bang morning, noon, and night. He would bang when I was with him and with my husband when he came home.

We continually redirected the play with the car or removed the car. He was a scientist, testing all variations on the banging theme. Fortunately, as he grew older he didn't need to check all rules and was satisfied with fewer repetitions. I am glad I was able to be consistent and kind, because he is now in graduate school and his persistence is paying off.

We have considered why we need limits, the language of limits, and how kids learn limits. Next, we will look at the three tools on this ***Set reasonable limits*** point of the STAR: ☆*Clear rules*, ☆*Consequences*, and ☆*A better way*.

Set reasonable limits point
☆*Clear rules* tool

The first tool in setting reasonable limits is a ☆*Clear rule*. Without clear rules that a child understands, limits may feel unreasonable and punitive.

Characteristics of clear rules

Clear rules are positive statements. They tell children what to do rather than what not to do. "Don't run" becomes "Walk." This is important because the mind cannot make a picture of "no" as in "no running." The first picture that comes to mind is running.

A linguist once said that eighty-five percent of adults will see the unwanted thing or action. So, when you say "No running. No running. No running. How many times must I tell you 'no running,'" the picture that comes to the child's mind is run, run, run, run. It is a little like the joke, "Don't think of a polar bear." The first image to flash into the mind is a polar bear!

Child guidance will be simpler if you stop and think of what you *want the child to do* instead of telling her to stop what she is doing. You might listen to yourself and make a list of the statements that begin: no, stop, don't, avoid, never, or quit.

Try rewriting them as positive statements. Here are some ideas to get you started.

Stop whining ➜	Talk pleasantly
No hitting ➜	Touch gently
Don't play with matches ➜	Bring me the matches
Don't leave the door open ➜	Close the door
Don't throw food ➜	Eat your food
Don't drop your pjs on the floor ➜	Put your pjs in the hamper

Occasionally, a parent will complain that it is hard to think of what to say that is not negative. While it is hard to find the positive statements in the beginning, it does get easier with practice. It seems unreasonable to expect children to think of what to do if an adult has trouble describing an alternative action!

The importance of stating positive limits was illustrated once by a student in a parenting class. Belinda reported that her delightful 20-month-old toddler had become a monster. "We're telling her 'No,' all the time. And she just does it anyway. I want my nice girl back. Any ideas?"

Before I could frame an answer, Belinda said, "I know what you're going to tell me." I looked at her questioningly. She said, "You are going to tell me to tell her what to do rather than saying 'No' all the time." I responded that that was a good place to begin. Two weeks later when I saw her next, she smiled proudly and said, "I've got my darling daughter back."

Clear rules are short. Short rules are easier to understand. The longer the rule, the more time and effort it takes for the child to figure out what part is important. Ask someone to read the sentences in the box "How many words does it take to convey an idea?" and see where the understanding becomes easier.

One guideline for short rules with young children is to use one word for each year of age. For example, with an 11-month-old use one word like "stop," "come," or "gentle." For a 20-month-old use two words, "come here," or "touch gently."

With older children, five or six words seem to be enough to get rules and requests across. "Bedtime is at eight o'clock." "Leave your shoes by the door." "Do homework before free time or TV."

The one-word-per-year-of-age guideline only applies to rules and points you want to emphasize. Babies and toddlers benefit from hearing longer and more complex sentences describing the world around them—it is how they pick up language.

Clear rules are appropriate for the child's age and temperament. It is not reasonable to expect a toddler to leave interesting items alone, or for an active 4-year-old to sit still at your friend's house and wait for you. Nor is it realistic to expect an 8- to 10-year-old to practice her instrument every day without attention or encouragement from an adult.

Young children are egocentric. Young children think the world revolves around them. When walking one evening, 4-year-old Tony announced, "The moon is following me." What this means for setting limits is that while some young children may understand rules when safety and cost are involved, few understand parental preference or convenience. They don't understand why you want them to get dressed. They operate as though what they want is all there is, even though they hear your words. This is why consistency and assisted compliance are so important.

How many words does it take to convey an idea?

Mommy wants you to stand beside her.

Stop fooling around and come here.

Get your butt over here.

Come here right now.

Please come here.

Come here.

Come.

Rules can change with age. For example, the toddler rule "Hold my hand in the parking lot" may change to "Walk beside me in the parking lot" for primary kids and "Stay alert in parking lots" for older school-age children. It may help to periodically review your rules and see if they need to be updated. You could do that on the child's birthday, the end of school, or the beginning of the year.

Some children object when older siblings have different rules. You can tie the rule to age or to ability of the child. When my kids were young, we had a tree outside that was fun to climb. We had the rule that to climb the tree, you had to be able to get in it all by yourself. This restricted the tree to kids who were tall enough to physically climb up and get down by themselves.

Rules can be negotiable or non-negotiable. Non-negotiable rules have no exception. Safety issues are not negotiable, such as, "Leave sharp knives alone," or "Wear your seat belt in the car." However, negotiable rules have exceptions occasionally. If bedtime is 7:30 P.M., your child might be permitted to stay up to 8:00 P.M. to greet a family friend or see a TV special. This flexibility allows you to adapt a rule as needed to increase options or extend privileges.

Rules are a bit like traffic lights. Some behaviors are never acceptable—red light rules. Some behaviors are always okay—green light rules. And some behaviors are okay sometimes and not other times—yellow light rules.

How to present rules and requests

For toddlers, actions speak louder than words. They are still learning self-restraint. They learn what rules mean by what you *do,* rather than what you say. However, eventually, if you are predictable, children develop some self-restraint. When children comply with verbal statements without assistance, you have entered a new era.

When compliance or cooperation is important, take the time to engage the child before saying what you want. Sometimes parents rush through the room saying, "Dinner-is-almost-ready. Put-away-your-toys-and-wash-your-hands," before the child has had time to switch his focus to the parent. The child may say, "Uh huh," but no communication has taken place.

Instead, get your child's attention, state your expectation clearly, and then check understanding.

Get attention. Go to the child, get down on her level, say her name, and look at her. Ask her to stop what she is doing and look at you if it helps. (Some children can either look *or* listen. For others, eye contact is not culturally appropriate.)

Explain clearly. Tell the child what is expected, including the time frame. Be both clear and succinct. "Get dressed, including your shoes and socks on, before eight o'clock." You may ask if help is needed. "Do you need any help choosing clothes or dressing today?" Sometimes you may want to add the consequence of compliance and noncompliance. "If you are ready on time today, you may watch televison while dressing tomorrow. If you are not ready by eight o'clock, you will need to finish dressing before watching television tomorrow."

Check understanding. Nine times out of ten, if you ask a child "Do you understand?" he will say "Yes" or "Uh huh" so another approach is needed. Instead, ask the child, "What do I want you to do?" and let him explain in his words. Then you can add, "What will happen when you're dressed on time?" and then, "What will happen if you're not dressed on time?" It may seem strange but children can say the rule without really understanding the rule, as José discovered.

Rules can be negotiable or non-negotiable.

We have a rule in our house that your room must be neat before you can have a friend visit. We consider this a safety issue as we don't want a guest to trip on a toy and hurt himself as one of our boys did.

Diego, our 8-year-old, asked if his friend Marco could come over and play. I said sure as long as your room is neat. Then, remembering that Diego has been dawdling a lot recently, I asked, "What will happen if Marco gets here and you're not done cleaning?"

"I don't know," he answered. José was surprised. Diego had been able to state the rule for three years, yet he didn't really understand it.

José explained, "Your room must be clear before he comes in the house. So if you're not finished, he will need to wait outside on the steps until you're done."

Activity 7–2: Make clear rules

Directions: Read the statement on the left. Identify the error and rewrite it to be an effective rule.

Example: [To a toddler] Don't get wet in that puddle.	☑ Negative, ☐ long, ☐ not age appropriate *Walk beside me.*
1. Stop pouring juice on your tray.	☐ Negative, ☐ long, ☐ not age appropriate
2. Remember to take your raincoat today because the weatherman said it might rain, and rain will cause your curls to wilt.	☐ Negative, ☐ long, ☐ not age appropriate
3. Don't leave your coat on the floor.	☐ Negative, ☐ long, ☐ not age appropriate
4. [To 30-month-old] Remember to feed the rabbit.	☐ Negative, ☐ long, ☐ not age appropriate
5. You can't go to the park if your room is a mess.	☐ Negative, ☐ long, ☐ not age appropriate
6. Don't throw balls inside the house.	☐ Negative, ☐ long, ☐ not age appropriate

Possible answers: **1.** Negative. Drink your juice. **2.** Too long. Dress for the weather. **3.** Negative. Hang your coat up when you come in. **4.** Not age appropriate. Wait several years. **5.** Negative. Work before play. Or, Room clean when we go to the park. **6.** Negative. Roll balls inside.

Family rules

In the ideal world, parents will have rules that they expect kids to follow and requests that kids may answer yes or no to, and the differences are clear. The real world is rarely that simple. Parents have primary rules that are extremely important that they always enforce, and secondary rules that are important and usually, but not always, enforced. There are also some pseudo-rules that parents desire but rarely enforce. Examples of these are listed in the table below.

Table 7–4: Rules and pseudo-rules

Primary rule	*Secondary rule*	*Pseudo-rule*
Extremely important, always enforced	Important, usually enforced	Desired, irregularly enforced
Possible examples		
• Touch gently • Wear a seat belt • Wash hands before eating	• Walk inside • Use inside voice • Say "please" and "thank you"	• Put toys away when asked • Get dressed the first time I ask • [To teen] Lights out at 10 P.M.

List the rules in your home. The clearer you are about what is really important to you, the easier it is to convey that information to children. You might begin by listing what is important. Keep a mental or paper log for several days to note what you say.

Review your family rules and note whether they are (1) positive—tell child what *to do,* (2) short—one word per year of age, but not more than seven, (3) age appropriate, and (4) enforced. If needed, rewrite any of your rules so they are positive, short, age-appropriate, and enforceable. You can use the exercise below or invent your own format.

Different families have different rules. I hope your rules reflect your values. It's worth checking and revising rules that don't reflect your values. Sometimes we have a rule because our parents had it, or because we think we should. Since different families have different values, they will have different rules too. It is often helpful to post the family rules, so that family members can be reminded of the house rules and so that guests can refer to them. Some people like to post them on the refrigerator, others on the back of the front door.

Activity 7–3: Consider family rules

Directions: Read each statement below. Decide if it is a rule you want for your family and how important it is—will you enforce it?	**Very important** *Always enforced*	**Important** *Usually enforced*	**Pseudo-rule** *Requested, but not enforced*	**Not a rule** *Not requested*
• Touch gently				
• Wear a seat belt				
• Wash hands before eating				
• Walk inside				

• Use inside voice				
• Say "please" and "thank you"				
• Put toys away when asked				
• Get dressed when asked the first time				
• Do homework before free time				
• Speak kindly/ respectfully to siblings and others				
• Ask before touching other people's belongings				
• Take care of your body—teeth, healthy food, sleep, etc.				

We have looked at the characteristics of ☆*Clear rules*. They are positive, short, age appropriate, and enforceable. We've seen how to present them. Next, we will look at ☆*Consequences*.

Set reasonable limits point
☆*Consequences* tool

The second tool on the **Set reasonable limits** point is ☆*Consequences*. When you have a rule, you need a consequence so children can find out what will happen if they ignore the rule. Children need to practice making decisions, and that will only happen if the consequences are reasonable and predictable. A consequence can be simply stepping back and letting the child find out what happens naturally, or planned, by stepping in to make something happen by design. Planned consequences will be meaningful to the child, just as natural ones are.

Types of consequences
There are two types of consequences—natural consequences and logical consequences. Natural consequences happen without adult involvement; logical consequences are planned.

Natural consequences let the child experience the results of his or her action. If she declines to tie a balloon on her wrist and then lets go, the balloon will fly away. It takes no effort from the adults to provide the consequence.

When you resist the temptation to rescue a child and let her experience disappointment, she can learn from her decision. In this case it's deciding not to tie the balloon on her wrist. If you solve her problem by buying her a new balloon, she learns to be dependent on others to solve her problems, rather than learning to think for herself.

Natural consequences are a powerful teaching tool. The drawback is that the results can be slow, erratic, or very serious. For example, a simple consequence might be "If you don't bring your hammer inside, it will rust," or, "If you continue to bend your walkie-talkie antenna, it will break." These are true consequences, and can be very good learning situations; however, they may take a long while to happen as the hammer won't rust overnight, nor will the antenna break off the first time it is bent.

A natural consequence may be very dangerous. For example, parents often warn children, "Don't run/play in the street, or you will get hit/hurt." When children check out this statement by going in the street, they are very rarely hurt. So kids often conclude that their parents are wrong, and that they can safely disregard them. Even when they are hit, they may discount the experience as a fluke as Adam did below.

Adam, 3, was drawn to the street and had been since he could walk. His parents continually reminded him to wait at the curb and take a grown-up's hand before stepping in the street, but he gravitated to the street. They even put a garbage bag full of trash in the street and ran over the bag with their car, but the demonstration had no impact.

Eventually, Adam was hit. He spent six weeks recovering in the hospital and at home. When he could move about outside on his own, the first thing he did was go into the street again. When he was questioned why he went back into the street, it appeared Adam believed that the injury was indeed a fluke and would not happen again.

Sometimes the simple natural consequence is too dangerous or inconsistent. In those cases, you can use a "logical" consequence.

Logical consequences are created by the adult and need follow-through. Logical consequences are most effective when they are immediate, related to the behavior, a true choice, and low energy.

Immediate. Making the connection between a child's behavior and the result is easier if the events are close in time. For example, when a child closes his finger in a door, he immediately hurts. It is easy to connect the pain with the door. If a child tries again, he will get the same result. However, if the child touched the door today and he didn't feel hurt until the evening or next day, it would be difficult to connect the events.

Related. When a parent provides a consequence that is related to the behavior, it feels more instructive and less punitive. "No dinner, no TV," is not related. However, "If you're not *hungry* enough for dinner, you're not *hungry* enough for dessert," is related. Finding consequences that are related takes effort, and it gets easier with practice. Making rules with related consequences is both easier and more important for ages 3 and older.

If you have trouble getting started thinking of consequences, Shari Steelsmith provides natural and logical consequences for more than fifty common misbehaviors

Logical consequences are immediate, related, a true choice, and low energy.

in her book, *Go to Your Room, Consequences That Teach.*

True choice. This means two things—first, that the child may choose the unwanted behavior with the consequence, and, second, that if he does the unwanted behavior, the parent will follow through with the consequence.

Before you state a consequence, be sure both parts of the choice are acceptable to you. You might want to modify, "If you don't pick up your toys, I will throw them away," to "If you don't pick up your toys, I will bag them for a week." Remember if you fail to follow through with a consequence, it loses its effectiveness.

Amanda came up to me after a talk to ask for help. She was having a tough time with her kids, ages 4, 7, 10. She told me that the house was a mess and the kids didn't listen to anything she said. She related that finally, in desperation, she told them if they didn't pick up their toys she would throw the toys away.

"Did they pick them up?" I asked.

She answered, "No."

Then I asked if she threw the toys away.

She said, "No."

I asked her if she had an idea what might be the problem. She looked puzzled and then said, "They don't believe me anymore." And she asked, "What can I do?"

We talked a bit and came up with several ideas. She left with a purposeful stride. I met her again in a parking lot about a month later. I asked how it went and she said, "Terrific."

She told her kids to put away their toys and said she would bag any toys that were left out and put them away for a week. The first night, she got a full black plastic bag of toys. The second night, she got another bag full of toys. The third night she got half a bag, and the fourth night, just a couple of toys.

I asked Amanda what she thought accounted for the change. "Well," she said with a grin. "Two things. First, I have become believable. And second, for a while they had a lot fewer toys."

Low energy. When your child disregards a rule, provide the consequence with minimal interactions. Often when a child disobeys a rule, the parent gets angry and goes on and on. Instead, calmly state, "I see you choose . . . " and let it go at that. When you go on and on, the child has to build an emotional shield to protect himself from your anger, so he is not learning what you wish. This was Eleanor's experience with her son.

*When my son Brendan was a toddler he loved to splash in the water puddles. He would get all wet and soggy. I would pick him up and take him home, ranting about his behavior the whole way. "I can't believe you splashed in the water **again!** You know what that means—we have to go home and change your clothes. If you just walked around the puddle like a nice boy we could both be outside, but no-o-o, you have to splash in the puddle so we have to go home and change your clothes. By the time we get back, if we do go back at all, there won't be anyone to play with." The more I talked, the less good it did.*

Fortunately, I enrolled in a parenting class where I learned the value of brevity. When we went out, I would remind him once, "Walk around the puddles." When he stepped in a puddle I would say, "I see you choose to go home and change clothes." He would cry and yell, but I would say nothing else. Interestingly, the less I talked, the more he learned. It was like all his energy went to defending himself

> *If you fail to follow through with a consequence, it loses its effectiveness*

from my tirade, so he had no energy left for learning. When he didn't need to defend himself from my anger, he could concentrate on learning what he needed to learn. Truly, less is more.

Effective consequences are immediate, related, a true choice, and low energy. Practice identifying and creating consequences in the activity below.

Activity 7–4: Identify natural and logical consequences

Directions: Read the behavior, then read a consequence and decide if it is a natural consequence or a logical consequence.

Behavior	Consequence	Natural	Logical
1. Throws food	A. Is put down from the table because he is done eating	☐	☐
	B. Has no food left, may get hungry	☐	☐
2. Grabs the toy from a younger sib	A. Returns the toy. Finds an alterative and tries to trade	☐	☐
	B. Make amends—does a kindness for sib to repair the relationship	☐	☐
3. Won't pick up toys	A. Toys get broken	☐	☐
	B. Parent removes unwanted toys	☐	☐
	C. Parent won't enter the cluttered room because it may hurt his feet	☐	☐
4. Dawdles getting ready for school	A. Takes the child to school in his pajamas	☐	☐
	B. Eats breakfast in the car (or bus) on the way to school	☐	☐
	C. No TV or computer time until the child is completely ready to leave	☐	☐
5. Says "I won't invite you to my birthday party."	A. Loses the friend	☐	☐
	B. Parent cancels party because child needs to learn to treat friends kindly before he can have a party	☐	☐
6. Watches TV instead of doing homework	A. No TV until all homework is completed	☐	☐
	B. TV put in a closet were it is not tempting	☐	☐
	C. Since schoolwork is most important, no distracting privileges (phone, computer, sports) until all homework is completed	☐	☐
7. Forgot her spelling words	A. Phones classmates and get the words	☐	☐
	B. Picks words from the dictionary and practices them instead of the spelling words on her list	☐	☐
8. Leaves his gloves at school	A. Gets cold hands	☐	☐
	B. Uses own money to buy new gloves	☐	☐

Effective consequences are immediate, related, a true choice, and low energy.

9. Forgets chores	A. Pays for someone else to do chores	☐	☐
	B. Chores help the family run smoothly. If you don't contribute (do chore), you may not benefit from the family (for example, go shopping at the mall)	☐	☐
10. Leaves her lunch at home	A. Goes hungry	☐	☐
	B. Borrows money from the office	☐	☐

Possible answers: **1.** A–logical, B–natural **2.** A–logical. B–logical **3.** A–natural, B–logical, C–natural **4.** A–natural, B–natural, C–logical **5.** A–natural, B–logical **6.** A–logical. B–logical, C–logical **7.** A–natural, B–logical, **8.** A–natural, B–logical **9.** A–logical, B–natural **10.** A–natural, B–natural

When can kids understand consequences?

Understanding the consequence of a behavior and the ability to regulate behavior are two different things. Young children can associate events and predict what may happen based on their experience. This is different from thinking about events, making a decision among several options, and regulating their behavior.

Babies and toddlers. Most babies and toddlers can make a connection between two events. The baby hits the mobile and it moves. A baby cries and a grown-up comes. Over time these events become connected. When the events are connected a child can predict what will happen.

Toddlers learn to associate two events, predict what will happen, and eventually modify their behavior accordingly. This process is governed largely by what the adult does—your actions, rather than what you say, help your child. This means that saying, "Sit on the chair, feet on the floor," has little or no effect alone. However, the words become more effective when combined with the action of putting the child on the floor.

The ability to understand a consequence is different from the ability to regulate one's behavior. This can be seen in the story below.

Josh just turned 2 and he loved to throw his toys. His parents thought that toys were to be treated gently. When Josh threw a truck or book, Mom would take the toy and put it in "time-out." This sequence happened over and over and over again. Josh clearly knew he was not supposed to throw a toy, but did it anyway. Occasionally, he would pick up a toy, arc his hand back, then stop mid throw, take the toy and put it in time-out himself.

Josh is in the process of learning. He knows what is expected, and does not yet have the self-restraint to comply all of the time. Most children need the parent to follow through between fifty and five hundred times. When you put the child back in bed over and over, you are developing the predictability that helps him learn self-restraint.

Preschoolers. Dr. Ann Corwin believes that children can understand consequences when they have developed reason and logic. This usually happens around 3 or 4. The two indicators that a child has this ability are (1) the child asks "why" about things and (2) the child engages in interactive play with another child or an adult. The interactive play might be, "Mommy, let's play tea party. I'll be the princess and you be the helper."

Children learn restraint from the outside before they develop self-restraint.

When children have the ability to question things and consider possible alternatives, they can then evaluate the consequences of different actions. Children can then decide to comply or not, depending on what best meets their needs. However, few preschoolers can see things from a perspective they have not experienced.

School-aged children like rules, and like them to apply equally to everyone, except perhaps themselves. Somewhere between 9 and 11, kids can begin to see things from another person's perspective. Up until then, children can only remember how people have responded.

Peer acceptance becomes increasingly important during the school-aged years. Friendships at this age tend to be mainly with members of the same sex. Younger school-aged children typically talk about members of the opposite sex as "weird." As they approach adolescence, they often show an increased interest by teasing, joking, and showing off.

Younger school-aged children (6 to 8 years old) have a strong desire to do things well, and they find criticism difficult to handle. They view things as good or bad, all or nothing, right or wrong, great or ghastly, with very little middle ground.

Older school-aged children (9 to 11 years old) generally like rituals, rules, and secret codes. They may belittle or defy adult authority. They still see things as right or wrong. These pre-adolescents may sometimes be verbally cruel to classmates.

Learning self-control is uneven for both children and adults. Children may comply a time or two or a day or two and then regress. Similarly, many adults find it difficult to maintain an exercise program, a healthier diet, or manage their temper without occasionally slipping.

Some children are easier than others. Temperament plays a large factor in how long a child will persist in unwanted behavior. If a child is highly adaptable, one or two reminders may be enough. If a child is very persistent, you may have to assist compliance several hundred times. Kathrine's twins illustrate this difference.

When Kathrine's twins, Sally and Sam, were a bit over 2½, they could sit on the stairs, reach through the railings, and touch the chandelier that hung in the entryway below. They quickly learned that if they pushed the light, it would swing back and forth. Kathrine told them not to touch the light, however, they did anyway. In exasperation, Kathrine swatted Sally's hand when she pushed the light. Sally looked shocked and didn't do it again. When Mom slapped Sam's hand, it made no difference. He continued to swing the lamp, and then he would slap his own hand after each time. The problem was only resolved when Dad got a ladder and shortened the chain, so Sam could not reach the light.

Sally and Sam had two very different temperaments. Sally was sensitive to people and adaptable. Sam was aware of others' wishes but very persistent in doing what he wished. He had not yet developed an internal sense of self-control.

To summarize, kids can understand about consequences when they begin to reason and use interactive play; however, they need to experience predictable consequences at all ages.

Consequences, punishment, and threats

People use consequences, punishment, and threats for the same purpose—to motivate the child to change his behavior. However, the process and the long- and short-term results are different for each method.

Consequences vs. punishment. The difference between the two is the method each uses and the way it is presented.

Consequences encourage change by building long-term decision making and responsibility. Parents clarify the child's options and the consequences of those options. Then parents follow through with action.

Punishment requires the child to obey now. That is done by intimidating or threatening to hurt the child physically or emotionally. Although threats and punishment may get the behavior you want in the short run, they often have long-term disadvantages. The more pain and fear children experience, the more distant they feel from the parent. The more distant they feel, the more likely they are to act out, especially when away from home. However, the more distant they feel, the more vulnerable they will be to delinquency or drug abuse later on.

Some of the differences parents report between punishments and consequences are listed below.

Punishments	Consequences
• encourage helplessness	• encourage responsibility
• teach "blind" obedience	• teach cause and effect
• are rigid, demeaning	• are respectful
• are arbitrary, without context	• offer choices
• coerce	• enhance self-esteem
• encourage guilt and shame	• are assertive
• are autocratic	

Consequences build competence; punishment builds resentment and shame

Punishment vs. threats. To me, the difference between punishment and threats is follow-through. With a threat, you say you will do something unpleasant, but rarely or never do. With punishment, a person both says she will do something unpleasant and then does it. If a person frequently threatens but does not carry out the threat, she loses credibility. Children believe they can disregard her wishes.

Is a time-out a punishment or a consequence? A time-out is a tool and can be used as either a consequence or a punishment. Delivery and intent distinguish between consequences and punishment. You can see the difference in the table below.

Table 7–5: Punishment vs. consequence

Situation: Ava hits Sophia when Sophia doesn't give her the toy she wants (both 3½).

Punishment	Consequence
"Shame on you, Ava. Bad, bad, bad. If I've told you once, I've told you a thousand times, 'No hitting.' Hitting is bad. You know better. Go to time-out. Sit there and think about what you did and how you hurt poor Sophia. You stay there until I tell you you can get up."	"Ava, we touch gently. You must find a gentle way to get what you want. Take a time-out and think what you could have done differently. Then you can go back and try again."
This is punishment. The tone is critical and it focuses on the wrongdoing.	This is a consequence. The tone is firm and kind. The focus is on growth and doing better.

Follow-through

I cannot overemphasize the need for follow-through. It is critical to setting limits. If you want your child to follow your rules, you must follow through with the consequences almost every time. It is your follow-through that tells the child you really mean business. For example, if you tell your toddler to get down off the table, you must go over and put him down if he doesn't scramble down himself. Toddlers, even more than children of other ages, learn much more by what you do than by what you say.

The quicker you follow through, the easier it will be for kids to learn. I remember Tracy, a friend, telling me about how her sister counted to ten after an order, and her nieces moved on number nine. My friend decided to count to three, her children move on number two.

Forewarning can be helpful. Many young children find warnings helpful. It gives them time to adjust to the transitions. "Two minutes to bedtime," "Five minutes to lunch," "Half an hour till your friend comes." With older children, it is helpful to ask them what help they would like or how they will remind themselves. Your goal is to gradually turn the responsibility over to the child.

Avoid sabotaging yourself. Sometimes parents unintentionally give away control by permitting extensions, excuses, or letting the child change his mind.

indulgent extensions tell the child she really doesn't have to comply. If you tell your child she must go to bed after one story, and then let her coax you into two more stories, you are teaching her that she really doesn't need to do what you say. This is a form of the unhealthy indulgent rules on the Limit Line presented earlier in this chapter. The parent's intentions are kindly; however, the action leads many children to believe that the rules really don't apply. In the long run, this inhibits the development of responsibility.

Notice the use of excuses. Some parents are tempted to ignore rules when they or their children are facing transitions or unpleasant events—the child is sick, starting a new school, Dad is traveling, Mom is stressed. An occasional indulgence is okay. However, note the overall pattern and avoid unconsciously slipping into indulgence. Angela found herself in this predicament.

How might you sabotage yourself?

> *Angela was concerned with her daughter Netta's behavior. Netta didn't obey the way Angela thought she should. Netta complied with her father a bit, but not much. When I asked Angela what their rules were and how they enforced them, she gave reasonable answers.*
>
> *As we talked, Angela shared that both she and her husband traveled a lot for work. Netta spent a lot of time with Aunt Nancy, who lived nearby—so they mostly saw her on weekends.*
>
> *After some thought, Angela realized that she was probably not very consistent when she came back from a trip because she wanted Netta to like her and to have fun with her. Further, when she mentally reviewed her behavior, Angela noticed that when she was tired, Netta had a cold, or the weather was grubby she relaxed the rules. As it turned out, there were more exceptions than times she followed through.*

It is easy to fall into the excuses trap, especially if you do not like conflict and know that your child will resist what you want.

Limit children's ability to change their minds. Certainly it is okay for kids to change their minds occasionally. We all do. However, when you permit children to change their minds frequently, there is no incentive for them to make wise decisions. For example,

Mark, 3½, resisted going to bed. Lauren said, "Mark, it is time to go to bed. Do you want to walk or be carried?" He did not acknowledge her question. She said, "I see you chose to be carried," and bent to pick him up. As she picked him up Mark said, "I want to walk," so she put him down. He slumped to the floor and began to fiddle with his foot.

After a moment Lauren repeated, "Do you want to walk or be carried?" He again ignored her. She picked him up and continued toward his room. After a moment, Mark said, "I want to walk," and she put him down again. This continued several more times before they finally got to his room.

Lauren became uncomfortable with this pattern—yes, Mark was going to bed, but it didn't feel right to have so much stopping and starting. After consulting with a friend she changed how she responded to Mark's wishy-washy tactics.

When Lauren told Mark it was time for bed, she added, "You may walk or be carried to bed. And tonight you get only one choice. Whatever you say first we will do."

When he declined to walk to bed Lauren picked him up and said he had chosen to be carried. He said, "No. I want to walk." She replied, "You wish you made a different choice. That's okay. Tomorrow you can choose again. For now you chose to be carried."

Within three nights Mark was walking to bed in a timely fashion. He had learned to make a thoughtful decision. Offering kids choices is helpful at times, and children need to know that some decisions are permanent.

We have looked at two tools of the **Set reasonable limits** STAR Parenting point, ☆*Clear rules* and ☆*Consequences*. Now we will look at the third tool, ☆*A better way.*

Set reasonable limits point
☆*A better way* tool

☆*A better way* is a simple technique for setting limits that uses negotiation. You can use ☆*A better way* with negotiable rules or to avoid a power struggle. ☆*A better way* has three parts: a statement of your wishes, a statement of the child's wishes, and a request for an idea that would work for both of you. You can see the parts in Mona's story.

Robin, 3½, had a skin problem requiring lotion to be put on daily. Bedtime had become a game of chase as I would try to put lotion on her. I was beginning to lose my cool and decided to try ☆A better way.

"Robin," I said, "My way is I put this lotion on you. Your way is I don't. What's a better way?"

Robin thought a minute and said, "Daddy do it." She took the lotion to her dad, and that was the end of it. A truly better way.

☆*A better way* involves the child, without compromising the parent's long view.

Needs vs. solutions. Often parents and children confuse needs and solutions. Because they want to do something a particular way, they consider it a "need," when it is really just one alternative. This can be seen in Beth's story.

Our family is committed to having only one car. From time to time, this creates problems. For example, yesterday I told my husband that I needed the car that night because I was teaching. He said that he needed the car because he had to work late.

We were stymied for a bit, until we realized that although we each used the word "need," our proposals were really "preferred solutions" and we had never considered options. When we started to look for alternatives, we found there were many. Among the more practical were I could take a bus, taxi, or get a ride from someone in the class and he also could take a bus, taxi, or bring some work home.

Focus on win-win ideas. This means that ideas must be acceptable to both you and your child. Unfortunately, sometimes parents have an idea in mind that they want and urge their child to agree to their idea. This negates the purpose of ☆A better way. Try ☆A better way only when you are willing to use a different solution.

Sometimes a child's "better way" is really his position restated. When that happens, clarify the position and restate the question as Heather does.

One evening when Heather told Max, 5, it was his bedtime, he replied, "I want to stay up late tonight." Heather had work to do that evening and did not have time to put a reluctant child to bed. She thought a couple of moments and decided to try ☆A better way. "My way is you go to bed now. Your way is you stay up late. What is a better way?"

Max replied promptly, "I go to bed at midnight."

Heather responded, "Midnight is late. That is your way. My way is for you go to bed now. What is something that works for both of us?"

Max thought a bit and said, "I go in ten minutes."

Mom agreed that ten minutes would work for her, and asked, "How will you know when ten minutes are up?" He thought again and said he would set a timer. Heather agreed to the plan. Max set the timer, and went off to bed when it rang.

A better way is powerful because the child proposes the idea. In the preceding story, how agreeable do you think Max would have been if Heather had suggested bed in ten minutes? Most children would reject the suggestion. The power comes because the parent accepts the child's idea. If you feel compelled to promote your idea, state it as an expectation, not ☆A better way, or try ☆Two yeses (chapter four).

Prerequisites. For ☆A better way to be successful, children need experience making decisions and following through. Most children can begin to use ☆A better way somewhere between ages 3 and 4. To begin, you can model the process out loud—generating ideas for difficulties you face and evaluating them.

Try ☆A better way only when you are willing to accept a different solution.

Activity 7–5: Create ☆A better way

Directions: Read each situation and create ☆A better way statement to offer the child.

1. You are making bread—in particular, you are kneading the dough, forming rolls with your hands. Your child demands that you get marking pens Now! You have explained that your hands are messy, but she still demands you get them.	My way:
	Your way:
	A better way:

2. You are trying to get going in the morning, and your daughter wants to watch a DVD. You know from experience once she gets started watching, it is hard for her to stop.	My way:
	Your way:
	A better way:

Possible answers: 1. My way is—to finish making the rolls. Your way is—for me to get the marking pens right now. What is a better way? Wait for child to answer. **2.** My way is—No screen time in the morning before school. Your way is—to watch TV when you get up. What is a better way? Wait for child to answer.

Activity 7–6: Identify errors with ☆*A better way*

Directions: Read the situation, identify the error, and revise the better way to remove the error.

1. *Background:* Margaret and her son, Kevin, were going shopping for athletic shoes for school. Kevin saw a toy that he really-really-really wants. Margaret brought only enough money for the shoes because money was very tight this month.

| Margaret said, "My way is you put the toy on your Christmas list. Your way is that we buy the toy instead of school shoes. A better way would be for us to come back tomorrow when you can bring your own money." | ☐ States child's position incorrectly or unkindly
☐ Parent suggests an idea
☐ Unwilling to negotiate |

Revise the statement:

2. *Background:* Company is coming for dinner this evening. Beth had agreed to vacuum the living room and tidy her room before she went to play with her friend, Ashley. However, she has spent most of the morning making bracelets. Ashley just arrived and invited Beth to come back with her to see their new puppy. Beth wanted to go immediately.

| Her father says to Beth, "I want you to stay home until your chores are done. You want to shirk your duty. What is a better way?" | ☐ States child's position incorrectly or unkindly
☐ Parent suggests an idea
☐ Unwilling to negotiate |

Revise the statement:

Possible answers: 1. Error: Parent suggests an idea. ***Revision:*** *My way is* you put the toy on your Christmas list. *Your way is* to use the money for your school shoes. What is *a better way?* **2. Error:** Dad states Beth's position unkindly. ***Revision:*** *My way is* that you finish your chores before you play or leave. *Your way is* to see the puppy now. What is *a better way?*

We have seen how you can use the tool ☆*A better way* to set limits and defuse power struggles. Next, we will look at how to incorporate this idea into setting limits.

Five steps for setting limits with young children

Effective limits make use of both ☆*Clear rules* and ☆*Consequences.* The following five steps will help you whether your child is 2, 6, or 10.

1. ***Make a clear, simple rule.*** As with other tools, the most effective rules are short and stated in the positive. "Don't run in the living room" becomes "Walk inside." "Don't hit" becomes "Touch gently." Using long sentences and negatives slows down comprehension and cooperation.

2. ***Choose an effective consequence.*** Many parents make rules and expect children to obey them automatically. Kids rarely do that. As soon as you make a rule, decide on a consequence rather than waiting for non-compliance. Sometimes the consequence can be as simple as letting the child find out what will happen naturally if she doesn't cooperate. For example, if she is not ready to leave promptly for the trip to the zoo with her preschool, she will be left behind.

3. ***Clarify the child's choice.*** For example, "Stephen, if you spend your allowance on candy today, you won't have money for the baseball cards you want. You can decide which is more important to you." Try to keep your manner neutral and not preachy. Remember, children sometimes learn more from their mistakes than from their successes.

4. ***Follow through with the consequence.*** If you tell your 5-year-old son that he can eat at dinnertime or wait until breakfast, you must remain firm. If your child pleads, "I'm hungry. I can't sleep," you still need to remain firm. Remind him of the rule, "We eat at mealtime. You chose to wait until breakfast." If you wish to make exceptions they should be negotiated *before* the rule is broken. If you back down, you will be teaching your child to ignore your rules.

5. ***Deal with the child's distress constructively.*** Children's distress is a natural part of the learning process. As soon as you choose the consequence, decide how you will deal with their distress. For example, you might say, "You're angry that you missed going to the zoo. You really wish that you were ready to go on time."

A key to effective limits is follow-through, follow-through, follow-through.

Avoid the temptation to preach or to relieve your child's distress. For example, if you say, "It's your own fault, you could have been ready if you hadn't watched cartoons," your child will probably get angrier and tune you out. If you try to reduce his distress by saying, "Don't cry, I can take you to meet your friends in the zoo," you rob him of a valuable learning tool and become increasingly responsible for his happiness. You can see how these steps work together in William's story.

When my son, Jeff, was a toddler, he was into throwing food at the table big time. I told him to stop but it wasn't working. I decided to use the STAR approach for setting limits.

   Clear rule: *Food is for eating.*
   Consequence: *Eat your food or get down from the table.*
   Clarify choice: *Do you want to eat or get down from the table?*
   Follow through: *If he throws food again say, "I see you chose to get down from the table," and then put him down.*
   Deal with distress. *If he cries, acknowledge his feelings. "You are sad you're on the floor by yourself."*
   We did exactly what we planned, and within a week the throwing was over.

You can use these five steps with any limit you wish to set. In the beginning, most children will need to test the limits to be sure you mean what you say. As you build credibility, children need to test less often. You can see how these steps work with an older child in Elena's story.

When my son, Paco, was in grade school, he was more interested in playing on the computer than doing his homework. I wanted him to finish all his homework before he played a computer game, but I recognized that it was hard for him to concentrate for that long without a break.

After talking with my husband, we decided that using the computer was a privilege that Paco earned by behaving responsibly. Finishing his homework before he played was considered responsibility. If he needed a break before his homework was done, he could run around outside or read to his little brother. He was to bring his homework to me for review when he was done, so I would know it was complete and correct. If he turned on the computer before his homework was checked, he would lose the privilege of computer use that day because his behavior was not responsible. If it happened again the same day, he would lose two days of computer use. For the weekend, we decided that he could do schoolwork or some family chore to earn computer privileges.

Clear rule: *Finish your homework and ask me to check it before you use the computer.*

Consequence: *Lose the privilege of computer use for a day.*

Clarify choices: *You have not shown me your homework. Do you want to take a break, return to your homework, or lose the computer privilege for today?*

Follow through: *If I came back later and found him at the computer before he had completed his homework, I would turn off the computer and say, "I see you have chosen no computer today." If he used the computer again that day before his homework was done, I would move the computer to our room.*

Deal with distress. *If he stomped around or yelled, I acknowledged his feelings, "You are upset or angry that you don't have any computer time today. You can make a different choice tomorrow." Or use ☆Simple listening: "Un-huh." "Really?" "Oh."*

We put a lot of thought into our plan and it paid off. In less than two weeks he accepted that he could only have computer time by earning it.

In the examples above the parent created the rules and consequences. As children grow older, it is helpful to involve them in establishing the limits.

You can set clear limits by making ☆*Clear rules,* ☆ *Consequences,* and following through with the consequences. When you are willing to negotiate a rule, you can use ☆*A better way.* However, even though you set a reasonable limit, it will not be effective if the child uses breaking the rule to get attention and gets it, or if the child does not have the skills.

After the summary and the STAR in Action Story, we will move on and look at the last STAR Parenting point, ***Teach new skills.***

Children don't need to like the rules, just follow them.

Summary of
Set Reasonable Limits

★ **Make a clear, simple rule.** Effective rules are short and stated in the positive. Using long sentences and negatives slows down comprehension.

★ **Choose an effective consequence.** The results should be immediate, related to the behavior, and a true choice.

★ **Clarify the child's choice.** Keep your manner neutral and not preachy. Remind yourself that children sometimes learn more from their mistakes than their successes.

★ **Follow through with the consequence.** Ignore pleading and requests for exceptions and extensions. If you back down, you will be teaching your child to ignore the rule.

★ **Deal with the child's distress constructively.** Acknowledge children's distress without reducing it. If you try to eliminate children's distress, you rob them of a valuable learning experience.

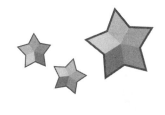

Bedtime for Maggie

My daughter, Maggie, 4½ , pushes her bedtime limit every night. We always seem to have a battle over getting pajamas on and teeth brushed. Most nights, I am falling asleep before she does. She is sleeping late in the morning, and we are having trouble getting out the door to preschool.

Maggie was doing great with her bedtime until we went to Florida on vacation. The problem began when we returned to west coast time. Being 4 years old, she needs to have a better routine and structure around bedtime.

Her little sister, Bea, 2, has also had some sleep issues since we have returned, but she is going to sleep at 7 P.M. and getting up at 4 A.M.! After getting up with Bea every morning, I don't have the energy or patience to help Maggie get to bed at night.

S—Stop and focus

This is how I have started STAR Parenting with this situation.

I didn't realize how big of a problem this had become until I took a minute to think things through. I had noticed my frustrations building with both kids—one getting up too early and the other going to bed too late. It took me a minute to realize that everything changed after our week in Florida, where we were on east coast time instead of west coast time.

Sleep is very important. I want Maggie to have a structured bedtime with clean teeth and some books before falling asleep. I want Maggie to know that there is a time for play and a time for bed. I want to give her some control over her bedtime schedule, but she also needs to know there is a clear bedtime. Also, I realized that I need to take better care of my own sleep needs.

Goal for me: To become more structured and disciplined in getting my kids to bed at 8:30 P.M. The hardest part is the extra energy it will take in the beginning. I hope it will save energy once we have a routine established. I definitely run out of energy in the early evening. A new skill for me will be better self-care during the day. Perhaps a short nap, sleeping in later in the morning, and having my spouse help out more with the kids.

The reality check for me is that Maggie is 4 and is really into her power. She took control of her bedtime and sleep habits. I like that she is finding her power in things—and I want her to use her power for better sleep. I can find ways to give her power over things like what pajamas to wear, what animal to sleep with, and what books to read. When I am tired, I tend to be a bit "my way or the highway," but if I'm rested I will have more patience.

Long view: I want her to be a strong, capable, cooperative young woman.

Temperament: Maggie likes variety and is persistent and strong willed.

Development: The task of a 3- to 6-year-old is to explore power. Maggie is doing a fine job of that.

Child's goal for self: To control her bedtime.

Parent's goal: To get enough rest to care for children and myself.

Desired behavior: Maggie go to bed at bedtime (8:30 P.M.) without a hassle.

T—Think of Ideas

I knew I had to change this issue and fast. We were becoming a very grumpy household. Maggie loved her extra freedom at night with Dad watching sports and Mom sound asleep. Maggie was playing computer games, dolls, and cars—anything but going to bed.

Referring to the STAR Parenting points and tools I made a list of ideas:

Set reasonable limits

☆*Clear rule:* Bedtime is at 8:30 P.M.; after dinner, our rule

---

1 There is a STAR in Action Story at the end of each chapter. Each story is written by a parent in his or her own words and shows how that person adapted the STAR Parenting process to his or her own life.

These stories use tools from all points, so some may be unfamiliar until you have read the appropriate chapter. You can see how different parents, with different values or kids with different temperaments, might make different choices.

is to brush your teeth and to put on pajamas, to have some quiet time, and then go to bed.

☆*A better way:* "I want you to go put on your pajamas now and you want to go play—what's a better way?" Maggie chose to put on her pajamas downstairs instead of in her room (fine by me!).

☆*Consequence:* "Put your pajamas on now or we will have no time to read books."

Avoid problems

☆*Reduce stress:* Give Maggie special time to play alone during the daytime while Bea is taking a nap.

☆*Change things:* Go outside and play during the day—run around the park or even go to the mall on a rainy day and find an empty area where the kids can run around a little. Place some special toys upstairs for quiet play after jammies are on and before bed.

☆*Two yeses:* "Do you want to put your jammies on by yourself or do you want me to help you?

Acknowledge feelings

☆*Simple listening:* When Maggie is upset about having to go to bed, just hug her and say, "Ohh, ummm, I see."

☆*Active listening:* Use some words to describe how she is feeling: "You are sad that it's time for bed, you want to play longer, you don't feel tired enough for bed yet."

☆*Grant in fantasy:* "What if we didn't ever have to go to bed?! We could stay up all night long and keep on playing with toys. We would never have to sleep— you could play and I could clean house! We would have so much extra time!"

Teach new skills

☆*Modeling:* After dinner, show Maggie what I do to get ready for bed and how comforting it feels to wash my face, brush my teeth, and put my pjs on. Talk to her about others in our family doing the same things.

☆*Shaping:* Walk Maggie through each step of the process and descriptions of what we are doing and why. First, we go and brush our teeth to get rid of the "sugar bugs," and then we go to the bathroom before we go to bed so we don't wake up in the middle of the night, and then we put on pajamas to stay warm and cozy.

☆*Re-do it right:* Help Maggie by taking her hand or walking with her back to her room or the bathroom and saying, "Whoops, we forgot to brush our teeth," or "Let's put our clothes in the hamper after we put

on our jammies," gently reminding her of our bedtime routine.

Reward cooperation

☆*Attention:* Notice when she is getting ready for bed with lots of smiles and nods of encouragement.

☆*Effective praise:* Tell her how well she is doing remembering our bedtime routine and getting to bed on time. "Wow. You remembered to get ready all by yourself."

☆*Rewards:* Give her a special reward of extra play time during the day or a special outing to the zoo or the kids' museum to celebrate her success and growing up. Maybe buy a special new pair of pajamas for doing such a great job. Say, "When your jammies are on early, we can play rag doll."

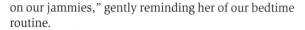

A—Act Effectively

The first thing I did was to get a handle on my younger daughter. I got her bedtime to be a bit later, giving her a later wake-up time. When I wasn't getting up with her at 4 A.M., I had a little more energy in the evening. Also, I got support from my husband. I told him what the issues seemed to be and asked for his help supporting all three of us on our process.

He works all day and loves to have some veg-out time in the evening, but we needed his attention to help with the bedtime problem. I did get a lot of resistance from Maggie. I realized that she needs to have some good quality time all by herself to explore her imagination with her toys. I talked about that playtime earlier in the day, saying: " Maggie— while Bea is asleep, this is your time to play with your toys however you'd like. When Bea wakes up, we'll all play together, but this is your special time to play."

The best options for me in the evening with Maggie turned out to be ☆*A better way* and ☆*Re-do it right.* Also having the ☆*Clear rule* about bedtime helped. (I really don't think I had ever made a clear bedtime rule until this process!) "In bed at 8:30 P.M.—we read two books and then you can have special imagination time before you fall a sleep. I want you to brush your teeth now and you want to do it later—what's a better way?" She came up with using a different toothbrush, having Daddy help her, brushing her teeth in a different room—fine options. Also, I would give ☆*Two yeses*—"You may brush your teeth and put on your pajamas now and play with Polly Pockets for twenty minutes before bed, or brush your teeth and put your pajamas on later and go straight to bed (no Polly Pocket time)."

R—Review and revise

Bea likes a definite routine and Maggie likes things to be a little different every day. It's hard to parent two kids so differently—but I realized it's important to stay flexible when changing the structure of our bedtime routine. Things got dramatically better after three nights, and it's not a smooth system yet. I'll continue to try new ideas and to go back to the STAR as we find the right routine and balance for us all.

Comment—I learned a lot about my kids and myself through this process. I also learned that I need more support from my husband. It's hard for me to ask for help, but I can do a lot more with a little help, so I learned a good lesson there. I am very thankful for learning these tools to help my kids (and myself) grow.

Chapter 8

Teach New Skills

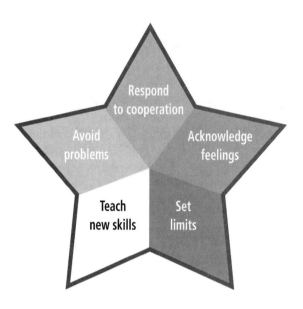

Offer children skills they need for the real world

You are your child's first and most important teacher. The skills you provide her will influence how she navigates the complexities of the world both now and as an adult. The last STAR Parenting point, ***Teach new skills***, offers three powerful tools to use: ☆*Modeling,* ☆*Re-do it right,* and ☆*Shaping*. First, however, I will share Vonnie's story that illustrates the value of teaching new skills.

> *Eric, 4½, was a creative, imaginative child; however, he was at the mercy of his friends. One day, I heard his friend, Paul, demand the toy Eric was playing with. Eric explained he was using it. Paul replied, "If you don't give it to me, I'll go home." Eric gave it.*
>
> *It was the same line Paul had used five times in the previous half hour. Each time I heard Eric give in I cringed, but I tried to stay out of it. Finally, I took Eric aside and coached my son on how to handle the situation. "When Paul threatens to go home say, 'Okay, I'll see you tomorrow,'" I instructed.*

"But I want him to s-s-stay," Eric wailed. "Try it this once," I urged. So we practiced and then he returned to play with Paul.

Soon, Paul demanded the truck Eric was playing with. When Eric declined, Paul said, "I'll go home." Eric replied as instructed, "Okay, I'll see you tomorrow." Paul was startled and repeated his demand and the threat to go home.

Again Eric replied, "Okay. I'll see you tomorrow." Paul frowned and grumbled, "Oh, well, I'll stay." In spite of my coaching success, it was a couple of years before I realized that Eric lacks people skills.

**Tools to
Teach new skills**
☆ *Modeling*
☆ *Re-do it right*
☆ *Shaping*

The goal of teaching new skills is for a parent to give children the skills they need to deal with life, rather than try to protect them from life. The three tools that *Teaching new skills* offers are ☆*Modeling*, ☆*Re-do it right*, and ☆*Shaping*. Teaching new skills may also involve tools from other points of the STAR.

Teaching new skills can be as simple as modeling how to zip a jacket, or as complex as coaching how to deal with anger constructively. Most parents expect to help their child learn to walk and dress. But few expect to teach children to share, keep track of time or their possessions, or solve problems.

Skills to consider building

There are four general categories of things parents may need to teach their children.

Temperament. In chapter three, you identified your child's temperament. Some children have temperament traits that are difficult for them and others to live with. The temperament traits are not inherently good or bad. They are helpful in some situations and difficult in others. For example, high activity level on a long hike is great. However, high activity in church is not.

You can teach children specific skills to cope with their temperament. We will look at several temperament traits that are often difficult and some strategies to cope with them.

High level of activity. At first, it is helpful if the parent arranges for the child to get enough activity. Talk about how the child's body feels before and after exercise. Then teach the child to notice his physical restlessness and find suitable outlets. If the child can run off the energy, great. If not, wiggling a foot or some other part of the body vigorously and quietly may help.

High intensity. High intensity can cause problems whether it is anger or excitement. *Dealing with Disappointment: Helping Kids Cope When Things Don't Go Their Way* offers a process for teaching children tools to manage their feelings and twenty-four self-calming tools. I describe the process on page 176.

High distractiblity. When children need to concentrate, they can learn ways to stay focused and avoid temptation, as you see in Felipe's story.

My son, Felipe, 7, has always been easily distracted. When he was little that was as asset since we could easily divert him by showing him something else interesting. However, now that he is older this distractibility has become a problem. He cannot stay focused long enough to put away his toys or do his homework. We have been working with him on monitoring his focus, using positive self-talk, and making an activity fun, hence easier to concentrate on.

I knew we were making headway when one Saturday he brought me a new dump truck that he really liked and asked me to keep it until he was done cleaning. He confided, "I can't seem to concentrate on putting things away with the truck calling, 'play with me.'" He had discovered that it was easier to work if the temptation was not visible.

Low persistence. Children with low persistence can be taught to persevere longer and reward themselves for persisting. To do this, the parent begins by encouraging persistence with praise or rewards. (See chapter five, "The Effort Effect." When the child can extend her persistence by external rewards, work with her to identify ways she can reward herself. Then gradually turn the process over to her.

Developing strategies to deal with temperament takes time and effort because you are working around the child's innate wiring.

Learning style. Each person has a preferred way of receiving and processing information—visually, aurally, kinesthetically, or conceptually. These differences can cause difficulties both at school and at home.

School challenges. When children get into school their natural learning styles may create challenges. Some teachers understand learning styles and strive to teach so all students learn. Unfortunately, not all teachers are successful. Your children may also need to deal with other people who process information differently, so it helps to teach them how to adapt. The table below briefly describes four learning styles and gives examples of general learning strategies, with tips on adapting to a teacher using a different style to give assignments.

Table 8–1: Learning style and strategies

	Description of learning styles	*General strategies for learning styles*	*Adaptive strategies to–*	
			record assignments	*learn spelling words*
Visual	Likes to see things. Learns through images. Likes drawing.	Use memory devices to create visual patterns. In reading, suggest visual clues.	Listen and visualize the parts of the assignment.	Memorize the letters and shapes of spelling words.
Auditory	Thinks in words. Verbalizes concepts. Fine memory for names, dates, and trivia.	Dictate a story. Explain facts to tape recorder. Create word problems to illustrate concepts.	Read the assignment and talk about it to oneself.	Spell the word out loud. Say each syllable.
Kinesthetic	Learns through physical movement. Very active, can't sit long. Communicates by gestures.	Movement is important. Let child wiggle foot, chew gum, touch things, walk around, or ride stationary bicycle while reading.	Wiggle foot while listening to the assignment and writing it down.	Clap hands for each letter. Snap fingers for hard parts.
Conceptual	Thinks in concepts. Explores patterns and relationships. Likes puzzles and learning how things work.	Offer context clues to help reading. Do experiments together and have child record results. Use learning games and word puzzles.	Listen to the assignment and look for the parts: description, how long, date due.	Look for patterns (visual and auditory). Make or use rules about spelling.

Many children need visual and kinesthetic presentations. Unfortunately, most classrooms rely on auditory presentations, with no support for either visual or kinesthetic learners. The focus on kinesthetic teaching may explain the success of Montessori schools.

Home challenges. These same learning styles can cause difficulty at home as well. This is illustrated by Anna Marie's story.

I have three kids, Geoffrey, 11, Ellen, 9, and Anthony, 7, and had a lot of trouble getting their cooperation until I learned about learning styles. What I discovered was that if I reminded Geoffrey of something, it went in one ear and out the other even if he was listening. However, when I took the time to write things down for him he got it and cooperated.

If I wrote a note for Ellen, it would be lost before she read it—I need to speak to her directly or leave a message on her phone. Anthony was entirely different. If I wanted him to remember something in the morning, I would need to tape a note over his light switch or to a chair in the path to the door—something that would involve movement. He would then notice the note, read it, and do it.

Further, if I want to teach them something, I need to show Geoffrey what to do, tell Ellen how to do the thing, and actually do it with Anthony a time or two.

Anna Marie found that when she took the time to adapt her style to the individual child things went much better; consequently, she actually saved time.

Levels of learning. Children go through three stages on their way to independence: helping with a task, being reminded, and doing it alone. The reminding stage can be misleading because a child can often do the task with no difficulty when the parent is present. However, the child cannot sustain the focus when the parent leaves, nor can he work alone the next time. There is a difference in the ability to do a task alone and the ability to be responsible for doing the task alone.

The process is illustrated in the Household job chart below. The letters refer to the average ages of stages mentioned above. You can see that it often takes kids years, rather than weeks or months, to move from one stage to the next.

Developmental, age-related challenges. In chapter three on expectations we looked at the task for each developmental age. In the ideal world, children would learn what they need and move on to the next stage with little direction from adults, in an orderly progression. But they do not.

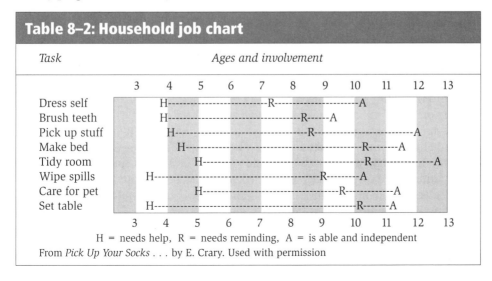

Table 8–2: Household job chart

Task	Ages and involvement

Task	3	4	5	6	7	8	9	10	11	12	13
Dress self		H					R		A		
Brush teeth		H					R	A			
Pick up stuff		H					R				A
Make bed			H						R	A	
Tidy room			H						R		A
Wipe spills		H					R	A			
Care for pet			H					R		A	
Set table		H							R	A	

H = needs help, R = needs reminding, A = is able and independent

From *Pick Up Your Socks . . .* by E. Crary. Used with permission

Aunt Beth's steps for writing a report

- Read a brief description of the topic (Norway) to get a general idea, perhaps from the encyclopedia or the Internet.
- Make a list of the topics you need or wish to cover. This can be from the assignment or ideas from the encyclopedia. (For example, history, geography, economics, government, and education)
- Choose one topic and read about it in one book. When you find an interesting fact, write it on a file card, and include the book title, author, and page number. Repeat with two other books.
- Write the section: spread the cards out, arrange them in a reasonable sequence, and write the section. Footnote material you quoted directly. Focus on getting the ideas down, rather than writing perfectly.
- Write the next sections using the same procedure.
- Write a paragraph (two or three sentences) summing up what you learned or like about the topic.
- Write an introductory paragraph explaining to the new reader what you wrote about.
- Review the whole paper and correct the grammar, spelling, and clarity of what you wrote. Note: Spell check and grammar check are a good start, however, you must read it (maybe even out loud) to catch all the errors.
- Have another person read it. Does it make sense? Can they find errors?
- Write the table of contents and bibliography.
- Let the report rest a bit, preferably overnight.
- Review the report again, correcting errors you or your reader missed.
- Print out the report. Bind it as the teacher likes, or if no instructions, staple it.
- Turn the report in.
- Celebrate completion of the task. Call someone and tell them you're done and what you learned or do something you really enjoy.

The toddlers' task is to begin to think and to manage their feelings. This often results in tantrums or defiance. Toddlers usually need help developing tools to calm themselves. Fortunately, self-soothing is a skill you can teach them. Note: Toddler tantrums are caused by lack of ability to manage feelings, rather than deliberately planning an uproar to make the parent miserable.

The preschoolers' task is to learn about power and identity. They often explore this by dawdling, and being bossy and demanding. Teaching them how to negotiate with others and find constructive ways to be powerful promotes a lifelong skill.

The first story in this chapter illustrated the benefit of teaching about intimidation and power. Paul had discovered that if he said he would leave, Eric would give him whatever he wanted. Mom taught Eric to retain his power by accepting Paul's statement with dignity.

Paul's mother, if told about the problem, might have taught Paul other tools to get what he wanted, like trading or bargaining. These and other strategies are offered in the Children's Problem Solving Books I have written: *I Want It, I Want to Play, I Can't Wait, and My Name Is Not Dummy.*

School-agers' developmental task is to learn about structure and to develop their own internal structure. They need to learn to collect information, make decisions, and experience and deal with the consequences of poor decisions. Ellen Galinsky describes seven essential life skills in *Mind in the Making.*

Sometimes parents of school-aged children are tempted to move in and solve their child's problems: however, that denies the child the opportunity to learn needed information. Steven had been teaching his son, Mike, 7, to check information before he acted on it. You can see the results of his effort in the following story.

Mike had just come home from school and wanted to play with someone. He asked his sister, Ava, 5, "Want to play ball outside?"

She said, "No." He thought she didn't want to play with him and felt hurt and angry. However, he could hear his dad's voice saying, "Mike, check your assumptions, collect information, and think of alternatives before you act."

So he turned back to Ava and asked, "Will you play with me?" "Sure," she answered, "as long as it's fun."

"What's wrong with playing ball outside?" Mike asked.

"I chased Puppy all afternoon with Anna. I'm tired," she responded.

"Well, what would you like to play?" he inquired.

"Checkers. So I don't have to move much." Mike agreed and went off to get the game.

Steve deliberately taught Mike how to think about a problem or conflict. Mike was able to tap into that structure when he was angry at his sister.

In addition to people skills, most children need academic skills. They need to know how to study to do their homework. Some kids are lucky enough to have teachers who teach them how to do their assignments, but many do not. These children can drift along quite a while before their lack of skill is noticed. You can see this in Katie's story.

Katie was a quiet girl who didn't like to draw attention to herself. She had somehow reached fifth grade without learning how to write a report. Her parents learned on the Friday before Memorial Day that a major report was due Tuesday. They were furious that Katie hadn't started. The more they yelled, the more she retreated into an uncommunicative shell.

Things were at a standstill until Katie agreed to spend the weekend with Aunt Beth and write the report. Aunt Beth was a former teacher with a very gentle manner. She asked Katie what she had been told about report writing. When Katie replied, "Nothing," Aunt Beth asked her to bring a stack of file cards and several books about Norway, the subject of the report.

When Katie arrived, Beth settled her at the table and showed her a list of the steps in writing a report (see page 164). She explained that she wanted Katie to know everything involved and added that although the list might look long, some of the steps were really short. For each step, Aunt Beth explained what to do, and then began each task with Katie to show her what she meant. She invited Katie to ask anything she was wondering about. Then Katie finished the step herself.

Beth also helped Katie pace herself by setting goals to accomplish within certain time frames. When Katie finished a section, they took a break and did something fun for a bit before returning to the report. By Saturday evening, all but the table of contents, bibliography, and final review were done. Katie went home

Seven essential life skills
- Focus and self-control
- Perspective taking
- Communicating
- Making connections
- Critical thinking
- Taking on challenges
- Self-directed, engaged learning

From *Mind in the Making* by E. Galinsky

Monday with a complete report and a sense of accomplishment. More importantly, she had a guide for future reports.

By dividing the process of writing a report into small pieces and modeling how to do each them, Beth was able to make the task much more manageable for Katie.

Blind spots. Many children have blind spots—information or skills that one would expect the child to have, but for some reason does not. This could be problem-solving or negotiation skills, time awareness, anger-management skills, or self-calming skills when the size of a task scares them. Parents may believe the child could do "it" if he would just try. In some cases that's true, but in others it is not.

If you find yourself getting really exasperated at something the child "should" be able to do, ask yourself, "What skills does the child need to be able to do this?" You may find that he does not have the needed skill, as Tony shows below.

Tony, 4, was supposed to put his shoes on so we could leave. I reminded him several times and nothing happened. Finally, I squatted down beside him and said, "I see your shoes and socks sitting by your feet. How come you haven't put them on?"

He replied, "Because the socks are wrong and I don't know how to fix them." They were inside out! I was dumbfounded! Such a simple, solvable problem. I showed him how to turn the socks right side out, he put them on, and soon we were on our way.

Sometimes, the skill the child needs is more complex. For example, Christine taught her son to be aware of the passage of time.

Christine was upset because Zack, her first grader, was getting sent to the principal's office frequently. He was not being disruptive in the usual sense. His offence was continuing to work on the math assignment when he should have switched to reading.

Christine decided that Zack was "time blind." In kindergarten this lack of time awareness had not been a problem because the program was flexible and someone would interrupt him if needed. Now, in first grade, he was expected to be aware of the passage of time and to switch by himself. So Christine decided to teach him to interrupt himself.

She bought two workbooks so he could switch from one to the other. Zack was to work for twenty to thirty minutes each evening after supper. Mom set a timer for six minutes. If he switched to the other workbook when the timer rang, he got one ticket. If he switched before the timer rang (between five and six minutes), he would get two tickets. The ticket could be exchanged for additional screen time.

It took a couple of weeks to develop an awareness of the passage of time, however, Zack got to the point where he could interrupt himself enough to switch books and then continue.

As we have seen, some children need help developing certain skills. Sometimes it is difficult for parents to determine whether the child is lacking a skill or is using the behavior as a way to get attention from the adults in his life. We will look at that in the "Identifying the problem" section in chapter ten.

Some skills are easy to teach. They are easy to see and understand. For example, it is easy to identify that a child can't crack an egg or make mashed potatoes. Other skills are more complex and not easily observed. For example, how do you solve a problem or calm yourself if you feel upset? You can see the results, but not the process. Jai Li's story illustrates this.

Ask yourself, "What does a child need to be able to do this?"

My son's teacher asked him how problems were solved in his family. Zhu thought a moment and said, "Momma gets quiet and then it's solved." I was pleased he noticed, but surprised he had no idea what I did. I decided to model talking myself through a problem so he could "see" what I do.

Keep in mind that you are your child's first teacher; with your help your child will grow competent and confident. The purpose of the **Teach new skills** point of STAR Parenting is to offer children the tools they need to be successful at home, at school, and in the world. Three tools to teach skills are ☆*Modeling*, ☆*Re-do it right*, and ☆*Shaping*.

Teach new skills point
☆*Modeling* tool

☆*Modeling* is the first tool we will look at on the **Teach new skills** point of the STAR. ☆*Modeling* is a powerful tool. Young children are natural mimics. They try to do the things they see the people around them do—read, cook, shave, drive cars.

Teach by modeling

Modeling is perhaps the most natural method of teaching. We are constantly modeling behavior for our children—for better or for worse. To model effectively, do exactly want you want your child to do and add an explanation when helpful.

Do what you want the child to do. If you want your child to stop whining, you need to speak pleasantly. If you want your son to hang his coat up, then hang your coat up. If a young child doesn't see you hang your coat up, he may conclude that it magically happens, like the sun rising in the morning. Children make judgments about what people do and don't do from what they observe. This is clear in the following story.

Nicholas and Jean split the household chores and childcare. For example, Jean made the meals and Nicholas did the dishes. Since he wasn't fond of doing dishes, he procrastinated and did them late in the evening after the kids were asleep.

One day, Jean asked their son, Leo, 4, to help clean up in the kitchen. He refused because "Men don't do the dishes." Since Leo had not seen his dad do the dishes, he concluded that males don't do them.

Explain what you are doing. Modeling is useful, however, children cannot see what you are thinking. It is often helpful to combine modeling with verbal description or explanation. When the behavior you want happens, encourage it with praise or attention, otherwise, it may disappear. You can see the process in the story below.

Jennifer wanted her son, Nathan, 3, to be helpful and was committed to finding ways to get involvement. They were out walking one afternoon and an older woman in front of them dropped a letter she was carrying. Jennifer picked the letter up and asked Nathan if he wanted to give it to the woman. He took the letter, ran up to the woman, and gave it to her. The woman smiled at him and said, "Thank you. That was very kind."

He returned to Mom smiling from ear to ear. Jennifer summed things up, "The woman dropped her letter. You took the letter and gave it to her. She liked that and thanked you. You were very helpful."

Avoid behavior you don't want your child to mimic. It is wise to remember that children may model everything they see or hear. They will pick up your bad habits as easily as your good habits. Most children will want to eat in the living room or smoke if they see adults doing it. Sometimes it takes many repetitions before a child picks something up, other times they learn after one exposure.

Seventeen-year-old Rico was staying with his Aunt Dorotea for a couple of weeks to take a summer class. She had warned him to watch what he said because her toddler, Nina, was picking up language rapidly and she didn't want her to learn any swear words.

One evening, Rico was working on a report. The stack of books beside him toppled and spilled the pop he was drinking all over his notes and the table, making a big mess. He started to swear, but caught himself in time to substitute the word "Fudge!"

Nina looked up at Rico startled, but said nothing and continued to play. The next day, however, she went around the house knocking things over and saying, "Fudge."

Many years ago, someone told me that children pick up eighty-five percent of their parents' attitude and habits—the question is, which eighty-five percent?

The next activity is to look at what you and your parenting partner are modeling. When you have done that, you can look at the next STAR Parenting tool, ☆*Re-do it right.*

Activity: 8–1: The good and the bad of modeling

Modeling or imitating can be helpful or frustrating, depending on the behaviors children copy. Below are behaviors that parents have noticed kids mimic.

Directions: Read each behavior and then decide if the behavior would be helpful or unhelpful for you.

Behavior	Helpful	Unhelpful
1. **Toddler**		
a. Pushes buttons on the keyboard like his mother	☐	☐
b. Says please and thank you like his mom and dad	☐	☐
c. Says inappropriate words heard from older sibling	☐	☐
d. Tries using his fork and spoon like mom and dad	☐	☐
2. **Preschooler**		
a. Waters the flowers	☐	☐
b. Picks up toys like his mother	☐	☐
c. Puts the laundry away like his sister	☐	☐
d. Rakes leaves with toy rake	☐	☐
e. Decides she wants to take showers like Mommy and Daddy	☐	☐

3. **2nd grader**		
a. Cries like her sister when she can't have her way	☐	☐
b. Scrapes his plate after dinner like his mother	☐	☐
c. Tells everyone to be polite, like her mother	☐	☐
d. Wants to dress like her aunt (age 24)	☐	☐
e. Sits quietly listening to the teacher explain an assignment (modeled by teacher)	☐	☐
4. **Older elementary**		
a. Starts to use foul language or argues with parents	☐	☐
b. Breathes calmly when upset	☐	☐
c. Teases someone on the playground (modeling peers)	☐	☐
d. Wants to be just like a movie star	☐	☐
e. Yells at cars on the freeway	☐	☐

Answers: People interpret these behaviors differently. Notice the behaviors you are modeling, then decide which to continue and which to change.

Teach new skills point
☆*Re-do it right* tool

The second tool for teaching new skills is ☆*Re-do it right*. This tool can be used to encourage physical habits. Each time you repeat a behavior or action, the likelihood of doing it again increases. That is because the neurological pathway in the brain is strengthened. So if you want your child to use an alternative behavior, you need to help him create an alternative path. The easiest way to do that is to take the child back to the same position and have him do the desired behavior.

How to ☆*Re-do it right*
☆*Re-do it right* involves gently returning the child to the place where the error was made, reminding or assisting him to do it right, and staying with him as he re-does the behavior correctly. For example, if your child forgot to close the door when he came in, walk over to him and say, "Oops, you forgot to close the door." Put your arm around him, and walk back with him and have him close the door. Since this process involves more time than doing it right the first time, most children quickly adapt.

This tool is much more effective in building a new habit than telling the child what to do. For some reason, physically going with the child makes the task seem more important. In the next section, there are several situations where ☆*Re-do it right* has been used. You can see what the parent did.

Examples of ☆*Re-do it right*
☆*Re-do it right* can be used to encourage a variety of physical activities—hanging up a towel, using a pleasant voice, making the bed, and walking indoors.

Hang up your towel. Rick was a single parent taking a STAR Parenting class to help him raise his 7-year-old son, Dylan.

One thing that really bugged Rick was that Dylan would drop his towel in the hall after taking a bath, no matter how many times Rick reminded him or fined him. And if he ordered him to do it, a power struggle ensued.

One evening, Dylan had just finished the bath and dropped the towel in the hall. On a whim, Rick decided to try ☆Re-do it right. He went over to Dylan, put his arm around him, and said, "Hey, Buddy, that towel belongs in the bathroom. Let's get it back there." Rick picked up the towel, gave it to Dylan, and they both walked to the bathroom. Dylan smiled as he hung the towel up. Rick reported to his class that he was astounded at the results—no hassle, no struggle.

Make your bed. Satomi had her standards and she wanted her kids to be able to make their beds so they looked nice.

As her son slipped out of his room, she noticed that his bed was not made. She put out her arm to corral him and said, "Oops, you forgot to make your bed. Let's do it right." Then she walked with him back into the room. He quickly pulled the covers and quilt up, and smoothed the pillow. She then smiled at him and remarked, "That was a good speedy bed-making job! You bed looks neat, and your room looks nicer."

Use a pleasant voice. Melissa was frustrated because her daughter used a whiney voice a lot. Nothing she did was helping.

Next time her daughter whined, Melissa smiled and said, "Whoops, Jasmine, where did your nice voice go? Re-say that pleasantly." Jasmine repeated the request in a pleasant voice.

Walk please. Mrs. D. was a Brownie scout leader with twenty-four girls in her troop. They met in a church that didn't want people running in the building. Each year when the troop began, the new girls would forget the rule, drop their stuff by the door, and run across the room to where the activity was.

As soon as Mrs. D. saw someone start to run, she would walk toward the girl, put her arm out to stop her, remind her of the rule, and then practice walking together. "Oh, dear, Anna, you forgot to walk. Let's re-do it right." They would turn and walk back to where Anna dropped her books, then turn around and walk back to where Anna was intercepted.

It was only a couple of weeks until all Mrs. D. needed to do was to take one step toward a girl and she would turn around, walk back to her books, turn again, and walk toward the group.

When using the tool ☆*Re-do it right*, you need to go to the child, remind him pleasantly of the correct behavior, and walk with him while he re-does it. It doesn't work to make the request from across the room or in a grumpy manner. Perhaps one reason why the tool works is the simple cheerfulness of the interaction.

Both tools we have talked about so far in this chapter are quite simple and take relatively little time. The next tool, ☆*Shaping*, takes more thought and planning.

Activity: 8–2: Correct ☆*Re-do it right*

Directions: Read each situation and the response. Identify the error in the adult's response. Write a new response that corrects the error.

Situation	Error and revision
1. Mom has just finished shampooing the carpet. To keep it looking good, she asks everyone to remove their shoes at the door. Her daughter, Elena, came home from school, and headed for the kitchen without taking off her shoes. *Mom calls from the desk where she is working, "Elena, remember to leave your shoes by the front door."	☐ Instructs the child from a distance ☐ Uses an angry voice ☐ Leaves child to finish *Revision:*
2. Mom is trying to teach her son, Chad, to put the lid down and flush the toilet when he is done. He has just forgotten again. *Mom scoots after him and says, "Chad, can't you ever remember to lower the lid and flush the toilet?" as she walks with him to the bathroom.	☐ Instructs the child from a distance ☐ Uses an angry voice ☐ Leaves child to finish *Revision:*
3. You have asked your kids to put their dirty dishes in the sink. Ming, your daughter, just left the kitchen without cleaning up. *You scoot after her, put your arm around her, point to the dishes and crumbs she left on the counter, and say, "Ming, please go back and finish cleaning up."	☐ Instructs the child from a distance ☐ Uses an angry voice ☐ Leaves child to finish *Revision:*
4. Your son Caleb just came in from playing outside and is leaving a trail of dirt behind him. *You grab the dust-buster in frustration and say, "Caleb, look at that mess you're making. When are you ever going to learn to watch what you're doing? Clean it up right now," as you hand him the dust-buster.	☐ Instructs the child from a distance ☐ Uses an angry voice ☐ Leaves child to finish *Revision:*

Possible answers: **1.** *Error:* Instructs Elena from a distance. *Revision:* Go to her and ask her to re-do it right. **2.** *Error:* Angry voice. *Revision:* "Whoops, you need to lower the lid and flush the toilet. Let's re-do it right." **3.** *Error:* Leaves the child to finish alone. *Revision:* Walk with her to put dishes away. **4.** *Error:* Angry voice and leaving child to finish himself. *Revision:* "Caleb, stop. Look, you are leaving dirt on the floor. It needs to be cleaned up. Let's re-do it right."

Teach new skills point
☆*Shaping* tool

The third tool on the **Teach new skills** point is ☆*Shaping*. ☆*Shaping* is a way to make a task or skill that feels overwhelming more manageable. You can use it to teach simple skills or more complicated behaviors. You can see the process in Mark's story.

Two-and-a-half year-old Amanda wanted to dress herself, but couldn't manage. She would scream "I do it, I do it" when I helped. Instead of continuing the battles, I decided to teach her how to dress herself.

When I watched what Amanda was doing, I noticed she tried to put her clothes on standing up like I do. She could not manage to balance and put her pants on. She needed to sit on the floor. I thought about how she could do it and made a five-step process out of it.

1. Lay her pants down flat on the floor.
2. Sit down on the floor facing the waistband.
3. Lift up the waistband and slip one foot in the opening and then the other.
4. Scoot the fabric up so her feet stick out.
5. Stand and pull the waistband up to her waist.

Then I showed her how to put her pants on seated on the floor. I sat on the floor beside her and demonstrated each step with my pants. It sounds kind of weird, but it really worked. I think it helped to divide the process into small steps.

When using shaping you can divide a skill into small steps or divide the process of teaching a skill into steps or levels. If you wanted to teach a child to wash his hands, you could use shaping to *describe* the skill or to *encourage* the action. The difference between using ☆*Shaping* to teach a skill or encourage a process is illustrated below.

Table 8–2: ☆*Shaping*

Teach the task *of hand washing*	**Encourage the process** *of hand washing*
1. Wet your hands 2. Put soap on your hands 3. Rub your hands together 4. Rinse your hands 5. Dry hands on towel 6. Hang the towel back up	1. Model (and comment on) the steps in washing your hands. Use steps at right. 2. Model the steps and ask the child to do them beside you. When the child can follow your lead, move to the next step. 3. Give verbal guidance only. Let him do it all. When he's skillful, move to next step. 4. Watch the child wash his hands. If he skips a step, give him a chance to remember. If he doesn't, then remind him. When no reminding is needed, move on. 5. Ask the child to wash hands without your presence.

How to get started

Divide the task into small steps and teach those steps. You can teach the steps by modeling or giving simple instructions. If you want to teach a complicated skill, two parts are needed. First, develop a plan and second, implement the plan. To develop the plan, (1) find out what the child can already do, (2) list what she needs to learn, and then (3) develop a plan. Second, implement the plan. We will look at each of these briefly, and then look at several examples of how parents have used the process with their children.

Find out what the child can already do. You can get information by watching the child, asking the child, or asking someone else for their impression. Mark watched his daughter to discover why she was having trouble putting her pants on. Tracy asked her son why he didn't have his shoes on and found that he didn't know how to turn a sock inside out. Other ways to get information are to schedule time to watch how a child handles the situation. You can also ask a friend to watch or ask your child's teacher for her ideas.

List what she needs to learn. The list may include both information and skills. Finding these involves going through the action you want step-by-step. You can do it mentally or physically. Some people find it helpful to imagine themselves as a sportscaster giving play-by-play descriptions of an event. Also note what information and vocabulary the child will need to be successful.

Develop a plan and implement it. Take your list and arrange the items in a reasonable sequence. Think about how you will introduce the material. In some cases you may want to invent the vocabulary or activities you will use.

This is the same process Aunt Beth used to help Katie write her report on Norway. First, Beth asked her niece what she knew. Then she listed the things that needed to be done, assembled the supplies, and demonstrated each step as Katie went.

Examples of shaping

The idea of shaping is to make a task that seems very difficult become easier. Sometimes shaping can be as quick and easy as it was when Mark taught his daughter to put her pants on. Other times it can take more time and effort. You can see this as Monica recalls helping her daughter learn to speak in a pleasant tone.

Every time Gina spoke it grated on my nerves. She whined about everything. When I thought about Gina's whining, I realized that part of the problem was that Gina really didn't know when she was whining and when she was speaking pleasantly. I thought about what was involved in noticing one's tone and changing it. I decided on three steps for change.

  1. Recognize the difference between a whiny voice and a pleasant voice.
  2. Notice when she is whining and switch tones.
  3. Start out with a pleasant voice.

The process took a couple of weeks, but this is what we did.

First, I taught Gina to recognize the difference between a whiny voice and a pleasant voice. I began with pleasant and whiny puppets. Then I invented a game called "Name That Sound" where I mixed whining and pleasant voices with animal sounds on a tape recorder. When she could identify the difference, we moved to stage two.

Second, I asked her to notice when she whined and to change to a pleasant voice. We began with changing pretend whining to pleasant talk. Then we moved to real life. I invited her to notice when I whined and ask me to change. And I told her I would do the same for her. I made a point to whine occasionally so she could catch me. When she could change easily, I moved to step three.

Finally, I asked Gina to start out with a pleasant voice. I told her that if she forgot I could ignore what she was saying or I could ask her to leave the room and count to five before returning. She decided that I should ask her to leave. She soon discovered that it took more time to leave and re-enter than it did to speak pleasantly in the first place. She quickly became more careful with her tone.

Shaping a physical skill. Five steps you can use to teach a physical skill are presented in the box below. Start by offering the least support you can and gradually increase the help if the child cannot do what you direct.

Find the right balance between patience and information. With *patience*, you need to allow the child enough time to think about your directions and do them. With *information*, you need to provide information in a timely fashion—before he or she gets too frustrated. The length of time you wait before moving to the next step varies from child to child depending on age, temperament, and experience. Start out with ten to fifteen seconds and then lengthen or shorten as needed.

Five steps to teach a physical action

1. Give attention. Do not offer help. Wait for ten to fifteen seconds for the child to begin the activity. If the child is stuck or having difficulty, move promptly to the next step.

- Reward success with continued attention or simple praise, "That's right." "You did it."
- Waiting more than fifteen seconds prolongs the agony with no benefit. Move to the next step.

2. Offer verbal information. Describe what needs to happen rather than giving instructions. Focus on *facts* rather than *direction*. For example, "Put the red box on the blue one," would become, "The red box is smaller than the blue one." Let your child use the new information to figure out what to do.

- Comment on actions that are successful. "You put the red box on the blue one."
- If words don't help quickly, move on to modeling the action.

3. Model the action. Show the child exactly what he needs to do. Get your own materials, for example, boxes, fruit, sock, scissors, so you have two sets. Stand (or sit) beside the child. As you show your child what to do, *explain* what you are doing. It helps to make the activity seem fun.

- Again, comment on successful actions. Give attention again.
- If the child doesn't pick up the activity quickly, give a physical cue.

4. Give a physical cue. Point, touch, twist, or reposition something so the child can see it. Give as little help as possible. Show the child where to look, how to hold, or when to push.

- Recognize success and return to giving attention.
- If this doesn't work, offer physical help.

5. Give physical help. Do the part that is hard for the child, not the whole thing. Again, the purpose is to help the child past the difficult part and on to more successful activities.

- Acknowledge completion. Remark on what you saw: "You put the red box on the blue one." Or remark that he succeeded: "You did it!"
- Acknowledge effort. "You really tried to stack the boxes." If your child still needs physical help, this piece of the activity is beyond the child's learning for now. Let the topic rest a couple of days or weeks before trying again.

Activity: 8–3: Steps in ☆*Shaping*

☆*Shaping* involves dividing a skill into several smaller steps or tasks, and then teaching each of those. Sometimes the step involves cognitive or mental information, sometimes physical skills, and sometimes it involves both.

Directions: Choose a skill and list several steps (four to six) to do the skill.

Choose a skill: ☐ speak pleasantly   ☐ clean the sink   ☐ negotiate with a sibling
List steps:

-

-

-

-

-

Possible answers:

Speak pleasantly	**Clean bathroom sink**	**Negotiate with sibling**
• Distinguish between a pleasant and a whining voice in other people • Notice when he or she is whining • Switch from a whining voice to a pleasant voice • Start speaking pleasantly • Speak pleasantly when upset	• Collect cleanser and sponge • Wet sink • Close the drain and sprinkle cleanser on sponge • Rub sponge over the whole sink • Rinse the sink • Check that all the sink shines, repeat as needed	• Gather data—what does the other child want? • Clarify the problem—I want . . . , Other wants . . . • Think of ideas • Evaluate ideas—which will work for both of us? • Make a decision and plan • Implement the plan

Shaping and chores. In *Children and Chores: The Surprising Impact of Chores on Kids' Futures*, I illustrate shaping by breaking the task of introducing chores into five steps: (1) make the job clear, (2) offer choices, (3) create a reminder system, (4) give support, and (5) establish consequences.

Shaping a self-calming strategy. In *Dealing With Disappointment: Helping Kids Cope When Things Don't Go Their Way*, I provide a five-step process for teaching children to calm themselves. The steps are in the box entitled "How to teach a self-calming strategy" on page 176. Stephanie used this shaping process to teach her son to take deep breaths when he was upset.

Our son, William, has always been volatile. When he was little, we accepted the crying and drama as a part of his age. However, he is 6 and he is still as intense as ever. My husband, Matthew, has been telling him to calm down. I had suggested that he take a breath or run around the house, but it had made no difference. We decided to choose one self-calming tool and teach it using the steps in Dealing with Disappointment. These are the steps.

Why bother with chores?

Marty Rossmann (University of Minnesota) has found that involving kids in chores beginning at 3 or 4 is the best single indicator of success in their mid-twenties.

How to teach a self-calming strategy

1. Introduce the skill
2. Link the skill to change in feelings
3. Practice using the skill when child is calm
4. Prompt child to use the strategy
5. Back out and let the child use the skill by himself

- **First we introduced the skill.** *Matthew showed William how to blow a tissue ball across the table. After William tried a couple of times, Matthew observed that the bigger the breath, the farther the tissue ball went. He encouraged William to blow the ball "real far." They continued to "play ball" until William could take deep breaths.*

- **Next we linked the action to a change <u>in feeling</u>.** *One evening when Matthew was feeling grouchy, he suggested playing tissue hockey. When they started, Matthew mentioned casually that he felt grumpy. After they played a while, Matthew turned to William and said, "William, guess what? I don't feel grumpy anymore."*

Matthew continued to comment on how he felt better after tissue hockey. Finally, one evening William was irritable but not in meltdown mode. Matthew suggested they play tissue hockey, but did not mention why. When William felt better, Dad casually commented, "You were upset when we started and now you seem better. Looks like tissue hockey might help you too." Matthew invited William to play when he looked irritated or restless until William could notice the feeling change himself.

- **Once William could notice the change in feelings, we began to practice using the tool in pretend.** *I asked William to help the characters in the stories we read. For example, when we read "Goldilocks and the Three Bears," the bears return and Goldilocks is scared and runs away. I said, "William, what could Goldilocks do to calm herself?" At first he looked blank, then grinned and said, "Take deep breaths."*

After a while, I started making up stories similar to situations that upset William. For example, the teddy bear was upset because the cereal he wanted was gone, and I asked William what Teddy could do. Soon he was able to coach Teddy on how to handle problems. Finally, I asked him to think back to a situation that day that infuriated him, and act out how he could have used the calming breaths.

- **Then I began to prompt William to use the strategy.** *I asked him what he wanted to call the calming breaths. He thought a moment and said, "Dragon breaths, because they like breathing out fire and getting rid of grumps."*

I asked if we could make that a special code for our family. If I needed to calm down, he could say, "dragon breath" to remind me. And, if he was getting upset, I would give him the same signal. I began to say "dragon breath" before he had totally "lost it," and surprisingly he cooperated most of the time. When he took breaths, I would comment, "Wow, you took a deep breath and you are more in control now."

- **Finally I backed out and let William be responsible for himself.** *After a couple of weeks of reminding, William was taking dragon breaths on his own. I was tempted to continue making suggestions, but I really did want him to do it on his own, so I reduced my reminders. The process took almost four months, but it was worth it. It is easier to be around him, and he feels better too.*

Stephanie and Matthew took the shaping steps from "How to teach a self-calming strategy" and applied them to their son's behavior. They were able to take a long-standing problem and make a change.

When you are teaching new skills, sometimes you need to develop standards. We will look at that next.

Establish a standard

When children are very young, letting them do something sloppily may be fine. As children grow older, you will want to teach standards for a task. **Again, teaching is different from telling.** To teach a standard, you need to determine the criteria, create a checklist, convey the criteria, and practice. Ask the child to do the task and check himself. Praise effort and success. You will notice that this is another example of shaping.

Determine the criteria. How will you and the child know when the job is satisfactory? The criteria should be clear and observable—things to which you can say yes or no. It is discouraging for children to do what the parent says, and then to be told it is not good enough, or more requirements have been added. You can see Satomi's criteria in the box "Making a bed."

When you have your list, think about whether is it reasonable for the child's age and temperament. The criteria can change as the child grows. For example, you might ask a 3½-year-old child to put the pillow at the top of the bed and pull the quilt up to touch it.

Create a checklist. When you have the criteria, make a list the child can use. It can be a simple list like Satomi's, a pictorial one if reading is difficult for the child, or a list with boxes to check off. The latter might help with the child who is learning the standard.

Convey the criteria and practice. The goal is to contrast a good job, a bad job, and an incomplete job. You can start with a task that is almost complete or a task that has yet to be done. It helps to read the criteria to the child one at a time and ask her to check them. Satomi explains how she presented the criteria to her son, Justin.

> **Making a bed**
> *Satomi's criteria for a 10-year-old:*
>
> **Sheets and blankets—**
> Hem or binding at top
> Even on both sides
> Smooth, with no wrinkles
> Tucked in at foot of bed
> **Pillows—**
> Fluffed and at head of bed
> **Bedspread—**
> Pulled to the top of bed
> Smooth, without wrinkles
> Even both sides and bottom

I wanted my kids to learn how to make a bed well. I picked a time when my daughter's bed was well made and asked her permission to use it as an example. When she agreed, I printed a list of the criteria and messed up my own bed a bit. Then I got Justin. We went into Jessica's room. I read him the criteria one-by-one and asked him to point them out and say if they were done.

Next, we went to my room and I repeated the process. The first item was the top of the sheet and blanket. The blanket was up on one side but not the other. He looked at me puzzled, expecting that it would be perfect. I asked, "Is it up and even all the way across?" He said, "No." I replied, "Good. You can tell what looks nice and what doesn't." We continued and he found the two other errors I made for his benefit. He was smiling, pleased he found them. If my bed had been perfect, he would not have learned to evaluate well.

One fun way to encourage children to use the criteria is to have them check the parent and find some errors. You might ask them to do this a couple of times with different errors each time. This is far more effective than evaluating a perfect room.

Ask the child to do the task and to check himself. Next time the child does the task, give him the checklist and ask him to check himself when he is done.

When we were done, I gave Justin the list and told him to make his bed and check his work. Then, when he was done, to call me and I would check his checking. He grinned and started to work. I left the room and waited. If I stayed, I was afraid I would make comments and I really wanted him to do the whole process by himself.

When he was done we both went back. I read each criterion, we both looked at it, and if it was correct I dramatically checked it off. The job was well done except for some small wrinkles in the bedspread. I said, "Whoops, you got a wrinkle here, let's re-do it right." The wrinkle was soon fixed and I put a big check mark on the list.

Praise when the task is well done. Focus on the positive. Tell children specifically what they did well. Here is how Satomi handed out praise.

"Wow, Justin, you did an excellent job. The sheets and blankets are neat. The pillow is fluffed and in the right place. The bedspread is even and wrinkle-free. Let's do a well-done dance." They joined hands and twirled around the room.

If your child invites negative attention like nagging and scolding, don't mention the aspects that are not good unless they happen a couple of times. Focus on what the child is doing well. Reminding her rewards unwanted behavior. You can refer to chapter six, "Respond to Cooperation," for ideas.

Activity: 8–4: Criteria for a clean room

Directions: Describe what you would expect a 4-year-old to do to clean his room. Describe how your expectations would differ for a 10-year-old.

	4-year-old	*10-year-old*
Bed		
Toys		
Dirty clothes		
Books		
Clean clothes		
Paper		
Floor		
Possible answers	*4-year-old*	*10-year-old*
Bed	Quilt pulled up Wrinkles acceptable	Bed made, no wrinkles (Satomi's list)
Toys	Off the floor—on the shelves or in a toy box	Neatly arranged on shelves
Clean clothes	In dresser or closet	Folded, in dresser or hung up in the closet
Dirty clothes	In a box in the closet	In the bathroom hamper or laundry bin
Books	On bookshelf	On a bookshelf. Arranged in an orderly fashion
Paper	Off the floor, in the trash	Put away or taken out to the recycle bin
Floor	Clear of "junk"	Clear of junk and swept or vacuumed

Create a teaching plan

If you wish to teach your child a skill or attitude, and she is having trouble with it, it may help to create a teaching plan. A teaching plan requires you to think about what is needed in a systematic, structured way. Decide what you want, list prerequisites, develop a plan, implement the plan, and review and revise as needed.

The plan is an adaptation of the STAR Parenting process. The **Stop and focus** step is divided into two parts—deciding what you want and considering the prerequisites. Looking at the prerequisites is important because sometimes children do not have the skills they need to learn to do what you wish. You can see how Patty used this process to potty train her daughter:

1. Decide what you want. State your goal in simple, positive language. Check that it is age appropriate. *Pee in the pot. No more diapers.* In *Is This a Phase?* Helen Neville writes that by 2½, half of the girls notice they need to go and get to the potty in time. For boys, the age is 3 years.
2. List prerequisite skills. Consider both physical skills and abstract ideas. *Physical skills:* Be able to get on the toilet. Pull pants up and down. Wipe herself. Wash her hands. *Abstract skills:* Feel when she needs to go. Interrupt herself. Relax and pee.
3. Develop a plan.

    Sequence the skills. Feel she needs to go. Interrupt herself. Go to the bathroom. Pull down her pants. Climb on the toilet. Pee in the potty. Wipe herself. Get off the potty. Pull up her pants. Wash her hands.

    Decide where to start. To begin with, I will start in the middle. I will take her when I think she might need to go, pull her pants down, and put her on the potty.

    Consider how to introduce the material. I will model the step I want her to do.

    Plan how to encourage cooperation. When she goes to the bathroom when I ask, I will thank her for cooperating. When she pees in the potty, I will give her a star.
4. Implement the plan. Follow through and remark on the child's progress. "Wow. You went in the potty again. Soon you will be able to wear big girl pants."
5. Review and revise. What is going well? What is difficult? Change what's not working—try another approach.

The focus of this chapter has been **Teach new skills.** Those skills can be mental, social, or physical. The tools were ☆*Modeling,* ☆*Re-do it right,* and ☆*Shaping.* We looked at how to create a teaching plan for more difficult skills.

In Part Two of this book, we have looked at the five STAR Parenting points and the fifteen tools. Right after the summary and the STAR in Action Story, in Part Three, we will look at how you can get started and how to avoid the dark side of the star.

Change challenging situations into learning opportunities.

Summary of
Teach New Skills

★ **Decide what you want.** State your goal in simple positive language. Check that it is age appropriate.

★ **List prerequisite skills.** Consider both physical skills and cognitive or thinking abilities children must have before they can learn to do what you wish.

★ **Develop a plan.**
Sequence the skills.
Decide where to start.
Consider how to introduce the material.
Plan how to encourage cooperation.

★ **Implement the plan.** Follow through. Remark on child's success and effort.

★ **Review and revise.** What is going well? What is difficult? How else can I teach it, if necessary?

STAR in Action Story[1]

Unwanted Gifts

My son's birthday is right after Thanksgiving. This year my family was all there for his birthday. Jonathan had an idea of what present he really, really wanted. He excitedly opened each present expecting it to be the one he wanted, looked at it, frowned, then tossed it aside. This was extremely embarrassing. This Christmas both sets of relatives, including my siblings, will be here for dinner and gift exchange. I'm afraid Jonathan will be disappointed with some of the gifts, and I don't want to have the same experience again. What can I do to prevent a scene?

Stop and focus

If I do nothing, I'm sure the gift exchange will be a disaster. I need to take a deep breath, stop fretting, and start thinking of what I can do. First, I do a reality check, then I will apply each STAR Parenting tool to the problem. If I get stuck, I'll ask my sister for help.

Long view: I want Jonathan to be an industrious, articulate, caring, and courteous young man.

Temperament: He is persistent, has trouble adapting, and has low emotional sensitivity to others. Once he gets an idea in his head, he goes for it regardless of whether it makes sense or not, and he is not affected by other peoples' feelings.

Development: The developmental task for 4-year-olds is "power and identity," although in this case, I think his behavior is influenced by inability to deal with his disappointment.

Desired behavior: Jonathan to receive gifts graciously. Before he can act graciously he may need (1) tools to deal with his disappointment, and (2) strategies for acting courteously.

Think of ideas

I didn't get very many ideas on my own, so I asked Joan, my sister, to help generate ideas. We put our heads together and came up with fifty ideas!

Acknowledge feelings

☆*Active listening* ① Say, "You're frustrated that you didn't get _____ ." ② "You are disappointed that it wasn't there."

☆*Grant in fantasy* ③ "Wouldn't it be great if you could see through the packages." or ④ "What if every box was IT?" Or, ⑤ "Wouldn't it be fun if you had a magic wand to make every present into an IT?"

☆*Simple listening* ⑥ Listen and say "Hmm," "Oh," "Really?" as appropriate.

Avoid problems

☆*Reduce stress* ⑦ Make sure (as much as possible) that Jonathan is well rested and fed. ⑧ Make sure the first gift he opens is the one he wants. ⑨ Give him a private hand signal to remind him to say, "Thank you."

☆*Change things* ⑩ Do a gift exchange instead of a bunch of gifts. ⑪ Do not open gifts in front of family. ⑫ Don't invite the relatives. ⑬ Tell relatives—no present. ⑭ Ask relatives to go together to buy one big gift. ⑮ Be gracious no matter what—and we will give some gifts to charity. ⑯ Make a game and focus on what he does get. Chart out what gifts he receives: gets four trucks, two cars, three coloring books.

☆*Two yeses* ⑰ He can thank them for the gift or thank them for the thought. ⑱ He can tell them why he likes it or he can just say "thank you for thinking of me." ⑲ He can tell them how he could use the gift or he can just say "thank you for thinking of me."

Respond to cooperation

☆*Attention* ⑳ When he is gracious, give him a "thumbs up." ㉑ Say "Thank you" in sign language. ㉒ Smile at him when he responds politely.

---

1 There is a STAR in Action Story at the end of each chapter. Each story is written by a parent in his or her own words and shows how that person adapted the STAR Parenting process to his or her own life.

These stories use tools from all points, so some may be unfamiliar until you have read the appropriate chapter. You can see how different parents, with different values or kids with different temperaments, might make different choices.

☆*Praise* ㉓ "You remembered to thank her for thinking of you." ㉔ "You were courteous. I'm proud of you." ㉕ "I noticed that you used a pleasant voice when you thanked Grandpa for his gift."

☆*Reward* ㉖ Give him a "Kind Ticket" each time he responds pleasantly. When he gets five Kind Tickets, Mom or Dad will do a kindness for him—like doing one of his chores. ㉗ Say, "If you are gracious with all the gifts, then you may go to the store and pick out a special present from Mom and Dad." (Consequence: If you are rude, you don't get it.)

Teach new skills

☆*Modeling* ㉘ Ask a friend to give you a gift you don't like. Model thanking the friend for thinking of you. When she leaves, explain to Jonathan that it is important to respond pleasantly whether you like the gift or not.

☆*Shaping* ㉙ Decide what specific skills he needs. Teach the skills he needs and then practice using them. 1. Calm himself down. 2. Choose two sentences he can say. 3. Practice the responses with puppets. 4. Practice the responses with Dad.

☆*Re-do it right* ㉚ If he opens a present and is rude, say, "Oops, you forgot the kind words. Let's try again. Let's show them what we've been working on."

• Ideas to teach dealing with feelings

Teach him to control his feelings when disappointed— take deep breaths.

Teach him to recognize other people's feelings by noticing their tone, expression, and language.

Ask him to choose two (or three) strategies to practice for dealing with disappointment. For example: take a deep breath, count to three, ask for a hug, use self-talk.

Use puppets to show one puppet getting a gift. If the "receiving puppet" is rude, then have another puppet discuss how the "giving puppet" might feel and how the receiving puppet might manage his feelings.

Teach facial expressions that are acceptable—eye contact, smile.

• Ideas to teach responding graciously

Discuss empathy: ㉛ Ask him to consider how he would feel watching another open a gift he gave. ㉜ Ask him why he might choose to be pleasant even if he didn't like the gift he got. Possible answers: He won't hurt their feelings. They will continue to give him gifts.

Demonstrate appropriate responses: ㉝ Model responding gracefully when someone gives you something.

Then later discuss how maybe you didn't really want it and you were gracious because that person gave you a gift. ㉞ At the dinner table model courtesy, saying, "I don't eat this very often but it could become my favorite." ㉟ "I will give it a try and see if I like it more now."

Suggest different forms of self-talk: ㊱ "If I don't get what I want I can add it to my Christmas list." ㊲ "If I don't like the gift myself, I can get the pleasure of giving it to a child who needs it." ㊳ "I will get some gifts I like and some gifts I don't. That is okay. I can cope." "If I don't like it now, I might like it later—don't burn my bridges." "I 'git' what I 'git' and I don't throw a fit."

Make a list of things to say. ㊴ Brainstorm ideas with Jonathan. ㊵ Create a list of kind things to say: Invite several of Jonathan's friends over for a get-together and then ask them, "What words do you want to hear when a person opens your gift?" Make a list of their ideas.

Practice acting graciously: ㊶ Ask Jonathan what phrases he likes or what he is more comfortable with. ㊷ Puppet receives the gifts and you have the puppet say all the right things ㊸ Practice food courtesy at dinnertime to address the issue of disappointment. Create a scenario where Jonathan wanted some other food and he is disappointed. Let him practice coping with his disappointment. ㊹ Open mock gifts over and over until Jonathan can say the right words in response to opening any gift.

Set limits

☆*Clear rules* ㊺ "Courtesy is required." ㊻ "It's okay to be disappointed and it's not okay to be disagreeable." ㊼ "You get what you get and you don't throw a fit." ㊽ "We are courteous and respectful." ㊾ "Show gratitude when receiving a gift."

☆*Consequences* ㊿ No more gifts are opened. They are put away for a set amount of time (weeks or a month).

☆*A better way* ㊿ "Your way is to throw the unwanted gift. My way is to say, 'Thank you for thinking of me.' What's a better way?"

Act effectively

I was so embarrassed by Jonathan's behavior on his birthday that I wanted to avoid a repeat. I was tempted to avoid the whole problem by giving him what he wanted early or requesting the guests bring no gifts. However, I knew that the problem would not go away without effort, so I might as well deal with it at age 4, rather than at 5 or 6.

☆Attention, ☆praise, and ☆rewards are fine, but he has to respond graciously first. I have already told him that I expect him to say "Thank you" for a gift and that didn't work, so there is no reason to expect it will work better this time. Further, acknowledging his feeling after he is upset doesn't help him respond appropriately. So that left **Teach new skills.**

I reviewed the brainstorming Joan and I did and pondered how I could teach a skill that seemed so obvious to me. I decided on four steps. 1. Model and practice taking a breath to calm down. 2. Ask Jonathan to choose a phrase to use to thank people when he receives a gift. 3. Have Jonathan practice opening a mock gift politely, and rewarding him when he is successful.

Jonathan chose the phrase, "Thank you for thinking of me." I wrapped one of his old toys in pretty paper with a bow. Then, I told him that when he opened the gift graciously three times, I would give him a gift he would like—not the large gift he wanted, but something he would like.

The first time he opened the gift, he hurled it across the room and shouted, "That's dumb." I remained neutral, said, "Fine," picked up the toy and rewrapped it. We tried the next day with similar results. The third time when he tried, he choked out, "Thank—you—for—thinking—of—me," and stared glumly at the gift. Uncivil as his manner was, this was major progress! I praised what he did do, "Wow, you used your polite words. That's great!" and gave him a hug. The next attempts went better, and he got his reward.

Review and revise

The process took longer than I expected, but it worked. I'm glad I was able to keep my cool when he threw the unwrapped gift and when he grudgingly said "Thank you." Oh, and he was able to respond politely at Christmas—what a relief.

Part Three

Using the Whole STAR

**Getting started with
STAR Parenting**

☆

**The dark side of
the STAR**

☆

**When things
don't work**

Chapter 9

How to Get Started

Planning helps progress

We have looked at the STAR Parenting process (chapter two), considered our values and expectations, and created a long view (chapter three). We have learned about the STAR Parenting points and tools (chapters four to eight). As you begin to use the STAR Parenting model you may find it feels as awkward as putting on skis or trying a musical instrument for the first time. This is common with any new skill and will pass with practice.

To see how we can get started, we will follow four parents as they choose and try the STAR Parenting points and tools.

Maryann's 5-year-old sons had gotten in the habit of demanding breakfast as though she were a short order cook. This began when they were sick and she was struggling to get them to eat anything. Now they were well, and still enjoyed demanding their food.

Kym's 26-month-old son's independent streak was frustrating her. He wanted to do things alone and didn't have the skills.

Cindy's son, Jesse, 17 months, hated car seats. He would arch his back and struggle to keep from being put in one. It wore her out just thinking about it.

Martina's dad, Jorge, was very concerned. Martina was in second grade and resisted doing her homework. She did her work at school, but at home she wouldn't cooperate.

There are two general approaches to using the tools. One is to randomly choose a tool and see what happens. The other is to systematically use the whole STAR Parenting process, considering a variety of options before deciding what to do. First, we will review the long view. Next, we will look at both approaches. Finally, we will consider some reasons why kids might misbehave.

Decide what you want

Step back; calm yourself if you're upset. This allows you to think and respond proactively, rather than simply react. You are about to analyze present behavior and imagine what you would like as future behavior.

Identify the problem. Choose a situation that annoys or angers you. Briefly describe it as if you were a reporter: who, what, when, where, why, and how the situation usually ends.

Create a behavioral goal. When you have identified the problem, decide what you want the child to do instead. Then consider how that relates to what you want your child to be like when grown (your vision), and what is realistic for your child's age, temperament, and your values. Revise the goal if needed.

Activity 9–1: Getting started—Create a goal

Goal (what I want my child to do instead) _____

_____

Does the goal advance my long view for my child? ☐ yes, ☐ no

Is the desired behavior age *appropriate*? ☐ yes, ☐ no, ☐ unsure

Is it realistic for my child's *temperament*? ☐ yes, ☐ no, ☐ unsure

Is it reasonable for my child's *experience*? ☐ yes, ☐ no, ☐ unsure

Is it in keeping with my *values*? ☐ yes, ☐ no, ☐ unsure

Revise the goal if needed: _____

Consider which approach to take. Once you have created a goal, you can decide whether to take a casual approach to solve the problem or a systematic one. One thing to remember when choosing an approach is that you need to handle things differently to have a different outcome. Be flexible. You can't expect a change if you do the same thing over and over.

With a casual approach, parents and caregivers consider a couple of alternatives for the problem. To keep from slipping back into their previous habits, they use a device to introduce new tools or rotate among them. Three possibilities are described in the casual approach section.

The systematic approach is more structured. Parents thoughtfully describe the problem and then systematically consider how to use each tool for the problem.

Then they choose the tools they think will be most effective and build a plan around them. They also consider what roadblocks might cause the plan to fail and how to cope with them.

Each approach has benefits and drawbacks. The casual approach is usually quick and simple. However, some parents tend to gravitate to the tools they already use rather than try a new one, or they get distracted or diverted and fail to follow through.

The systematic approach takes more time and thought. For hurried parents (and who's not hurried nowadays?), this approach takes commitment. One strength of the systematic approach is that parents generate many ways to handle a problem—some new, some familiar—and the act of generating ideas increases the parent's skills even when he or she does not use the tools. A second benefit is that the parent anticipates possible roadblocks and how they might be prevented or handled.

Activity 9–2: Getting started—Choose an approach

Approach I will try: ☐ casual ☐ systematic

If casual: Tool (or tools) I will try: _____,

_____ , and/or _____

If systematic, use the STAR Parenting planning worksheet, page 232.

I will reassess this approach (date): _____

When you resolve a problem, it is useful to take a moment or two and reflect on what went right and what still needs improvement.

Casual approach

Many parents find that they need a way to help them choose new tools. There are several ways you can pick a new tool: open *STAR Parenting Tales and Tools* to a page and use the tool, draw the name of a tool for the day, or roll dice.

Open to a tool. The simplest way to get started is to clarify your problem, describe the behavior that you want in a short and positive statement, and then open the book somewhere in Part Two (which covers points and tools) and use the tool you open to.

Now let's look at Maryann, Kym, Cindy, and Jorge to see how they chose to select a tool (or tools) and what they did to get the new behavior they were aiming for.

Draw a tool. Write each of the fifteen STAR Parenting tools on slips of paper and put the strips in a container. Every few days draw a slip. Try to apply the new tool as your first response to a situation. Use the tool for a couple of days, so you have a chance to practice the tool before picking a new one.

Maryann, whose twin boys were in the habit of demanding breakfast, decided that she was done as a short order cook.

One evening after the twins went to bed, she went to the kitchen and drew a STAR Parenting tool to use. It was ☆Clear rules. She thought about what she wanted and decided on the rule, "Breakfast will be served to pleasant people."

The implied consequence was, "If you are not pleasant, I will not fix you breakfast." She also drew a second tool (☆Active listening) for backup if she needed it.

Mom met the boys in the hall before they came to the kitchen and said, "We have a new rule about breakfast. 'Breakfast will be served to pleasant people.'" The boys seated themselves at the table, looked at each other, and began to chant, "We want waf-fles. We want waf-fles. We want waf-fles."

Maryann turned to the boys and said, "Chanting is not pleasant. What do you think that means about breakfast?"

"You won't fix breakfast?" one twin ventured.

"You're right," Maryann replied.

"But we'll starve," they cried simultaneously.

"Breakfast will be served to pleasant people. You may act pleasantly or fix yourself cereal."

"But, Mom, we want waffles," they complained.

Maryann switched to ☆Active listening, "You're disappointed that there are no waffles for breakfast this morning."

The twins looked at each other. One said, "Will you fix eggs?"

Mom thought a moment and said, "That was a pleasant request. Yes, I will fix eggs." Maryann was relieved it went so well, although she expected that she would be challenged again the next day.

Although the primary tool Maryann planned to use was a ☆*Clear rule*, she actually used five STAR Parenting tools. See if you can identify them.* We will talk more about using the whole STAR to change behavior in the next chapter.

Roll the dice. Kym, who needed to teach her independent little boy new skills, liked variety. To make a game of choosing a tool, she carried dice in her pocket—one red and one blue. When she found herself getting irritated, she would take a deep breath, pull out her dice and roll them. She used the red die to determine the STAR Parenting point and the blue die to determine the specific tool.

On the *red die*, Kym assigned numbers one through five to the STAR Parenting points, starting with one for **Avoid problems** and progressing clockwise. Number six became free choice or throw again, depending on her mood.

The numbers on the *blue die* were linked to

> ### Roll of the dice decision
> #### STAR points
> 1 = Avoid problems
> 2 = Respond to cooperation
> 3 = Acknowledge feelings
> 4 = Set limits
> 5 = Teach new skills
> 6 = Free choice
>
> #### STAR tools
> 1 & 4 refer to the first tools (change things, attention, simple listening, clear rule, model)
> 2 & 5 refer to the second tools (reduce stress, praise, active listening, consequences, re-do it right)
> 3 & 6 refer to the third tools (two yeses, rewards, grant in fantasy, a better way, shaping)

---

*Answers: *Change things, Clear rules, Consequences, Acknowledge feelings,* and *Rewards the STAR Parenting tools. Since there are six numbers and three tools, two numbers referred to each tool. (See box on page 188.)

*When Kym's preschooler was upset because he was having trouble putting his pants on by himself, she rolled her dice. She rolled a three on red (**Acknowledge feelings** point) and a six on blue (☆Grant in fantasy tool). She turned to Cam and said, "Wouldn't it be fun if you had magic powers and your pants would hop on your body when you snapped your fingers?" He stopped whining but was still struggling unsuccessfully to put his pants on.*

*Kym rolled again. This time she rolled a one on red (**Avoid problems** point) and a three on blue (☆Two yeses tool). She thought a moment and said, "Looks like you're having trouble with your pants today. Do you want me to put them on you, or do you want to do it together?" Cam thought a minute and said, "You do it."*

Kym had never used ☆*Grant in fantasy* before. She tried it simply because the number came up and was surprised at how her son calmed down.

We looked at three random ways to use the tools: opening the book, drawing a tool, and throwing dice. You might try a random approach if you are stuck in a rut or don't have the time to sit and plan. However, if the behavior is very frustrating or is serious, people usually get better results with the systematic approach.

Systematic approach to using STAR Parenting

Below you can see how two parents used the entire process in different ways. Cindy, the mom with the car seat challenges, sat down with a friend and talked things through. Her description of the process is below. Jorge used the problem-solving chart (page 191) and filled it in.

Cindy explains her experience. *Jesse, 17 months, hated car seats. He would arch his back and struggle to keep from being put in one. It wore me out even thinking about it. One day I decided I needed a plan before I took him anywhere again. My friend Maryann came over. We brainstormed ideas, and then I mentally walked through the process.*

Stop and focus. When he got upset, I could take three deep breaths. And I could remind myself that although I want him to climb into the car seat pleasantly, it was not reasonable to expect an active toddler to be confined happily. Since I wanted him to be safe and to feel good about himself, I needed to keep both goals in mind.

Think of ideas. Maryann and I generated seventeen ideas using all points of the star. We didn't use the ☆Simple listening tool or ☆A better way because a 17-month-old child is too young. [Ideas they came up with are listed in the following table.]

Look before you leap, think before you speak.

Table 9–1: Cindy's ideas for the car seat trouble

STAR point	Ideas on each point
Avoid problems	*Take Jesse fewer places:* ① *Leave him with my spouse,* ② *Get a babysitter,* ③ *Plan shopping so I make fewer trips. Other ideas:* ④ *Get something new he can play with in the car seat.* ⑤ *Tell him where I am going and what we will do there that might interest him.* ⑥ *Take him outside and let him run around until he's tired and then put him in the car seat.*
Reward cooperation	⑦ *Praise him if he gets in cooperatively, "Wow, you got in yourself."* ⑧ *When he is in the seat, give him attention by singing songs he likes in the car.* ⑨ *Give him a "car toy" he can play with only when he is buckled in.* ⑩ *Give him a sticker when he gets in cooperatively.*
Acknowledge feelings	*When he gets upset, say,* ⑪ *"Yeah, it is frustrating to sit when you want to be running around." Or,* ⑫ *"You feel angry that you need to sit in the car seat."*
Set reasonable limits	*Make a rule:* ⑬ *"Seat belts on in the car." Explain the consequence,* ⑭ *"You can get in the seat yourself or I can put you in." If he doesn't get in, put him in and remark "I see you chose for me to put you in." Cindy's note to herself: Ignore his protests or use active listening. A 16-month-old child is too young for the tool "☆A better way."*
Teach new skills	*Teach him some ways to occupy himself in the car seat.* ⑮ *Make a soft tetherball and tie it to his car seat. (Be sure the string is too short to choke him.)* ⑯ *Get a book with interesting pictures to look at.* ⑰ *Give him a soft truck to drive on the chair and window.*

Act effectively. *I decided to start with three points. Since it is typical for toddlers to fight seat belts, I will try to avoid the problem and reduce the number of trips I take. I planned to set a firm limit: "Seat belts on in the car," and let him get in by himself. If he didn't get in, I planned to put him in and explain that it was his choice for me to put him in. I would encourage him by talking with him and singing songs when he is quiet.*

Review, revise, reward. *If that didn't work, I planned to acknowledge his feelings and get some new things that he could play with. Then I would put him in gently, whether he was crying or not. To reduce my stress, I would tell myself, "Jesse is lucky to have me. We are learning together."*

As it turned out, Cindy needed to use tools from all points. It took about two weeks of deep breathing and persistence on Cindy's part and noisy resistence on Jesse's part, but Cindy felt resolving the problem was worth the effort. Now her son gets in the car seat pleasantly on most days.

Jorge's approach. Some people like to use a chart or planning sheet to get started generating ideas and planning what they will do. Below is the sheet that Jorge used to deal with his daughter's reluctance to do homework.

★ STAR Parenting planning sheet—Jorge's example

Background: Describe last time the behavior happened	*My daughter, Martina, is in second grade. We're all having a tough time. Last year was fine, but all of a sudden she resists doing her homework. She does her work at school, but at home would rather read, draw, or bead bracelets. I am constantly reminding her to return to the table and do her work.*

Stop and focus

Collect data: • Age of the child • Length of the problem • Frequency of behavior	Child's age: *7 years* How long has behavior been a problem: *6 weeks* Frequency: *every day*
Values: List two that may be related to the behavior	*In my family we value* 1. *Persistence* 2. *Curiosity*
Development: What is the child's developmental task? How might it apply *here*?	Task: *structure and skills* Possible relation to behavior: *To find out how things are done in the wider world and develop a structure for how her world works.*
Temperament: List three traits that might affect this behavior and how intense the traits are	Trait and strength (high, low, moderate) 1. *Uncomfortable in school this year—low approach* 2. *Slow to adapt—low adaptability* 3. *Gives up easily—low persistence*
Desired behavior: What you want the child to do *instead* of what she is doing	Specific behavior: *I want her to work on her homework until she is done, even if it is hard. I want her to be able to motivate herself and work without reminding.*

Think of ideas

Avoid problem ☆*Change things* ☆*Reduce stress* ☆*Two yeses*	• *Remove distractions (books and beading) from study area OR Give her a snack before starting.* • *Encourage Martina to run around outside before starting.* • "*You can have thirty minutes of down time (snack, running around, bathroom) before you start your homework, or start your homework right away and have an extra thirty minutes after your homework is done.*"
Respond to cooperation ☆*Attention* ☆*Praise* ☆*Rewards*	• *Keep an eye on her and each time she finishes a page smile at her.* • *Each time she finishes a couple of problems, say, "Wow, you have finished two problems." Or, "You have done two more problems—what persistence." Or, "You are moving along. Look at all the problems you have done."* • *Give her a small bead or chocolate chip to put in a bowl each time she finishes a problem. Gradually increase the effort needed.*
Acknowledge feelings ☆*Simple listening* ☆*Active listening* ☆*Grant in fantasy*	• *When she complains about homework, I will make non-committal comments like "oh?" "Humm", "I see."* • "*You feel overwhelmed by the idea of homework.*" • "*Wouldn't it be fun if you had a magic set of help-phones that you could put on your head that would give you the information you needed for that day?*"

Set reasonable limits ☆Clear rules ☆Consequences ☆A better way	• *Homework first, then play* • *"Each time I remind you to return to the table, you lose five minutes of screen time."* • *"I want you to do all your homework when you get home from school. You want to do it when the mood strikes. What is an idea that will work for both of us?"*
Teach new skills ☆Model ☆Re-do it right ☆Shaping	• *Model positive self-talk and problem solving. Beat her record. Balance the check book at the table with Martina and say, "This is hard. I can figure it out. If I get too frustrated I can take a deep breath."* • *When she wanders from the table I can go to her, turn her to face the table, and gently say, "Oops, you need to finish your homework," as we walk to the table.* • *Shaping. Gradually increase the effort required for a reward. See example below.*

Act effectively

Ideas: What will you try first?	*I will remove distractions, give her attention, and praise her when she focuses on her homework.*
Roadblocks: What might interfere with your success?	*Getting distracted myself and not noticing when she is working.*
Support: How can you protect yourself from the problem?	*I could set a timer for myself to remind me to check on her, or I could do something at the table myself while she works.*
Make a plan. What will you need? Who will get it? Do you need anyone's help?	*I will need to get snacks. And tidy the area around the kitchen table. I will also need to get a timer with a soft ring so I don't disturb Martina.*
How long will you continue this plan?	*One week.*

Review and revise

What went well?	*She was able to do her homework while I was beside her.*
What needs to change?	*She stopped when I left. We will need to work on her motivating herself.*
What will you try next? For how long?	*Shaping. I will need to get small beads and chocolate chips. I will try for two weeks.*
What have you learned for the future?	*Patience. If I want Martina to learn something hard, I must do my part and be patient.*

Jorge's planning sheet is the process that he used to help Martina do her homework (planning sheet for you on page 193). When he did what he planned, she would do her homework as long as he was beside her. This was an improvement, but not where he wanted to be. His next goal was to teach her to be persistent by shaping. He began by rewarding Martina for small steps, and gradually turned responsibility for the process over to her. This can be seen in the box on page 193.

☆*Shaping:* **Persistence with homework**

Begin by rewarding small successes and gradually increase the effort required for the reward.

1. Give the child a bead or chocolate chip to put in a small bowl each time she finishes a problem. **2.** Three problems for one chocolate chip. **3.** Ask her to select an incentive for finishing the whole assignment from a short list you provide. (For example, points for a trip to the zoo or a new book, the privilege of choosing the dinner menu, or staying up later on the weekend, etc. If she wants something large that is not on the list, say, "That's a good idea for when you can do all your homework by yourself for a whole month.") **4.** Let her choose an incentive for three days. Then for a week. Then two weeks. **5.** Ask her what incentive she would like for finishing her homework by herself for a month. **6.** Ask her how she will reward herself (or celebrate) after completing a second month.

✎STAR Parenting planning worksheet

Background: Describe last time the behavior happened	
Stop and focus	
Collect data: • Age of the child • Length of the problem • Frequency of behavior	Child's age: _____ How long has behavior been a problem? _____ Frequency: _____ times an hour ☐, a day ☐, week ☐ , or month ☐.
Values: List three that may be related to the behaviors	1. 2. 3.
Development: What is the child's developmental task? How might it apply here?	Task: Possible relation to behavior:

Temperament: List three traits that might affect this behavior and how intense the traits are	*Trait* *Intensity* 1. _____ _____ 2. _____ _____ 3. _____ _____
Desired behavior: What you want the child to do *instead* of what he/she is doing	Specific behavior:

Think of ideas

Avoid problem ☆*Change things* ☆*Reduce stress* ☆*Two yeses*	• • •
Respond to cooperation ☆*Attention* ☆*Praise* ☆*Rewards*	• • •
Acknowledge feelings ☆*Simple listening* ☆*Active listening* ☆*Grant in fantasy*	• • •
Set limits ☆*Clear rules* ☆*Consequences* ☆*A better way*	• • •
Teach new skills ☆*Model* ☆*Re-do it right* ☆*Shaping*	• • •

Act effectively

Ideas: What will you try first?	
Roadblocks: What might interfere with your success?	

Support: How can you protect yourself from the problem?	
Make a plan. What will you need? Who will get it? Do you need anyone's help?	
How long will you continue this plan?	
Review, revise, and reward	
What went well?	
What needs to change?	
What will you try next? For how long?	
What have you learned for the future?	

Both the casual approach and the systematic approach depend on understanding the problem. This may be easier if you first understand what is driving the behavior.

Identifying the problem

In addition to age and temperament, there are some other things to consider. An unwanted behavior may be due to a skill deficiency, desire for attention, bid for power, or something else entirely. Ask yourself the following questions to help decide if your child has a "blind spot" or if he is using the behavior for another purpose.

- *Has the behavior been consistent for a long time?* For example, has he always been physically active? Has she been reluctant to try most new things all along? Has she always been "a drama queen"—responding intensely whether happy or mad? If the problem has been consistent, you may be dealing with a temperament trait.

  Temperament traits are consistent over time, and only shift slowly with much parental guidance and support. In their book, *Temperament Tools: Working with Your Child's Inborn Traits,* Helen F. Neville and Diane Clark Johnson offer strategies for dealing with different temperaments. In the section "Working with challenging traits" in chapter three you can get some ideas of skills kids need to cope with their temperament.

- *Is the behavior typical for the child's age?* Some examples of age-typical behavior are—Toddler throwing food; pulling the cat's tail; standing on the table; or more annoying, looking at you while he does the forbidden action. A 2-year-old upset because there is no more cereal, or the dress she wants is dirty. A preschooler dawdling, or telling a friend, "I won't invite you to my birthday party." A school-aged child forgetting to take his lunch or bring home spelling words, or resisting making her bed since her friend doesn't have to. Regardless of how unpleasant an age-typical behavior is, teach the child the skills he or she needs. You can do that with the ***Teach new skills*** point. If the behavior is very annoying, you can use tools from the ***Avoid problems*** point to reduce the problem while you are teaching needed skills.

- ***Is the child using the misbehavior to get attention?*** For example, he eats the dog food or hits his sister to get attention. If a child can't get attention by being nice, he will be difficult. Use tools on the ***Respond to cooperation*** point so he doesn't need to misbehave in order to get attention.

- ***Are rules unclear or inconsistently enforced?*** When you say "I hate it when you whine" it's unclear. Is this a rule? When you say "Speak pleasantly" that is clear. When you say, "No whining," and then give her what she wants to stop the whining, you are actually rewarding the whining. This inconsistency encourages the negative behavior. If your response is inconsistent, take some time to figure out what situations are important enough that you will always follow through. Once you are clear, your child can learn from you.

- ***Is the child overstressed?*** For example, has the family recently moved, is there a new baby, or has a grandparent died? Feelings of confusion or jealousy make it difficult for a child to function. If your child feels stressed, acknowledge his feelings and reduce the stress before expecting success in changing his habits. If you can't change the situation, then teach skills so the child can cope with the situation.

- ***Does the child have the skills to do what you want?*** For example, expecting a child to calm himself down when he has no skills will fail. Expecting him to share when you haven't taught him to negotiate will not work. If the child does not have the needed skills, then teach the child the skills he or she needs.

Note: A problem can also be an indicator of a serious underlying issue such as abuse, illness, or relationship conflicts. If you've ruled out other possible causes, and made a good effort to solve the problem, you may want to seek professional help if it persists.

Consider all STAR Parenting points

As you may have noticed, both the casual and the systematic approaches encourage use of a variety of tools. This is for several reasons.

The best tool for a situation may be one you don't consider. Some parents resist using a specific guidance tool because of a belief about that tool. Their concern may be in response to one expert's opinion, or may arise from overuse or misuse in their childhood. Some people don't acknowledge feelings because it is too "touchy-feely." Others dislike rules and consequences because they seem too rigid or mean to them. Still others avoid praise or rewards because they are afraid the child may become dependent on them or because they don't believe a person should be rewarded for "doing what they're supposed to do anyway." Unfortunately, the shunned tool may be the best one for the job. That happened to Shelly.

Blind spots are skills a child has not learned yet.

Shelly really wanted her preschool son to put his coat on by himself. She was taking a STAR Parenting class, so she tried each of the tools, except rewards. She didn't like rewards and didn't want to use them. Her classmates suggested she give it a try since nothing else had worked.

Because her son loved chocolate, Shelly decided to offer him one half of a chocolate chip if he put his coat on when asked. When she returned the next week, everyone was curious how things went. She sheepishly replied that he was now putting his coat on by himself, and it only took three times. He does it without fuss or chocolate. She finished by saying it was definitely worth one and a half chocolate chips.

There is another example of the effectiveness of rewards in the STAR in Action Story, "Don't hurt the baby," on page 109.

Sometimes you need to use several tools to change a behavior. For example, when you are teaching a new skill, it is often helpful to praise the child's effort. When you make an unpopular rule such as "Homework before television," you may need to acknowledge the child's feelings, "You're angry/disappointed that you have to finish your math before watching TV." You may need to reduce a child's stress level before you can teach him a self-calming strategy.

When you consider how you could apply each of the fifteen tools to a given problem in the brainstorming stage, it is easier to see how to combine the tools if you need them. You can get ideas on how the tools can be used together by reading the STAR in Action stories.

Tools may lose effectiveness. Sometimes, overuse causes a tool to become ineffective. Other times, a change in the child is the cause. The following stories illustrate how ineffectiveness played out in three families.

Martin and Alexis frequently distracted their young children when they were upset, rather than teaching them self-soothing skills. After a while, distraction failed to work, and they were left in a difficult place.

Bethany praised almost everything her son did with the hope of encouraging his self-esteem. That worked when he was little, but by the time he was in school, he expected it from everyone and got discouraged when the teacher and kids in class did not provide it.

Luke wanted his daughter to obey and to know the difference between right and wrong. He made rules for everything and enforced them consistently. When she was little she tried to comply. But as she grew, the rules felt overwhelming and she always seemed to be in trouble for something. Eventually, she gave up trying to follow all the rules.

Most parents find it *most* effective in the long run to use a variety of tools. You don't have to like all the tools, but you want to be able to use them when the situation calls for them.

Question and answers

This seems like STAR Parenting takes a lot of time and energy. How can I realistically do all this? It's true. There are no shortcuts to good parenting—it takes time and energy. You will find that you already spend—and will continue to spend— lots and lots of time and energy reacting (acting ineffectively) to problems.

There are no shortcuts to good parenting. You relearn what works at each new stage

You really don't have a choice whether or not your parenting will be challenging or exhausting. You do have a choice how to spend the time and the energy. You can choose to take charge by adopting a proactive approach.

STAR Parenting can make your life much easier in the long run. However, in the beginning you may find the STAR steps awkward and unnatural. That is okay. As you use the STAR, you will become more skillful.

I am trying to use the tools and process, but I find the most appalling things come out of my mouth. Is this normal? It is common. At first, you may notice yourself doing things you don't like. Slowly, you will begin to think of ideas while you are speaking. Eventually, the ideas will surface before you speak. Many people believe it takes twenty-one days to learn a new habit, so hang in there and keep trying.

We have seen how to get started using the STAR Parenting points and tools and acknowledged that good parenting takes effort. You relearn what works with each child at each new stage.

In this chapter, you may have noticed that several parents combined tools to change a child's behavior. Following the summary and after the STAR in Action Story, chapter ten will address the dark side of the STAR. It will explain how any tool that can be used to help can also be used to discourage.

Summary of
How to Get Started

★ **Create and review a behavioral goal.** Is the desired behavior appropriate for the child's age and experience? Is it compatible with your values and long view? How does his or her age and temperament affect the goal?

★ **Decide if you will approach the problem casually or systematically.** A casual approach is appropriate for day-to-day frustration and annoyances. The systematic approach is helpful when you are learning the process and to deal with behaviors that frustrate you or are serious.

★ **When you have trouble, identify what is going on.** What is the need that is driving the behavior? Skill deficiency? Desire for attention? Power? Circumstantial stress? Cry for help? Behavior related to temperament or the child's developmental stage? Are the rules inconsistently enforced?

STAR in Action Story [1]

Dressing—Staying Focused

Getting my daughter, Naoko, 3, dressed and out in the morning is extremely frustrating. She gets distracted and wants to play with any toy she sees, she changes her mind about what to wear again and again, or she runs away to either start a game of chase or for the joy of being naked.

Stop and focus

Naoko's delays are exhausting my patience—not a good way to start the day. Some thoughts about the situation are below, then on to thinking of ideas.

Temperament: Naoko is easily distracted which is often helpful, but not during dressing.

Development: I know it is unrealistic to expect a 3-year-old to dress by herself consistently, and I still want to work on it. [*Note from author:* Many children between 2½ and 3 often go through a stage where they cannot make and act on a decision.]

Parent's goal for the child: I would really like her to dress herself, but I will settle for her staying focused on dressing while I dress her so we can finish in a timely manner.

Think of ideas

I called a friend who took the STAR Parenting class with me and asked her to come over. When we sat down to brainstorm we came up with a lot of ideas, more than could be used at one time.

Avoid problems

☆*Change expectations* ① Expect dressing to take a while and consider it a gift when it is quick. ② Let her go to day care in her pjs. ③ Explain why I want her to get dressed. ④ Let her wear whatever she wants.

☆*Change things* ⑤ Turn off the TV until she is dressed. ⑥ Remove toys that distract her. ⑦ Dress in a dull place, like the hall. ⑧ Dress in the kitchen or in a warm place.

☆*Change the schedule* ⑨ Get dressed before breakfast or playing. ⑩ Get dressed before going to bed.

☆*Reduce stress* ⑪ Give a five- or ten-minute warning. ⑫ Allow enough time for her to dress without rushing. ⑬ Limit the number of clothing choices. ⑭ Make sure she gets enough sleep.

☆*Two yeses* ⑮ "Do you want to put your shirt on first or your pants on first?"

Respond to cooperation

☆*Attention* ⑯ Watch her as she tries to dress herself. ⑰ Make up and sing a dressing song to help her remain focused.

☆*Praise* ⑱ When she puts her shirt on, "Good job. You did it by yourself." ⑲ "I'm proud you put your shirt on by yourself." ⑳ "I bet you're proud you put your shirt on yourself." ㉑ Notice and comment on what she does well. "You held your foot still so I could tie your shoe. Thank you."

☆*Reward* ㉒ "When you are dressed, we will go to the park." ㉓ Set a timer for thirty minutes. Tell her that as soon as she is dressed, I will spend the rest of the time playing or reading to her.

Acknowledge feelings

☆*Clarify my feelings* ㉔ Explain that I am frustrated because I need her to dress now.

---

1 There is a STAR in Action Story at the end of each chapter. Each story is written by a parent in his or her own words and shows how that person adapted the STAR Parenting process to his or her own life.

These stories use tools from all points, so some may be unfamiliar until you have read the appropriate chapter. You can see how different parents, with different values or kids with different temperaments, might make different choices.

☆*Grant in fantasy* ㉕ "Wouldn't it be fun if we had a magic wand that we could wave to change your clothes so you didn't have to stop playing?"

☆*Active listening* ㉖ "You're disappointed/frustrated that you can't play right now."

☆*Simple listening* ㉗ "Oh." "Umm" "I see" (Not effective for this age)

Teach new skills

☆*Modeling* ㉘ As you dress yourself and pretend to get distracted, say, "Oops, I was distracted. I need to keep dressing." ㉙ Model and verbalize getting distracted, noticing, and refocusing yourself.

☆*Shaping* ㉚ (a) Parent takes the child to a dull place to dress. (b) When dressing is smooth, ask the child if she wants to dress in room or hall. (c) Let the child decide, without prompting, where she will dress.

☆*Re-do it right* ㉛ When she gets distracted, gently return her to the task, "Oops, you need to finish dressing."

Set limits

☆*Make rule* ㉜ "Wear pants, socks, and shoes outside." ㉝ "Choose clothes once and stick with it." ㉞ "Stay inside until your shoes are on."

☆*Consequence* ㉟ "If you change your mind, I decide." ㊱ "If you go outside without shoes, I will bring you back."

☆*A better way* ㊲ "I want you to dress now. You want to dress later. What's a better way?"

~~~~~~~~~~~~~~~~~~~~~~~~~~~~~~~~~

Act effectively

Thirty-seven ideas—Wow! To narrow the choices, I thought about what irritates me most in the morning. There are two elements. One, Naoko's inability to choose an outfit for the day and stick with her choice. And, two, her distractability when I try to dress her in her room.

Until we master these two elements, there is no point expecting her to dress alone.

Choose clothes. This is my plan. *A rule:* Select your clothes the night before. Put what you want to wear on the small chair in the hall. *Consequence*: If Naoko does not put clothes on the chair before she goes to bed, I will select the clothes for Naoko and put them on the chair. *Two yeses:* If Naoko is goofing around before bed and has not put her clothes out, I will ask, "Would you rather stop playing and choose your clothes for tomorrow, or play now and wear what I choose for you tomorrow?" *Acknowledge feelings:* In the morning, if Naoko is upset about her choice, I'll say, "You're sad that you chose to play and didn't choose your clothes for today. Tonight you get another chance to choose. What do you want to put out for tomorrow?"

Getting dressed promptly. This is my plan for staying focused to dress. Instead of dressing her in her room or in the living room, I will dress her at the end of the hall so there will be little to distract her. Her clothes, chosen the night before, will be on a small chair there. When she cooperates, I will praise her. If she is restless, I will help her focus by asking, "Do you want to put your pants on by yourself or would you like help?" I will start on Saturday so I have two days to work the kinks out before work on Monday.

~~~~~~~~~~~~~~~~~~~~~~~~~~~~~~~~~

Review and revise

Choosing the clothes the night before worked once I convinced her that she could not change her mind. At the end of the week, dressing was better but not good. I allotted ten minutes to dress Naoko. I set a timer for five minutes. I said when the timer rang, the time would be half up. If she was dressed, we could go read a story. When it rang the second time, it would be time to leave. If she was not dressed, I would take her and her clothes to daycare. This is working better. She is usually cooperative. so we have time for a story or cuddle before we leave.

Chapter 10

The Dark Side of the STAR

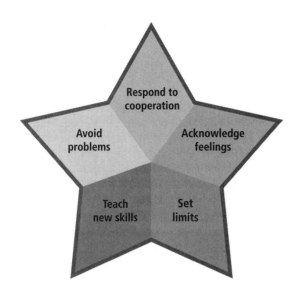

*Anything you can use for good,
you can also use for ill*

Any tool or process that can be used for good can also be misused. For example, a hammer can be used to build a house or destroy it. Similarly, consequences can be used to guide a child to appropriate behavior or to break the child's spirit or feeling of self-worth.

We will look at the dark side of the STAR Parenting process, points, and tools. Then we will look at some reasons why people may use the dark side.

Dark side of the STAR Parenting points

Avoid problems. The purpose of this point is to reduce hassles so you can concentrate on your goal. The dark side of avoiding problems is that it may deny problems, accommodate the child when it is inappropriate, or ignore issues that should be addressed.

On the way home from day care, Patricia took her 3-year-old twins, Matt and Mara, to the store to get Halloween costumes. Mara quickly chose a princess costume. Matt wanted a pirate costume—compete with hat, sword, and parrot.

The pirate costume was too expensive, and Patricia was reluctant to bring a plastic sword into the house. The more she explained, the louder Matt screamed. She told him that if he couldn't find a costume they agreed on in five minutes, then they would leave and come back another day.

When the five minutes was up, Matt refused to go. He was so intense that Patricia bought the expensive costume rather than deal with his "disappointment" all the way home.

Matt had a very strong temper and needed tools to manage his feelings. We all avoid problems from time to time; however, with the dark side of the STAR, people consistently avoid issues that need to be addressed.

Respond to cooperation. The purpose of responding to cooperation is to notice and acknowledge positive behavior. The dark side of the STAR encourages unwanted behavior. Parents do this by giving attention to negative behavior by nagging or scolding, or by building a dependence on rewards or praise. They may also reward unwanted behavior by letting the child hear them talking about it to someone else.

Children will do what is needed to connect with people. There is a saying, "If a child can't get a kiss, he will take a kick." Put another way, "angry attention" is better than no attention. This is why some parents find themselves nagging their child more and more as the child increases the pressure.

You can create unwanted dependence on external motivation by using rewards or praise as your only or even primary way to get your child to do something. Praise and rewards are an important part of healthy parenting; however, they can be overdone.

Acknowledge feelings. The purpose of this point is to reflect children's feelings without judging or changing them. When you do that, children feel heard and connected, and can often move on to other activities. The dark side discourages feelings. There are several ways you can discourage feelings:

- Use the roadblocks (deny, discount, decrease, and resolve)
- Forget to reflect pleasant feelings
- Acknowledge mostly unwanted feelings
- Take control: ask questions, give advice, fix the situation

Set reasonable limits. The purpose of the reasonable limits point is to provide clear boundaries and let children test them. The dark side focuses attention on undesired behavior. The parent interacts with a child primarily when he or she breaks a rule. This is another example of the child's desire for attention at any cost.

Another characteristic of the dark side is lack of consistent follow-through.

One woman asked for help because she was having trouble with her son. When she explained the problem, it sounded like limits were not consistently enforced. When asked about that, she said she was very careful to follow through.

However, she added that occasionally she made exceptions: when her son was sick, when she was tired, when her husband was traveling (because that was stressful for their son). When she logged her behavior, she found that she was enforcing rules between one quarter and one third of the time.

The dark side of limits sometimes requires skills a child does not have due to age or temperament. Some parents assume that once the child can talk, you can reason with her. They make rules and expect compliance before the child understands or has developed sufficient self-restraint.

Teach new skills. The purpose of teaching new skills is to prepare the child for living in the real world. The dark side of the STAR acts as though the child is incompetent and will continue to be so. Parents do this by continuing to teach a child after he or she has the skill, or by belittling the child for her inability to learn as fast as they believe she should learn.

Behaviors of people guiding children from the dark side are summarized in the table below.

Table 10–1: Summary of the dark side points

STAR point	Purpose	Dark side action
Avoid problems	Reduce hassles so you can concentrate on your goal	Ignore issues that should be addressed Accommodate a child when it is inappropriate
Respond to cooperation	Notice and encourage positive behavior	Give attention to negative behavior (nagging, scolding) Build a dependence on rewards or praise
Acknowledge feelings	Reflect children's feelings without judging or changing them	Forget to reflect pleasant feelings Acknowledge mostly unwanted feelings Take control: ask questions, give advice, fix the situation
Set reasonable limits	Provide clear boundaries and let children test them	Focus attention on undesired behavior Interact with children primarily when they break a rule Do not follow through Require skills a child does not have due to age or temperament
Teach new skills	Offer skills needed for living in the real world	Act as though the child is incompetent Continue to teach after the child has the skill Belittle the child for inability to learn

Dark side of the STAR Parenting process

The STAR Parenting process has a dark side just as the STAR Parenting points and tools do. We will look at each step.

Stop and focus. The idea of this step is to disengage emotionally from the conflict and clarify the problem and what you want your child to do instead. One way parents can sabotage this step is to discount the importance of reviewing values, developmental stage, and temperament. This sometimes happens if a parent has two children and tries what worked with the first on the second without considering the different ages, temperaments, and experiences.

One mom had let her older daughter "cry it out" when she got in the habit of waking at night. The process took three days, with the third day of crying lasting only five minutes. When her second daughter started waking in the night, she let her cry as well. However, it did not work.

The younger girl cried for two hours the first night and five the second night. Both parents and the child were exhausted the next day. Mom had forgotten that her younger daughter always had trouble going to sleep when she was tired. So when she was crying, she missed sleep and was even more tired. No wonder she could not fall asleep the next night.

Another way people court the dark side is by failing to create a clear idea of the desired behavior. For example, one dad wanted his 5-year-old son to stop sucking his thumb. The act of sucking, either thumb or pacifier, is a powerful self-calming tool. However, it did not occur to Dad to decide what self-comforting habit the son could substitute. As a result, they went through three years and six alternative habits before the boy found something that was acceptable to his father.

Think of ideas. The purpose of this step is to generate a wide variety of ideas. One way people sabotage themselves is to stop brainstorming when they think of an idea that might work, rather than to list a variety. Another way to misuse the STAR is to focus on one point or to discount a point or tool. It is natural to have favorite tools, but it is important to be able to use all points and tools because they are helpful in different kinds of situations and they teach children different things.

Act effectively. This is the step that puts life into the ideas—you select ideas, collect needed support from others, and predict possible problems. A dark side approach is to use one of the first ideas generated and give the process little thought.

Limiting the number of tools you are willing to try often leads to frustration and failure. This can result in failure to follow through. You'll probably keep trying if you have generated many ideas you are willing to try.

Review and revise. The purpose of this step is to learn and grow as a parent. It's a "dark side mistake" to rush on without reviewing what worked or what needs to be changed. The parent continues to use tools or approaches that may no longer be effective with a child. Also, since there is no official recognition that the behavior improved, parents often feel as though it continues.

By making dark side mistakes, parents make life more difficult for both themselves and their child. The dark side of the steps is summarized in the table below.

Table 10–2: Summary of the dark side process

STAR step	Purpose of step	Dark side action
Stop and focus	Clarify the problem and what you want	Discount the impact of temperament, developmental stage, and values Lack clear vision of desired behavior
Think of ideas	Generate a variety of ideas	Stop generating ideas too soon Focus on one point Discount a point or tool Lack new ideas

| Act effectively | Plan your approach | Give preparation little thought
Lack of follow-though |
| Review and revise | Evaluate and update if needed | No evaluation or revision
No closure |

Examples of dark and light tools

We have looked at the dark side of the points and process. Next let's see what light and dark side actions might look like for two situations. As you read the chart, notice your reaction to the parents' responses. You may find yourself gravitating to dark side mistakes in some situations. Some of the dark responses may feel good to the child at the moment, but take you off course in the long run.

Table 10–3: Examples of light and dark tools—"Cookie please"

Situation:
Child: Mommy/Daddy. Can I have a cookie? Please? Pretty please?
Parent: No. It's too close to supper.
Child: I'm hungry. My tummy aches. Plea-e-e-se, Mommy/Daddy?

Point	Dark side	Light side
Respond to cooperation	***Criticize.*** Whine. Whine. Whine. All you ever do is whine. Nothing ever makes you happy. If I give you one cookie now, you'll want another in a minute.	***Praise.*** Thank you for telling me you're hungry. Let's see if you have time for a snack before supper. (Check the clock for the time.) Oh darn! The clock says it's too late for a snack. What do you want to do instead?
Acknowledge feelings	***Deny feeling.*** You're not hungry—you're bored. Now quit bugging me! ***Fix things:*** Poor dear, you must be starving. Yes, you can have a cookie now.	***Active listening.*** You're disappointed that you have to wait until after supper for a cookie.
Avoid problems	***Ignore rule.*** Okay, but it might spoil your appetite for dinner.	***Two yeses.*** Dinner is in half an hour. You can have a cookie for dessert, or have carrots now if you're very hungry.
Set reasonable limits	***Criticize.*** No. No. No. How many times do I have to say No? ***Threaten.*** Ask once more and I'll swat your bottom to help you remember.	***Clear rule.*** Only water the half hour before dinner. ***Consequence.*** No snacks

Teach new skills	**Lecture.** Hungry? You don't know what real hunger is. Hunger is when you don't have enough food for days or weeks, not just minutes or hours. In Africa millions of people are too poor to buy enough food. *They* are hungry, not you.	**Modeling.** When I'm hungry and have to fix dinner, I think about something else. Thinking of something else takes my mind off feeling hungry. For example, "What would I do if a lion knocked at our door?"

Table 10–4: Examples of light and dark tools—"He hit me"

Situation:
Parent is working at the table.
Child (Ava): Mommy/Daddy, Tommy hit me.

Point	*Dark side*	*Light side*
Respond to cooperation	**Criticize.** Fight. Fight. Fight. All you kids ever do is fight. If it's not one thing, it's another. Can't you guys ever solve anything without involving me?	**Praise.** Thanks for telling me. — OR — **Attention.** How did you try to handle the situation?
Acknowledge feelings	**Gushes.** Oh, you poor baby. Where did he hit you? I know how that must hurt. You stay away from that horrid brother of yours.	**Simple listening.** Oh. I see. Really? Hmm-m-m.
Avoid problems	**Deny issue.** Forget about it. As soon as I'm done here, we will go out shopping and get you something really great.	**Reduce stress.** All three go for a run around the block before the parent tries to work at the table.
Set reasonable limits	**Sarcasm.** Are you bleeding? Is your bone broken? You know not to interrupt me unless something serious is happening. Now scram!	I will remind Tommy of our rule about touching and the consequence. **To Tommy:** **Clear rule.** We touch gently. Hitting is never okay. **Consequence.** You must re-do it right or do a kindness.
Teach new skills	**Sarcasm.** Yeah? And what did you do to him? **Orders.** Stop. I don't want to hear. You guys need to learn to play together. Get back there and be nice to each other.	**Re-do it right.** I can see you guys are having trouble cooperating today. Let's go back. I'll help you two kids problem-solve together.

Now you can practice identifying "dark" and "light" statements in Activity 10–1.

Activity 10–1: Identify dark side statements

Directions: Read a pair of statements. Star the light side response. Cross out the dark side response and explain why it is dark in the space below.

Point	Parent says
Avoid problems Reduce hassles and work on what is important **Dark side** Ignore issues that should be addressed	1-A. *"That's okay. I know you didn't mean to hurt your sister."* 1-B. *"I'm glad you didn't mean to hurt your sister, and you need to do a kindness."*
Respond to cooperation Notice and acknowledge desired behavior **Dark side** Respond to undesirable behavior and encourage dependence on external rewards	2-A. At the grocery store, *"When you speak pleasantly, you may choose a box of cereal."* 2-B. At the grocery store, *"Stop crying, here's the cereal you want."*
	3-A. Reminding the child every five minutes to get dressed for school. 3-B. *"I see you put your socks on."*
	4-A. *"I'm impressed. You guys decided on who gets in the front seat."* 4-B. *"Bicker, bicker, bicker. All you ever do is quarrel."*
Acknowledge feelings Accept children's feelings **Dark side** Discount and ignore feelings or confuse with their own	5-A. *"You don't hate your brother."* 5-B. *"You're frustrated that your brother won't leave you alone."*
	6-A. *"You feel disappointed that you didn't get the part you wanted in the play."* 6-B. *"I'm sorry you didn't get a part in the play."*

Set limits Provide boundaries and let kids test them Dark side Focus primarily on unwanted behavior or unrealistic expectation	7-A. Rule for 2-year-old, *"No lying."* 7-B. No age-appropriate rule. Two-year-olds have no concept of being honest or lying.
	8-A. *"Ask for help if you have trouble with your sister."* 8-B. *"How many times do I have to send you to your room before you stop picking on your sister?"*
Teach new skills Offer skills needed for living in the world Dark side Act as though the child is incompetent or belittle the child	9-A. *"I don't know why you can't learn to ride a bike [use the potty or read]. Your brother could at your age."* 9-B. *"You will learn to ride a bike. You just need to learn how to balance."*

Answers: **1-A:** *Dark side.* Does not deal with hurting a person. **1-B:** *Light side.* **2-A:** *Light side.* Tells the child what to do. **2-B:** *Dark side.* Rewards unwanted behavior. **3-A:** *Dark side.* Rewards dawdling with attention. **3-B:** *Light side.* Comments on progress. **4-A:** *Light side.* Comments on success. **4-B:** *Dark side.* Comments on unwanted behavior. **5-A:** *Dark side.* Denys child's feeling. **5-B:** *Light side.* Acknowledge feelings. **6-A:** *Light side.* Acknowledge feelings. **6-B:** *Dark side.* States parent's feeling. **7-A:** *Dark side.* Not developmentally appropriate. **7-B:** Correct. **8-A:** *Light side.* Tells the child what to do. **8-B:** *Dark side.* Talks about what not to do. **9-A:** *Dark side.* Focuses on incompetence. **9-B:** *Light side.* Focuses on what to do.

We have seen examples of the dark side of the STAR. Now we will look at why someone might use the dark side.

Reasons for misuse of parenting tools

The misuse can be unconscious, misguided, or deliberate.

Unconscious misuse. Parents love their children and want them to be happy and successful. They can, unfortunately, use a tool in such a way that it compounds the problem or even creates a new one. You can see the effect of too much "nurture" in Rosalina's story.

Rosalina grew up in a harsh household and found it difficult to say "No" to her daughter or to resist her pleading. As a result, her daughter grew up expecting others to make life pleasant for her, and she did not learn the skills she needed to make herself happy.

Rosalina was unaware of the effects of her day-to-day decisions on the long-term quality of her child's life.

Misguided use. Most people who make poor decisions are unaware of the possible effects of their decisions.

Gwen wanted her son to be independent and self-motivated. She believed that if she made rules about when to do homework, helped him figure things out, or offered incentives for completing schoolwork, he would be dependent on her rather than become self-reliant. So, she left it up to him. He could do it, or not.

This worked okay in early elementary school when the expectations were minimal. However, as the work increased, her son fell behind and his grades dropped. Gwen was concerned but still believed that the natural consequence of not turning assignments in on time or at all (Ds and Fs) would motivate him into working. Eventually, he began skipping school and finally dropped out.

The sad part is that Gwen made her decisions based on information she read, but she did not consider how it applied to her son's temperament and interests, nor did she review her decision and revise her approach when the results were not what she expected. This is why we have the ***Review and revise*** step in the STAR Parenting process.

Deliberate misuse. There are some people who are deliberately hurtful. They enjoy embarrassing people or inflicting pain. Some people may believe that lecturing, belittling, or using sarcasm are effective ways to change behavior. You may have met one or two in school or at work. Needless to say, these people can use good parenting tools in unhealthy ways.

There are probably as many ways to misuse the tools as there are to use them wisely. Fortunately, most parents are not as extreme as the ones described above. If you find yourself gravitating toward the dark side, use the STAR Parenting process to get yourself back on track.

In this chapter we have seen how anything you can use for good can also be used for ill. Right after the summary and the STAR in Action Story, we will look at what parents can do when things don't work.

Summary of
The Dark Side of the STAR

★ **Anything that can be used for good can also be misused.**

★ **Dark side use.** The dark side avoids dealing with problems that need to be addressed. It gives attention to undesirable behavior, ignores or discounts children's feelings, and treats children as incompetent.

★ **People misuse parenting tools for various reasons.** Some do it unconsciously. Some misguidedly expect the good they hope for to outweigh the bad. A few people use the dark side to deliberately hurt children.

STAR in Action Story[1]

Phone Interruptions

Making calls is always a great challenge, as my 2½-year-old daughter, Lola, is constantly interrupting. She wants my attention and she wants the phone.

I have tried giving her a toy phone but only a real one will do. And her whining just gets louder the longer I try to stay on the phone. It doesn't matter if I pleasantly ask her to be quiet or if I ignore her. It makes talking on the phone almost impossible, and losing my temper only makes everything worse.

How do I teach my child skills to respect my phone time, to wait and not interrupt?

Stop and focus

Since Lola's behavior was bothering me more and more, I decided that I needed to sit down and think about the problem.

Long view: For the long term I want Lola to be assertive about her needs and wishes (which she is); however, she needs to realize that others have needs too (which she does not) and learn to cooperate.

Development: Two-and-a-half-year-olds are still learning to deal with their feelings and have not mastered self-restraint, so I know it is not reasonable to expect Lola to be respectful all the time. However, I would like her to let me talk some of the time.

Temperament: Lola is persistent and intense. Both traits make the behavior more difficult to deal with.

Parent's goal for the child: Ultimately, to let me finish my phone call. Right now, to let me talk five minutes without interrupting.

Think of ideas

Using points on the star, I came up with these ideas.

Avoid problems

☆*Reduce stress* ① Tell Lola beforehand that she can talk when I am done.

☆*Change schedule* ② Take two minutes up front for her to talk or ③ Play before calling so she has an adequate reserve in her "positive feelings" bank.

☆*Change time* ④ Call after she goes to bed.

☆*Change environment* ⑤ Set up an activity while I am on the phone.

☆*Change things* ⑥ "What do you need to play by yourself?"

☆*Two yeses* ⑦ "You may play with play dough or play kitchen until it is your turn to talk."

Respond to cooperation

☆*Attention* ⑧ Let Lola be with me, as I'm stroking her arm (so she won't feel ignored).

☆*Praise* ⑨ Make my call very short and say, "Thank you for waiting."

☆*Reward* ⑩ Reward her for waiting for me.

Reasonable limits

☆*Clear rule* ⑪ Sit or play quietly while I am on the phone.

⑫ Use a timer to time five minutes and then talk two minutes.

⑬ Bring and set timer. When the alarm goes off, call is over.

☆*Consequence* ⑭ "If you whine, then you don't get a turn to talk."

---

1 There is a STAR in Action Story at the end of each chapter. Each story is written by a parent in his or her own words and shows how that person adapted the STAR Parenting process to his or her own life.

These stories use tools from all points, so some may be unfamiliar until you have read the appropriate chapter. You can see how different parents, with different values or kids with different temperaments, might make different choices.

☆**A better way** ⑮ "Your way is to talk now; my way is to finish, then you talk. What is a better way?" (May not be age appropriate.)

Acknowledge feelings

☆*Active listening* ⑯ "You feel frustrated because my attention is elsewhere."

☆*Grant in fantasy* ⑰ "Wouldn't it be great if we had ten phones and they all could be used at the same time?" (May not be age appropriate.)

☆*Simple listening* ⑱ Nod and sympathize with Lola as she screams out her frustrations.

Teach new skills

☆*Shaping* ⑲ Practice waiting for turns by first teaching Lola a counting song. Then pick up the phone and pretend to talk, while singing the counting song. Then let Lola pick up the phone while I sing the song. Then practice for longer by repeating the song.

☆*Modeling* ⑳ Role play with my husband waiting for a turn with the phone.

☆*Re-do it right* ㉑ Say "Oops, you aren't waiting patiently for your turn. Let's try to re-do it right and wait patiently for a turn."

Act effectively

I decided to pick three different tools: ☆*Modeling,* ☆*Active listening,* and ☆*Two yeses.*

☆*Modeling.* I had to enlist my husband. For one week, each morning, before he left for work, he would pick up the phone and pretend he was calling someone (*e.g.,* Grandma). Then I would interrupt and whine. He would say to the phone, "Excuse me for a moment." Then he would turn to me and say, "Wow. You are really excited to talk on the phone *(Active listening).* You may read the newspaper or skip around the coffee table while I finish *(Two yeses).* Then you can have a turn." I would pick one option, "I am going to read my newspaper," while he continued to "talk" on the phone. Then after a couple

of minutes my husband would say, "Thanks for waiting quietly while I talked. Now you can talk to Grandma," I would pretend to talk and then hang up.

☆*Two yeses.* During the same week I would try calling someone every day for two minutes (telling them it was for Lola) to see Lola's reaction. The first day she jumped at me and whined for "my turn" the second I picked up the phone. As my husband had done, I excused myself from the phone and said to Lola, "You are really eager to talk on the phone. You may play with play dough or with your kitchen while you wait for your turn with the phone." Lola looked at me, started jumping up and down again and reaching for the phone saying, "My turn, my turn."

☆*Active listening.* "Wow, it is hard to wait," I said. I walked over to her table and took out the play dough. "I'll finish my turn soon." I played with play dough while finishing the conversation. Lola watched me then poked at the play dough. Then I said, "My turn is done and you calmed down. It is your turn."

We practiced these three ideas for a week each day with different levels of success. The next three weeks there were no planned phone calls. Lola calmed down at some point during the phone calls, and initially it still took a great deal of prompting. It really depended on how tired or hungry she was. Toward the end of the two weeks, on a good day, Lola would start to jump then run to the play dough table. On the bad days she would just jump and whine.

Review and revise

I was making headway but it was very slow. I decided I would limit, as best I could, the use of the phone to times she was not hungry or tired, so she could be as successful as possible.

Note to self: When running counter to a child's developmental stage, it takes extra time and effort. Maybe planning my calls while Lola is asleep or away, then trying again in a few months, would be best.

Chapter 11

When Things Don't Work

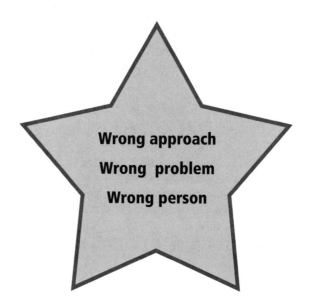

*If things aren't working,
try something else*

So you did it all and it didn't work—what can you do now? There are three reasons why STAR Parenting (or any other parenting material) might not work. The parent focuses on the—

- wrong tool or point
- wrong problem
- wrong person

Let's check these out, then learn two or three things you can do.

Wrong tool or approach

The approach chosen is not suited to the problem. You think that a particular tool is called for and neglect to consider any others. We have seen this in a couple of examples.

Not enough attention. Sometimes parents underestimate a child's need for attention or to connect with a parent.

Daniel had a new baby sister (STAR in Action Story, page 109) and felt displaced. He did not bear ill will toward his sister, but he hurt her to get his mom's attention. Daniel's mom wanted a "better consequence," but no consequence would work because Daniel needed attention and would do whatever was necessary to get it.

When Daniel got enough attention, the hurtful behavior vanished.
No skills. Children need to have the prerequisite skills before they can comply.

Benjamin would strike out whenever he was angry. Mom would acknowledge his feelings, but there was no change in his behavior. She then tried time-outs with a similar lack of success.

In this family there were two role models for anger—Dad smashed things and Mom was totally passive. Benjamin and his parents needed to learn strategies to manage anger and self-calming tools.

Wrong problem

Occasionally, the problem a parent sees is the presenting or immediate problem, not the underlying or on-going problem. This can happen a couple of ways.
Wrong issue. Sometimes parenting is more effective if you look behind the annoying behavior and deal with the underlying issues.

Chang's parents attended a parent lecture and wanted a "good consequence" for when their son slammed his bedroom door. To better understand the situation, the instructor asked, "Why did he slam the door?" The mom answered, "Because he was sent to time-out." The instructor asked, "Why was he in time-out?" "Because he hit his sister," she answered. "And why did he hit his sister?" the instructor continued. "I don't know," Mom replied.

Children hit for many reasons—to draw attention, express anger, or get what they want. Knowing why Chang hit would be helpful information, because even if he remained quiet in his room, they would still have the problem of hitting his sister. However, if they solved the hitting problem, they would solve or improve both problems.

Three-year-old Brittany didn't want to use the potty, try new food, or take swimming lessons. Once her parents discovered that her behavior resulted from her temperament ("slow approach" and "slow to adapt") rather than "stubbornness" or "defiance," they were able to relax and teach her concrete skills to manage her temperament.

Once Brittany had some coping skills to deal with change, she made strides in all three areas—using the potty, tasting new foods, and swimming.
Medical issues, known or unidentified, can complicate children's behavior.

Thomas's parents were furious that he still wet his bed at age 7. They were sure it was intentional. At a friend's suggestion, they took him to a specialist who discovered that Thomas did not have an enzyme that slowed down urine production at night, so his body made urine at a very fast rate, filling his bladder to overflowing. It was no wonder he was having trouble.

Life too stressful. When a child is severely stressed, he or she may not have the personal resources to make wise decisions or comply with parents. This is true for both young children and teens.

Courtney couldn't understand what had come over her kindergartner, Alissa. Normally, Allissa was a pleasant, cooperative child. Recently, she had begun to steal things from her teacher's desk and to bully some children. Mom made her return the items and apologize to the teacher and children, but the behavior continued.

Diane, a neighbor, also noticed the sudden change. She knew that Alissa's grandfather has just died and that Courtney was contemplating taking a two-week trip alone during summer break in six weeks. Diane suggested that Courtney talk with Alissa to find out how she was feeling and what was going on.

Courtney was surprised to find out that Alissa was terrified that if her mother went on the trip she would be left alone and that Mom would die like her grandad did and never come back. Courtney explained that if she went on the trip, Alissa's Aunt Mary would come and stay with her, so she would not be alone. Second, that Granddad had been sick for a long, long time before he died and Mom was healthy, and expected to live for a long, long time. And third, if she did die, Alissa would go to live with Aunt Mary.

Amazingly, the behaviors ceased immediately. Courtney thanked Diane for the idea, and added, "I didn't know you needed to be a detective to be a good parent."

Alissa's challenging behavior stopped as soon as her stress was reduced. This can also happen with teens.

Mitchell was always in trouble at home and in school. Somehow he managed to get by—just barely. When he entered middle school, he had the good fortune to have an English teacher who discovered that he could not see very well. She arranged for Mitchell to get glasses, and his disruptive actions declined dramatically.

Stress can result when a family moves, a sibling is born, parents divorce, or a family member dies or is hospitalized. Similarly, when a child is being teased or bullied or has an undiagnosed learning disability, life feels overwhelming. It can also result when a child has an allergy or medical condition that puts stress on the body. Once the underlying problem is addressed, the unwanted behavior may vanish.

Wrong person

Sometimes the problem is not the child at all, it is the parent. A parent's feelings from the past intrude in current situations or the parent lacks follow-through.

Parent's past. A parent's birth order and past experience influence his or her experience as a parent. This can be seen in the two stories below.

Tracy had two children—Sonya, 4½, and Ryan, 2¾. Whenever Tracy heard her son cry, she was sure that her daughter Sonya was doing something mean to him. Mom told Sonya to be kind over and over, but she could still hear Ryan's cry from time to time.

Tracy enrolled in a parenting class to learn how to deal with her kids' conflicts. The first assignment was to observe her children for twenty minutes and log the frequency of unpleasant interactions and how they started.

The first time she observed, the only unpleasantness occurred when Ryan grabbed the teddy bear Sonya was playing with and yelled, "Mine." Tracy was surprised that Ryan grabbed the toy without provocation so she decided to observe again. The second time was similar—Ryan grabbed a doll out of Sonya's hand.

Still convinced Sonya was the problem, Tracy observed another twenty minutes. This time Ryan was more demanding. Whatever Sonya touched, he wanted. When she began to draw, he wanted the red crayon that she was using. She said he could use it when she was done, but he wanted it "Now." When she refused to give it to him, he tried to grab it. When she moved it out of his reach, he hit her.

In the parenting class Tracy shared that Ryan was not the poor, innocent victim she has believed. When asked why she had been so sure Sonya was picking on Ryan, Tracy shared that while growing up her older sister always picked on her, so she assumed Ryan's older sister was pestering him too.

Tracy discovered she had been focusing on the wrong person two ways: First, her son was causing the conflict, rather than her daughter, and second, her judgment had been clouded by identifying so strongly with her son's birth order.

Alice was a very skillful mom. She had taken several classes I offer and had been in a mom-and-tots class with me. One day she asked for help thinking of what to do when Sean, her son, 3½, took the pepperoni off her pizza.

I was surprised because there are several simple things she could do. To find out why she hadn't thought of them I asked, "Has anything like this happened to you before?"

She looked startled for a moment and said, "Yes. When I was a child, my brothers would take food from my plate and my parents didn't protect me." Then she smiled and added, "I'm a grown-up now. I can handle it."

Her experience of helplessness as a child interfered with her ability to deal with her son. Once she realized that she was the primary problem, not her son, it was easy for her to handle her problem.

Inattention or poor follow-through. Sometimes parents cause the problem they are frustrated with by their lack of attention or follow-though.

Amber complained that her son never did as she asked. She had been visiting a friend's house and was getting ready to go. Amber told her son, Cole, 3, to put his coat on, then she got distracted. Cole put his coat on, waited patiently for a bit, then, when she continued to talk, he took it off and returned to play.

A few minutes later, Amber noticed that his coat was not on and told him again to put his coat on because it was time to go. Again Cole put his coat on. Amber continued to talk, and he finally took off his coat and returned to play.

A third time, she noticed his coat was off and told him to put it on immediately. This time, however, he continued to play. Amber got mad and said, "See, he never does what I ask him to."

In this case, the root of the problem was not Cole's unwillingness to do as Amber requested, but her failure to notice that he had complied and then leave the house. In addition, parents sometimes fail to follow through because they are afraid the child will get angry or be unhappy if they remain firm and enforce limits.

What you can do

When you have a problem that you cannot deal with, you can return to the beginning and start again, check your level of self-care, or get professional help.

Return to basics. As you have seen above, sometimes it helps to start the problem-solving process all over.

Focus on your expectations. Check your values, your child's temperament, and her developmental stage. Challenge your assumptions and ask why you think they are true.

Focus on yourself. Does the behavior *always* bother you? Do you always react the same? If not, what is the difference? Is there something in your past or a relationship with another person that is making the problem more difficult? Do you need more self-care or support?

Focus on the problem. Collect data: when does it happen? How long has the behavior been happening? How long does an episode last? What is the context—what happened *before* the behavior? Who owns the problem? What, specifically, do you want the child to do differently?

Once you have reviewed the situation, then you can generate ideas. Think of at least two ways to use each tool—even if you think it is silly. The purpose is to expand your thinking and get you out of the habit you are in. You can also ask several people what they do to find different ways to use the tools.

Next, make a plan, remembering to consider personal road blocks and how you will get around them. Decide how long you will use the plan, and then do it. Finally, review your plan, revise as needed, or get outside help.

Review self-care efforts and options. If you find yourself getting upset at one time and not another, look at your self-care and see what you need. Also, if you find yourself angry or discouraged much of the time, get some respite time or get some outside help (see below).

Get outside help. Everyone gets stuck sometimes. One problem with a book is that the book cannot give you feedback on what you are doing. Also, there are some special circumstances, like children with autism, ADHD, and bipolar characteristics, that require more information and skill than most families have.

So, when you have problems you cannot resolve, it is helpful to consult outside help. This could be a class, a child development specialist, a counselor or therapist, a doctor, or perhaps a parenting coach. The goal is to get someone who has more information or experience than you have.

Classes. The advantage of a class is that it is interactive. You can ask questions and get feedback. You also meet other parents and find that they have issues and concerns too. Look for classes at community centers, mental health groups, or the local community college.

Child development specialist. Sometimes parents have problems because their expectations are not realistic. Some parents may look at another person's child who is their child's age and decide that their child is being defiant because she isn't doing what the other child is. They don't realize the two children have different experiences, temperaments, and genetic make-up. Some childcare centers have staff trained in child development, or you may be able to get a referral from your doctor's office.

Parenting coach. A good parenting coach has been trained to listen nonjudgmentally, ask you questions to get you thinking, give you new, relevant information, and offer you specific suggestions to help you deal with yourself and your children. Look for someone who has received extensive training and has experience dealing with situations similar to yours.

Health care professional. Some doctors and practitioners can help you determine if there is a physiological basis for a child's problem, as we saw with Thomas. Also, when some children have allergies, it can make them irritable and prone to outbursts. Another medical problem that can cause challenges is childhood sleep apnea. You can ask your child's doctor for information.

Counselor or therapist. Sometimes the problem may have its origins in something from the past or an unconscious belief that is driving the parent's or child's current behavior. In these cases, seeing a counselor or therapist may be helpful. To find one, ask friends or co-workers who they have heard is good or who to avoid. Check with your church, mental health groups, or the phone book to get ideas. When you find some possibilities, check that they have training and experience related to your concern.

In this chapter, we have seen three reasons why things do not work—wrong approach, problem, or person. I've suggested several things you can do to get unstuck. In the next chapter, after the STAR in Action Story, we say goodbye.

Summary of
When Things Don't Work

★ **Three reasons why things may not work.** The *wrong approach:* parent uses the wrong approach or has little skill. The *wrong problem:* child lacks skill, is too stressed, or is scared. The *wrong person:* parent is scared, reacting from the past, or inattentive.

★ **What you can do.** When you are unable to solve the problem, get help. *Return to STAR Parenting* and use the process more thoughtfully. *Review your self-care* and get the help you need, or *get outside help* by contacting a parenting class, child development specialist, parenting coach, health care professional, or counselor.

STAR in Action Story[1]

Getting the Toys Cleaned Up

Peter, 6, and Lori, 4, leave their toys all over the floor in the family room and sometimes in the dining room and living room. I was getting tired of stepping around their toys, and I was concerned that if we didn't address the issue, the problem would get worse and be harder to correct later when they're older.

My initial approach to the problem was to establish a limit. My first tendency in dealing with parenting issues is to impose a limit. Limits by themselves do not work, and I know this. This story illustrates the importance of incorporating the whole STAR.

First try—with limit alone

My limit was: *Any toys on the floor at the end of the day will be put away for one week.* Every evening I would pick up the toys left out and put them up on top of the bookshelf. I would remind the kids to pick up their toys, but it was like pulling teeth. This wasn't working. After about a month there was no improvement and I was tired of picking up the toys and putting them on the bookshelf. Time to **Review and revise.** I will go back to the beginning, start again, and use the whole process.

Stop and focus

I am frustrated with having to either walk around my kids' toys or pick them up. I am going to put in the time up front to deal with the problem.

Long view: I want my kids to appreciate living in a neat space and to know how to clean up their belongings.
Development: At 6 and 4, Peter and Lori should be able to do the majority of the work, although they may need some reminding.

Temperament: Peter is easily distracted. Lori is intense and persistent.
Parent's goal: Kids to clean up every evening before they go to bed.

Second try—all around the STAR

I started over. On a large sheet of paper I wrote down the five points of the STAR. Under each point I wrote down as many ideas as I could think of. A couple of days later I filled in the missing tools. After refining the list, I typed it up and put it on the refrigerator.

Think of ideas

Avoid problem

☆*Change things* ① Go through the toys in the family room and remove the toys that Peter and Lori have outgrown. ② Put toys that they don't play with much upstairs in their rooms. ③ Put a bin in the dining room that they can use for putting toys away in that area.

☆*Reduce stress* ④ Make sure Peter and Lori get enough exercise and sleep.

☆*Two yeses* ⑤ I can help you pick up your toys or you may pick them up yourself and have an extra story at bedtime.

Set limits

☆*Rule* ⑥ When you are finished playing with something, put it away so that it is not sitting out on the floor. ⑦ Pick up toys you were playing with before you start something new.

☆*Consequence* ⑧ At the end of the day, any toys left on the floor will be put in your room. You can play with those toys upstairs. In one week, you can bring the toy downstairs again if you want.

☆*A better way* ⑨ Say to child: "My way is you pick up your toys from the floor when you're no longer playing with them. Your way is you leave them on the floor. What is a better way?"

---

1 There is a STAR in Action Story at the end of each chapter. Each story is written by a parent in his or her own words and shows how that person adapted the STAR Parenting process to his or her own life.

These stories use tools from all points, so some may be unfamiliar until you have read the appropriate chapter. You can see how different parents, with different values or kids with different temperaments, might make different choices.

Teach new skills

☆**Shaping** Here are some skills Peter and Lori will need to leave a space neat.

⑩ *Notice what needs to be picked up.* When you start to play with something, look around to see if there is anything that you're not playing with anymore.

⑪ *Reward yourself.* Think of something you can reward yourself with when you finish picking up. Some ideas:

⑫ Play with something in the clean spot you just cleaned up.

⑬ Draw a picture of a prize for yourself and hang it on the refrigerator.

⑭ Play the piano.

⑮ Look at a book.

⑯ Play a game on the computer.

⑰ Go outside and swing, or slide, or play on the climber or in the sandbox.

⑱ *Keep from getting distracted while cleaning up.* If you start to play with a toy while you're trying to clean up, put the toy on a table or in another room so that it doesn't distract you. When you finish cleaning up, go get the toy and play with it to reward yourself.

⑲ *Break chore up into smaller pieces.* Separate toys into piles. Pick up one pile and put it away. Pick up another pile and put it away. Repeat until all piles are picked up.

⑳ *Use tools that make it easier to clean up.* Use a game board or box lid to scoop up small pieces (such as Legos®), then pour them into the bin or box that they belong in. ㉑ Put toys in a box. Carry them to where they belong, put them away, and then fill box with more toys.

㉒ *Make the job more fun by making it a game.* For example, say a letter of the alphabet each time you pick up something and each time you put it down where it belongs.

☆**Modeling** ㉓ Parent says, "I better clean up this project before I start _____," and puts away project.

☆**Re-do it right** ㉔ If something was missed, gently say, "Look, some Legos® are hiding. Let's finish the job."

Respond to cooperation

☆**Praise** ㉕ Compliment kids when they pick up their toys or when they start to pick up their toys. Reward effort also.

☆**Reward** ㉖ Give out "Helper Tickets" as rewards when I think appropriate. They can use Helper Tickets to enlist our help when they have toys they need to pick up. Child gives Helper Ticket to parent. Parent helps child pick up some toys.

☆**Attention** ㉗ Give attention to children when they are cleaning up by helping them. Then tell them why I'm helping them. "I appreciate your remembering to clean up all by yourself."

Acknowledge feelings

☆**Active listening** ㉘ When a child complains about having to clean up toys, say, "You're frustrated *(feeling)* that you have to share the floor space with the rest of the family *(situation)*."

☆**Grant in fantasy** ㉙ "Wouldn't it be great if we had two family rooms? When one gets too messy, we could just switch rooms and send a robot in to clean up the messy one."

☆**Simple listening** ㉚ If a child complains, respond noncommittally with, "Oh" "I see," "Really?"

Act Effectively

This list really pointed out how lopsided my original approach had been. And my new consequence is more directly related: *If you are not responsible for your toys in the communal part of the house, you'll need to play with them in your room.*

I decided to pretty much do it all. I commented when I cleaned up (modeling). I began to teach Peter and Lori the skills they would need to be successful. I watched carefully so I could acknowledge their cooperation. If they were upset, I acknowledged their feelings.

Review and revise

The plan has been in effect for about two months and it's been very successful. The other day Peter announced he was going to play with play dough. Lori was sorting and organizing juice can lids in the family room. She had them spread out on the floor and was putting stickers on each lid. Lori came into the kitchen to join Peter playing with play dough. Then she said, "But wait! First, I need to clean up my project!" Wow! I rewarded her with a hug and a Helper Ticket, then I picked up juice can lids with her.

Closing Thoughts

~~~~~~

A STAR parent is a growing parent, not a perfect parent

~~~~~~

Congratulations for making it this far—that shows concern, interest, and perseverance. All three are useful traits for parents.

Looking back in *STAR Parenting Tales and Tools,* we have seen how the STAR Parenting process, points, and tools work. You have had a chance to practice many of the STAR Parenting tools. And you have read stories of people who have used the STAR Parenting process to solve their problems. The next step, if you have not already begun, is to experiment with process and tools in your own family.

We have a saying that "A STAR parent is a growing parent—not a perfect parent."

Why focus on growing? I believe keeping an open mind is important because life is always changing. Your child is growing and changing, so you must grow in response. This might involve learning new ways to use the STAR Parenting tools you have or learning new information to deal with the world or challenges that face you.

Why not perfection? Perfection is not attainable. The stress of continually researching information and worrying whether or not you're doing exactly the right thing can undermine your own observations and intuition about your child. And the pursuit of perfection can drive everyone around you crazy.

For me, being good enough, is good enough. Really! It models how to handle mistakes, and it helps children realize that the world will not fall apart if *they* make a mistake. That is very comforting to children.

Good enough is good enough. Really!

Consider developing a STAR Parenting community

The STAR Parenting process, points, and tools work with kids of all ages. It is easier to parent well when you have people to bounce ideas around with. If you have a common language, problems and solutions are easier to discuss. You can form a study-support group to help apply the STAR Parenting principles to your child's current age and to brainstorm ideas for the challenges you face. Some things you can do together are:

- Use the STAR Parenting Study Guide Qwik Sheet from ParentingPress.com.
- Create your own STAR Parenting ideas bank for common issues.
- Check out STARparent.com to see the interactive stars, classes available, and Ideas Bank.
- Start a STAR Parenting cluster (group of trained STAR parents) at your church, your child's school, or your neighborhood center.

Some intriguing topics

There are a number of interesting topics that are beyond the scope of this book. I will share three.

How much is enough?—The problem of overindulgence and what to do instead. Jean Illsley Clarke, Connie Dawson, and David Bredehoft have done research into childhood overindulgence and how it affects adults' lives. They have identified three styles of overindulgence: (1) too many things (toys, clothes) and too many activities (sports, music lessons, scouts, play dates, etc.), (2) over-nurture (doing things for children that they should be doing for themselves, such as helicopter parents), and (3) weak structure (not enough chores, limits, or responsibility for the child's own action). Further, they have found that childhood overindulgence is very debilitating in adulthood in surprising ways.

You can read more about this in their book, *How Much Is Enough? Everything You Need to Know to Steer Clear of Overindulgence and Raise Likeable, Responsible and Respectful Children from Toddlers to Teens.*

Encourage independence and responsibility—If you want your children to be independent and responsible as teens or adults, you need to change your level of support as they grow. There are four stages: nurturer, teacher, coach, consultant. For example, the way you establish rules and consequences would be different at each stage.

You can find out more about this in my book, *Am I Doing Too Much for My Child? Getting Your Child on the Road to Responsibility and Independence.*

Thinking styles and family life. How you think and how you process information has a profound effect on your relationships—with your partner, your children, your extended family. Some of the problems parents and older children have are caused or complicated by not respecting different thinking styles. *Why Don't You Understand? Improve Family Communication with the 4 Thinking Styles,* by Susie Leonard Weller, provides a fascinating answer to why this happens and how to communicate more effectively.

My wish for you is that you will—

- *Enjoy your children where they are.* Every age has it joys and its challenges. When you spend enjoyable time with your children, you create memories for yourself and your child that can be recalled when your children are grown and on their own.
- *Be curious.* Notice what is going on around you. Ask yourself, "What might happen if I tried . . . ?" Learn one new thing each day. When you are open to new information and ideas, it is easier to find new solutions when you need them.
- *Make your own decisions.* You are the expert on your child and you are your child's strongest advocate. Several times when my children were young, I made the mistake of using someone else's judgment when it was contrary to my own. In one case it was a friend and another it was a professional. In both cases it was wrong for my children.
- *Hunt for solutions that work for all involved.* The more ideas you consider, the more likely you are to find something that works for everyone. It is not always possible to find something that will work for everyone, but the process of hunting is helpful.
- *Take time to smell the roses.* It is easier to give your children the nurture and structure (love and limits) they need when your own needs are met. That can involve taking a walk in the woods, getting a massage, curling up with a good book, or talking with a friend. Do what energizes, refreshes, and calms you.

I invite you to take the STAR Parenting tools you have learned and tales you have read and try them out.

A STAR parent is a growing parent, not a perfect parent. You now are a STAR parent by virtue of taking the time and thought to read *STAR Parenting Tales and Tools.*

Best wishes on your parenting journey!

Appendix A
Poster, Tables, and Forms

Poster—Summary of STAR Parenting

STAR Parenting

A STAR parent is a growing parent—not a perfect parent

Stop and focus
- Calm yourself
- Consider your values
- Consider your child
- Consider the situation

Think of ideas
- Go for volume
- Add variety
- Hunt for new ideas

Act effectively
- Evaluate ideas
- Make a plan
- Strengthen your plan
- DO IT

Review and revise
- Review what's working
- Revise unresolved areas
- Reward yourself for success or effort

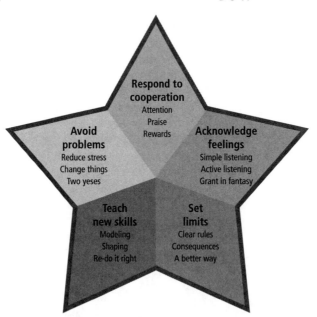

Respond to cooperation
Attention
Praise
Rewards

Avoid problems
Reduce stress
Change things
Two yeses

Acknowledge feelings
Simple listening
Active listening
Grant in fantasy

Teach new skills
Modeling
Shaping
Re-do it right

Set limits
Clear rules
Consequences
A better way

STAR Parenting points

Avoid problems—Reduce hassles so you can work on what is important.
Set limits—Give boundaries and let kids test them.
Teach new skills—Offer skills needed for dealing with the world.
Acknowledge feelings—Accept feelings without judging or changing them.
Respond to cooperation—Encourage desirable behavior by noticing it.

Summary of STAR Parenting points and tools

Avoid problems—Reduce hassles so you can work on what is important.

☆*Reduce stress*	Provide outlets for stress. Foreshadow transitions. Look for ways to simplify the child's life.
☆*Change things*	Consider when and why behavior occurs. Change environment, schedule, or expectations to reduce the problem.
☆*Two yeses*	Tell child what he/she may do. Change tool, time, or location to find acceptable behavior.

Respond to cooperation—Encourage desirable behavior by noticing it.

☆*Attention*	Notice behavior you want. Give recognition with nearness, touching, smiling, nodding, okay sign, etc.
☆*Praise*	Notice desired behavior and comment on it. Effective praise is specific, immediate, and sincere.
☆*Rewards*	Look for desired behavior. Reward the behavior as soon as he/she does it. Use something the child wants or needs.

Acknowledge feelings—Accept feelings without judging or changing them.

☆*Simple listening*	Listen. Respond with neutral statements like: "Uh-huh," "Okay," "Yeah," "Tell me more," "Really?"
☆*Active listening*	Reflect the feelings and describe the situation. No judgment, no questions, no advice. Leave the problem with the child.
☆*Grant in fantasy*	Grant in pretend what you cannot give in real life. Be outrageous enough so that child knows it is pretend.

Set limits—Give boundaries and let kids test them.

☆*Clear rules*	Tell child what to do, rather than what to stop. Rules are positive, short, and age appropriate.
☆*Consequences*	Consequences strengthen rules. Logical consequences are related to behavior, a true choice, and low energy.
☆*A better way*	Find a solution that works for both parent and child. "My way is . . ., your way is . . . What will work for both of us?"

Teach new skills—Offer skills needed for dealing with the world.

☆*Modeling*	Do exactly what you want the child to do. Explain what you are doing and why you are doing it.
☆*Shaping*	Divide the skill or task into small steps. Introduce those steps. This can be done with both simple and complex tasks.
☆*Re-do it right*	Pleasantly return with the child to the site of unwanted behavior and help the child re-do correctly.

Desirable children's traits

Directions: Imagine that you find that the preschool child you are planning to adopt has the characteristics listed below. Check your reaction to each statement listed below under the appropriate letter.

O = *outraged,* *C* = *concerned,* *N* = *neutral,* *P* = *pleased,* *E* = *elated*

Your new child:	Your response:	O	C	N	P	E
1. is very active, always on the go.		—	—	—	—	—
2. takes whatever she or he wants.		—	—	—	—	—
3. can throw and catch a ball very well.		—	—	—	—	—
4. is a very beautiful child.		—	—	—	—	—
5. has a smile for everyone.		—	—	—	—	—
6. doesn't want to be dirty or messy.		—	—	—	—	—
7. can do "physical" things easily (*e.g.*, run, climb, ride a trike).		—	—	—	—	—
8. faces unpleasant situations (*e.g.*, doctor's shots) without flinching.		—	—	—	—	—
9. asks questions about everything.		—	—	—	—	—
10. can do things a variety of ways.		—	—	—	—	—
11. always turns out lights when leaving a room.		—	—	—	—	—
12. gives toys away to anyone who asks.		—	—	—	—	—
13. sees what needs to be done and helps without being asked.		—	—	—	—	—
14. tells the truth even when it is to his or her disadvantage.		—	—	—	—	—
15. always wants to do things by him- or herself.		—	—	—	—	—
16. is tested as academically gifted.		—	—	—	—	—
17. does what anyone says.		—	—	—	—	—
18. lets another child bite him or her.		—	—	—	—	—
19. doesn't like activities interrupted.		—	—	—	—	—
20. always thanks people.		—	—	—	—	—
21. is always sought out by playmates.		—	—	—	—	—
22. says prayers every night.		—	—	—	—	—
23. can be trusted to leave tempting items alone.		—	—	—	—	—
24. comforts a sad child at preschool.		—	—	—	—	—
25. gets own snack whenever hungry.		—	—	—	—	—

Ranking children's traits

Directions: Rank the personality traits listed below. Begin with 1 as the most important to you.

Note: The traits are the same as were presented in Activity 3–1. The numbers in parentheses indicate the corresponding statement in Activity 3–1.

____ **Active,** lots of energy, always moving (1)

____ **Aggressive,** competitive (2)

____ **Athletic,** does well in sports (3)

____ **Attractive,** physically nice looking (4)

____ **Cheerful,** pleasant, friendly (5)

____ **Clean,** neat, uncluttered (6)

____ **Coordinated,** physically coordinated (7)

____ **Courageous,** stands up for own beliefs (8)

____ **Curious,** inquisitive (9)

____ **Flexible,** resourceful, innovative (10)

____ **Frugal,** conserves resources and energy (11)

____ **Generous,** shares with others (12)

____ **Helpful to others,** altruistic (13)

____ **Honest,** truthful (14)

____ **Independent,** self-reliant (15 & 25)

____ **Intelligent,** intellectual (16)

____ **Obedient,** compliant (17)

____ **Passive,** not aggressive (18)

____ **Persistent,** has "finishing power" (19)

____ **Polite,** well mannered (20)

____ **Popular,** liked by peers (21)

____ **Religious,** respects God (22)

____ **Self-controlled,** self-restraint\ed (23)

____ **Sensitive,** considerate of others' feelings (24)

Identify your child's temperament traits

Directions: For each trait, read the description, and then mark where your child fits on the scale provided.

1. **Activity level.** How active is your child? If you were on a desert island, would your child be "on the go" or "laid back and idle?" Are her movements quick or slow?

   Physically active . . . . Physically quiet

2. **Adaptability.** How quickly does your child adjust to changes in plans? How quickly does she adapt to new places, foods, or things?

   Quick to adapt . . . . Resists change

3. **Approach.** What is your child's first reaction to new people, places, or experiences? Is he or she eager or reluctant for new experiences?

   Curious . . . . Cautious

4. **Distractibility.** Is your child easily interrupted by things going on around him? Does he continue to work or play when noise is present?

   Hard to distract . . . . Easy to distract

5. **Emotional connection.** How readily does your child understand other people's feelings? How much is your child affected by other people's feelings?

   Unaware of feelings . . . . Very aware of feelings

6. **Intensity.** How much energy does your child use to express emotions? Does she laugh or cry vigorously? Or, does she smile and fuss mildly?

   High intensity . . . . Low intensity

7. **Mood.** What mood does your child usually display? Does your child see the world as a pleasant or an unpleasant place?

   Somber/Grumpy . . . . Sunny/Cheerful

8. **Persistence.** How long does your child continue with a difficult activity? Can he continue when frustrated? Can he stop when asked?

   Very persistent . . . . Stops easily

9. **Regularity.** Does your child have a predictable internal clock? Does he or she generally get hungry at the same time everyday? . . . sleep at the same time? . . . have bowel movements at the same time?

   Irregular schedule . . . . Regular schedule

10. **Sensory awareness.** How aware is your child of his or her physical world? How sensitive to changes in sound, light, touch, pain, taste, and odor? Note: Kids can be sensitive to one sense and less so to another.

    Physically insensitive . . . . Physically very sensitive

Family rules with preschoolers

Take care of your body
> Eat nutritious foods • Take baths regularly • Get enough exercise
> Brush teeth daily • Take medicine when needed • Get enough sleep
> Wash hands before eating • Act safely (see below)

Treat people pleasantly/respectfully
> Ask for what you want. (No whining, screaming, pouting, hinting, or
>   complaining) • Accept "No" gracefully.
> Touch gently. (No hurting, threatening, mean names, or uncomfortable
>   teasing)
> Problem-solve differences. Find solutions that meet everyone's needs.
> Ask permission before using something that belongs to someone else.
>   Return it in good shape. • Say please and thank you.

Contribute to the family
> Clean up your own messes • Do your chores promptly.
> Offer to help when you see ways to do so.

Use good meal manners
> Eat and drink in the kitchen and dining room only.
> Try one bite of everything before seconds, dessert, or saying you don't
>   like it.
> Get permission before leaving the table.
> When you are excused from the table, take your plate to the kitchen and
>   wash your hands and face.

Act safely at home
> Food only in mouth. (No toys, pens, etc.) If you are chewing, sit down.
> Walk inside. (No running inside)
> Ask to touch sharp items, hot items, or things plugged in. (No playing
>   with knives, sharp scissors, with stove, fireplace)
> Keep the gates shut (so dog/little kids won't get out).
> Sit with bottom on chairs and sofas.

Act safely outside
> Stay with Mama or Daddy, or other adults in charge. (Never leave the
>   store or your home without a parent.)
> Tell the person in charge before leaving the house.
> Stay where you can see me and I can see you.
> Hold hands when crossing the street and in other unsafe places. (Don't
>   play in the street)
> Wear helmet when using bike, skiis, scooter, skates, skateboard, etc.

Family rules with school-aged kids

Treat people and property with respect
Treat ourselves and others' things, feelings, and bodies with respect
    If we don't, we make amends promptly by checking to see if they are okay and doing something to help them feel better or fixing what is broken. Only apologize if you mean it.

Speak respectfully to others
    Whine and sassy are not languages we speak in our house.

Problem-solve differences
    Find solutions that meet everyone's needs.

Be truthful and believe others unless there is proof otherwise

Act safely
    Helmets are required for skiing, snowboarding, skateboarding, and biking. No exceptions!
    Walk in parking lots next to an adult. Cars cannot see you.
    Ask/check in with the parent/person in charge before leaving the house.
    When away from the house, always stay within sight of the parent/ person in charge. They need to be able to see you too.

Be courteous
    Always say "goodnight" to each other.
    Use manners and proper table etiquette.
    No computer/online/TV without permission.

Contribute to the family
    Do your daily chores.
    Clean up your own messes.

Family rules with teenagers

Treat people and property with respect
No hurting, threatening, name calling, or uncomfortable teasing.
Ask permission before using something belonging to someone else.
When you use other people's property, leave it in as good shape as you found it.
Tell parents where you are or where you want to go. Come home at agreed-upon time.

Ask for what you want. Accept "No" gracefully
No hinting, whining, pouting, or complaining.

Problem-solve differences with people
Find solutions that meet everyone's needs.

Clean up your own messes
Mop up spills. Wash dishes you use. Hang up your clothes.
Leave common areas (living room, dining room, bathrooms) neat.

Respect sleep and work schedules
No incoming calls or loud noises between 10 P.M. and 8 A.M.
If people are working, ask if it is an okay time to interrupt.
Get enough sleep and nutritious food to be pleasant and healthy.

Maintain supplies list and equipment
If something you use is low, put it on the shopping list.
Check with the cook before opening a box/can of food if there are no others.
If you break something, fix it or let others know it needs to be fixed.

Contribute to the family
Offer to help when you see ways to do so.
Do your chores promptly.

Coordinate schedules regularly
Let the cook know if you will not be eating dinner.
Arrange to get school supplies, etc. before the assignment is due.
Negotiate rides or car use (and other stuff) before you need it.

Maintain a safe and drug-free home
Report things that need repair or are unsafe to a parent.
No smoking inside. If someone smokes outside, see that their butts are disposed of in garbage can (not on the ground).
No alcohol, drugs (except prescribed medicine), or weapons on the property.

Be responsible for your guests' actions
Be sure they honor family rules. If they don't, ask them to leave or ask an adult for help.

✐ STAR Parenting planning worksheet

Background: Describe last time the behavior happened	

Stop and focus

Collect data: • Age of the child • Length of the problem • Frequency of behavior	Child's age: _____ How long has the behavior been a problem? _____ Frequency: _____ times an hour □, day □, week □ , or month □.
Values: List three that may be related to the behaviors.	1. 2. 3.
Development: What is the child's developmental task? How might it apply here?	Task: Possible relation to behavior:
Temperament: List three traits that might affect this behavior and how intense the traits are.	_Trait_ _Intensity_ 1. _____ _____ 2. _____ _____ 3. _____ _____
Desired behavior: What you want the child to do _instead_ of what he/she is doing.	Specific behavior:

Think of ideas

Avoid problem ☆_Change things_ ☆_Reduce stress_ ☆_Two yeses_	• • •
Respond to cooperation ☆_Attention_ ☆_Praise_ ☆_Rewards_	• • •
Acknowledge feelings ☆_Simple listening_ ☆_Active listening_ ☆_Grant in fantasy_	• • •

Set limits ☆Clear rules ☆Consequences ☆A better way	• • •
Teach new skills ☆Model ☆Re-do it right ☆Shaping	• • •

Act effectively

Ideas: What will you try first?	
Roadblocks: What might interfere with your success?	
Support: How can you protect yourself from the problem?	
Make a plan. What will you need? Who will get it? Do you need anyone's help?	
How long will you continue this plan?	

Review and revise

What went well?	
What needs to change?	
What will you try next? For how long?	
What have you learned for the future?	

Values—225 desirable attributes of people

1. Read the attributes and check those you would like your child to have when he or she is grown.
2. Circle the five attributes that are most important to you.
3. Underline the five that are least desirable.

Accepting	Confident	Family-oriented
Accurate	Conforming	Farsighted
Active	Conscientious	Fatherly
Adaptable	Conservative	Feels for others
Adventurous	Considerate	Feminine
Affectionate	Contented	Firm
Aggressive	Conventional	Flexible
Alert	Cooperative	Forceful
Aloof	Courageous	Forgiving
Ambitious	Creative	Formal
Amusing	Critical	Frank
Anticipates consequences	Curious	Friendly
Argumentative	Daring	Fun-loving
Artistic	Dedicated	Generous
Attractive	Deep interests	Gentle
Authoritative	Deep ethical sense	Genuine
Aware	Deliberate	Giving
Bold	Demanding	Good judgment
Broad-minded	Democratic	Good-natured
Businesslike	Dependable	Happy
Calm	Depends on other opinions	Happy-go-lucky
Can make decisions	Determined	Hard working
Can say no	Dignified	Healthy
Capable	Discreet	Helpful
Careful	Dominating	Honest
Caring	Eager	Humorous
Cautious	Easy-going	Idealistic
Cheerful	Effective	Imaginative
Clear-thinking	Efficient	Independent
Clever	Emotional	Individualistic
Coherent	Empathetic	Industrious
Common sense	Encouraging	Informal
Community oriented	Energetic	Ingenious
Compassionate	Enterprising	Initiative
Competent	Expressive	Insightful
Competitive	Fair-minded	Integrated
Completes plans	Faithful	Intellectual

Based on Using Your Values to Raise Your Child to Be an Adult You Admire *by Harriet Heath, Ph.D.*

Intelligent
Inventive
Involved
Joyful
Kind
Knowledgeable
Leisurely
Lethargic
Liberal
Light-hearted
Likeable
Logical
Loves nature
Loving
Loyal
Masculine
Mature
Methodical
Meticulous
Mild
Moderate
Modest
Motherly
Motivated
Natural
Nurturing
Obliging
Open
Opportunistic
Optimistic
Orderly
Organized
Original
Other-centered
Outgoing
Painstaking
Patient
Peaceful
Perfectionist
Persistent
Plans ahead
Playful
Plays it safe
Pleasant

Poised
Polite
Popular
Practical
Precise
Progressive
Proud
Purposeful
Quick
Quiet
Rational
Realistic
Reasonable
Robust
Reflective
Relaxed
Reliable
Religious
Reserved
Resourceful
Responsible
Retiring
Self-centered
Self-confident
Self-controlled
Self-driving
Self-educated
Self-reliant
Self-respectful
Self-sufficient
Sensible
Sensitive
Serious
Sharp-witted
Sincere
Skillful
Sociable
Sophisticated
Spiritual
Spontaneous
Spunky
Stable
Steady
Strong

Strong convictions
Strong-minded
Sympathetic
Tactful
Talkative
Teachable
Tenacious
Tender
Thirst for knowledge
Thorough
Thoughtful
Tolerant
Tough
Trusting
Trustworthy
Truthful
Unaffected
Unassuming
Uncritical of others
Understanding
Uninhibited
Verbal
Versatile
Warm
Well informed
Wholesome
Zealous

Look at your top ten values and notice if any of the values conflict with others.

Appendix B
STAR Ideas Bank

Ideas for common issues and challenges
Topics contain ideas generated during STAR Parenting classes.

Each idea is followed by two letters indicating which tool was used. Here is a list of the STAR Parenting points with the tools and their two-letter identifiers:

Avoid problems: CT = *Change things,* RS = *Reduce stress,* 2Y = *Two yeses*

Respond to cooperation: AT = *Attention,* PR = *Praise,* RW = *Rewards*

Set reasonable limits: CR = *Clear rules,* CN = *Consequences,* BW = *A better way*

Teach new skills: MD = *Modeling,* SH = *Shaping,* RD = *Re-do it right*

Acknowledge feelings: AL = *Active listening,* SL = *Simple listening,* GF = *Grant in fantasy*

More ideas in the STAR in Action stories

STAR Ideas Bank—**Whining**

Problems:
☆Two-and-a half-year-old daughter whines whenever she can't have what she wants. It can be a puzzle she can't quite do or my refusal to give her a cookie right before supper.
☆Five-year-old whines when he can't find the toy or book he wants.
☆Nine-year-old whines because he is hungry and wants a snack NOW, even though dinner is twenty minutes away.
Goal: For children to use a pleasant voice when asking for something, and to accept 'No" gracefully when told "No."
Reality check: Whining is a very common complaint. Some parents unintentionally teach children to whine by ignoring them when they speak pleasantly. Children learn to whine because it gets through to their parents. You may want to notice what happens before the whining. Children (and adults) often whine when tired, hungry, or stressed.

Lots of ideas

Avoid problems

1. Make sure child isn't whining because hungry or tired. **RS**
2. Add fifteen minutes to prep time (dinner or departure) so you can respond thoughtfully when child whines. **RS**
3. Take the child outside (change of scenery). **CT**
4. Schedule a nutritious snack so child doesn't get overly hungry. **CT**
5. Involve child in what you are doing (fixing dinner, changing the baby's diaper, etc.) **CT**
6. Use ear plugs to reduce the whine sound. **CT**
7. Change your expectations. When your toddler whines, take a deep breath and remind yourself that kids are just learning to control their responses. **CT**
8. Import another person to cook or distract child (like older sib, or mother's helper). **CT**
9. Say, "You can speak pleasantly or whine elsewhere." **2Y**
10. Say, "You can work the puzzle pleasantly here, or do it in your room and whine." **2Y**
11. Say, "If you don't want to use your inside voice, you can whisper or sing." **2Y**

Respond to cooperation

12. Withhold attention when the child whines. Do not comment on whining or ask child to speak pleasantly. See number 6. **AT**
13. Respond immediately when the child stops whining. **AT**
14. Plan "quality time" each day. **AT**
15. Praise the pleasant voice, "That was a pleasant request—nice tone, medium volume, and polite words." **PR**
16. Notice and compliment the child when she accepts "no" gracefully. **PR**
17. Say, "I can understand you so much

better when you use your words. Thank you!" **PR**
18. Reward your child when she speaks pleasantly in a situation when she usually whines. Give her a hug and a special non-whining sticker. **RW**
19. Each time you notice she increases the pleasantness of her voice, reward her effort. You could use cooperation tickets, stickers, silly bands—something that is important to your child. **RW**

Acknowledge feelings

20. Say, "Sounds like you're frustrated that I won't give you a cookie right now." **AL**
21. Say, "You're sad that the toy you want isn't here." **AL**
22. Say, "You feel left out when Momma plays with your little sister." **AL**
23. Listen to the child and respond with supportive statements like: "Oh," "I see." **SL**
24. Give in pretend. Say, "Wouldn't it be fun if we had a magic wand? When you had trouble, you could tap the puzzle with the wand and the pieces would zoom back to their places." **GF**

Set limits

25. Make a clear rule. "If you want something, ask pleasantly." **CR**
26. Explain, "When you ask pleasantly and get a "No," accept the 'No' gracefully." **CR**
27. Clarify, "Only nutritious snacks the hour before meals." **CR**
28. Say, "You can whine only once a day." Give child one whine ticket each morning. When he starts to whine, ask, "Is this your one whine time?" **CR**
29. Explain, "When you whine the answer is 'No.'" **CN**
30. Clarify, "When you whine, I will leave the room until you're pleasant." **CN**
31. Say, "You want to use a whiny voice. I want you to speak pleasantly so I can understand you. What is a better way

to get what you need?" **BW**

Teach new skills

32. Use a pleasant tone of voice when you are asking the child for something—even when you are rushed. **MD**
33. Start to whine, change to a nice voice, and comment, "I started to whine, but remembered to change to a pleasant voice." **MD**
34. Say, "Oops, that was a whiny voice. Try again with a nice voice." **RD**
35. Divide learning into several steps. Tell the child to (1) take a deep breath, (2) think of words to use, and (3) then say what he is thinking in a pleasant voice. **SH**
36. To teach the difference between a whiny voice and a pleasant voice you could break the task into three steps. (1) Notice tones in other people's voices and discuss them. (2) Ask the child to notice when he or she is whining and change to a pleasant voice. (3) Invite her to start out with a pleasant voice (and acknowledge her effort when she does). **SH**

Ideas for toddlers

- Use signs for specific needs. "More," "drink," "eat," "hug"
- Tell the child to raise her hand when she needs something.

Ideas for older kids

- Have the child whine into a tape recorder so she can hear how it sounds.
- Ask the child to make a puppet show (play or story) for a younger sibling, cousin, or neighbor that illustrates two benefits of speaking pleasantly (not whining).

STAR Ideas Bank—Grocery store tantrums

Problem: I hate grocery shopping. If it's not one thing, it's another. If I put Jenny, 3½, in the cart, she cries to get down. If I put her down, she runs away. The few times she stays near me, she begs for everything she sees.

Goal: To be able to go grocery shopping with Jenny and have it be a pleasant experience. Specifically, to have Jenny stay in the cart or next to me to be safe while I am shopping. Looking at *values*, courtesy and safety are important to me.

Reality check: Developmentally she is in the power and identity stage. Jenny wants to be her own person, and do what she wants. She often doesn't like to do what she is told. By *temperament* Jenny is physically active, intense, and persistent. No matter how often I say "no" she'll ask "why" and keep trying the same thing, over and over again.

Lots of ideas

Avoid problems

1. Bring a small bag of toys for Jenny that she only gets to play with in the store. **CT**
2. Go in the morning, when she's more agreeable, instead of when she's tired. **CT**
3. Say, "You're the driver. Tell me which way to turn the cart and we'll drive around and find the items we need!" **CT**
4. Go as a family and make a game. Mom gives Dad and Jenny an item to hunt for. When they bring it back she gives them another item. When done they go for lunch or a treat together. **CT**
5. Say, "Jenny, you can go grocery shopping with me and stay in the cart or I can have a sitter come over and you can stay here." **2Y**
6. Say, "You can sit in the cart and eat a nutritious snack, or you can walk beside the cart and hand me items we need." **2Y**
7. Before you go grocery shopping, take her to the park to run off energy. **RS**
8. When she wiggles and whines, take deep breaths and remain calm when you respond. **RS**
9. Shop when you have someone to watch Jenny and can leave her at home. **RS**

Respond to cooperation

10. Each time she gets something and puts it in the cart, give her a thumbs-up sign and ruffle her hair. **AT**
11. Reinforce positive behavior at the grocery store with a treat from home that can be eaten in the cart. Start with a whole small box of kid crackers; then a container with a couple slices of fruit. If the problem behavior starts in the store, tell her you will put the snack away and it will only come out after a few minutes of good behavior. **RW & CN**

12. Jenny likes stickers. You can set up a system where she gets stickers when she sits calmly in the cart and/or walks pleasantly beside the cart. After she earns four stickers, she'll get an ice cream cone. You could do this two times and then taper off. She could earn only stickers, then just praise. And, eventually, you can drop the praise. **RW**
13. When she helps you find something from the shopping list, say, "You are a good helper. It's easier to find all the items with your help." **PR**

Acknowledge feelings

14. Say, "Wouldn't it be super if all the grocery items could understand our language? Then I could just call out their names and they would jump into our basket right away!" **GF**
15. Comment, "Wouldn't it be wonderful if all the foods in the store came to life and played with you?" **GF**
16. When she does sit in the cart well, say, "You must be very proud of yourself for staying in the cart all the time!" **AL**
17. When Jenny says, "Mommy, I want out!" Respond with simple words like, "Hmm," "Really," "I see," and smile, and keep walking. **SL**
18. When she gets restless, say, "Looks like you feel bored sitting in the cart." **AL**

Set reasonable limits

19. Clarify the rules: "Jenny, at the grocery store, you either sit quietly in the cart or walk next to me pleasantly." **CR**
20. Remind Jenny, "If you want to ride in the cart, you must sit still. **CR**
21. Explain the consequences. "If you walk out of my sight in the grocery store, I will put you in the cart so I will know you are safe." **CN**
22. Say, "Jenny, you may get out of the cart if you walk by me, otherwise you will have to go back in the cart." **CN**
23. Say, "Jenny, I want you to sit in the cart quietly, you want to walk on

your own and explore the store. What would be a better way?" **CR**

Teach new skills

24. Show her how you find each item on the shopping list. **MD**
25. Model decision making. Say, "I really want a candy bar right now, but it's not on my list and it isn't good for me. So I'm not going to buy one, instead I'll get a healthy snack that is on our list." **MD**
26. You could teach her to use a shopping list. (1) Give Jenny a copy of the shopping list with pictures. When you get something show it to her to cross off the list. (2) Tell her you can only buy things on the list. Occasionally show her something that is not on the list for her to reject. (3) Give her a couple of items from the list to find. **SH**
27. When she whines, say, "Whoops. That was a whiny voice. Try again in a pleasant voice." **RD**
28. When she wanders away, say, "Uh-oh, you forgot. Re-do it right and walk beside the cart." **RD**

STAR Ideas Bank—**Trouble leaving a play date**

Problem: Amy, my 4-year-old daughter, is dreadful when leaving a friend's house. Yesterday, when I went to pick her up after a play date, she yelled and screamed and refused to go. I had to bodily pick her up and carry her out under my arm. She was screaming, flailing, and trying to hit me. The tantrum continued most of the way home. It doesn't happen when someone else drops her off at our house—only when I pick her up. It happens every time I pick her up and it has been getting worse for the last month or two.

Goal: I want her to thank her hostess for inviting her and to walk out quietly. She doesn't have to be cheerful, just civil. *Values:* Being polite both as a guest and host is important to me.

Reality check. Temperament. It sounds as though Amy may be both intense and a natural planner. Natural planners (slow to adapt) have trouble adapting to plans that are not their own. *Development:* Four-year-olds are into power and identity, which makes the clash stronger.

Lots of ideas

Avoid problems

1. Set expectations—talk beforehand about expected behavior. **RS**
2. Give a five-minute warning before leaving the friend's house. **CT**
3. Create (with your child) a "coming home" tradition. **CT**
4. Call the friend's house to warn that you will be coming in five minutes. **CT**
5. Say, "It's time to go and I'm glad you are thinking about saying goodbye and leaving." **CT**
6. Reduce general stress by seeing she (and you) get enough exercise. **RS**
7. Say, "Do you want to leave the easy way or the hard way?"(Mom carries you.)" **2Y**
8. Say, "Do you want to say goodbye to your friend or shall I?" **2Y**

Respond to cooperation

9. Reinforce good behavior with a "treat" waiting at home. Something to look forward to, *e.g.,* baking cookies, watching a video. **RW**
10. When you show up, and before your daughter has a tantrum, smile and say pleasantly, "You are considering your options." **PR**
11. Smile and remind her, "When you come gracefully, you can choose the music to listen to on the way home." **RW**
12. Give attention when she is pleasant, *e.g.,* give her a "thumbs-up" or "okay" sign. **AT**
13. Say, "Thank you for coming quietly." **PR**
14. Say, "You were very courteous leaving today." **PR**

Acknowledge feelings

15. "You feel disappointed/angry that we have to go home now." **AL**
16. When she starts to complain, simply listen to her frustration. For example: Amy says. "I don't want to go home." Parent replies, "Oh."

A. "I want to stay here," P. "Really?"
A. "I don't like you. You're mean." P. "I see."
A. "Go away." P. "Hmm."
A. "I want to play more." P. "Really."
A. "I mean it." P. "I see."
A. "Can I come back tomorrow?" P. "We can ask." **SL**

17. Give support by pretend. "Wouldn't it be fun to have a machine that magically sends you where you want to go when you want?" **GF**

Set limits

18. Clarify rule, "Guests leave their friend's house pleasantly." **CR**
19. Give choices, "It is time to go. You can walk pleasantly or I can carry you. You decide." **CR**
20. Clarify expectations, "If you behaved badly, write (or draw) an apology." **CN**
21. Consequence—Stay home the next time she's invited to a play date. **CN**
22. Say, "You want to stay and play. I want to leave now so I can fix supper. What is something that will work for both of us?" **BW**

Teach new skills

23. Model dealing with your disappointment, "Charlene's baby is sick so we can't go to the concert tonight. I am so-o-o disappointed." **MD**
24. Ask her, "What can you do to make yourself feel better if you don't want to leave?" Three starter ideas:
    • Shake out mad feelings.
    • Talk about how sad you feel.
    • Call your friend when you get home. **SH**
25. Role play options with puppets. Or, play, "What would you do if . . ." to rehearse different exit strategies. **MD**
26. Divide getting oneself together into steps. (a) losing it, (b) calming yourself, (c) assessing the situation, (d) reflecting on your options, and (e) finding the positive. **SH**
27. Model correcting yourself using the shaping steps above. (Have a tantrum, stop, and re-do it right.) For example, after an unpleasant phone call you could yell: (a) "I can't believe he was so rude. He promised to deliver the new dryer here this afternoon but his schedule is too full to deliver it as he promised." (b) Then stop, take a deep breath, and say, "Okay [your name], get a grip. It is okay to be mad, and not okay to be unpleasant." (c) Assess the situation out loud, "No matter how big a tantrum I have, the dryer is not coming, so I might as well make the best of it." (d) Next, model reflecting on what you can do. "Okay, I'll re-do this right. I'm very frustrated that the new dryer is not coming today. However, I can take the wet clothes to a laundromat and dry them." (e) Find an upside. "My kids have never been to a laundromat so it can be an educational experience. While we wait for the stuff to dry we can have an ice cream cone in the store next door." **MD**
28. When Amy starts to have a tantrum, go to her and gently invite her to re-do it right. "Oops, Amy. You forgot to leave pleasantly. Let's re-do it right." **RD**

STAR Ideas Bank—Getting out in the morning

Problems:

☆Dressing always seems to take twice as long as it should. For example, today while my kids finished eating, I collected my things, Julieanne's school bag, and got the daycare stuff (diapers, food, and toys) ready. Then I dressed Luke (2)—tedious because he wanted to play chase. Next my daughter, 6, desperately needed help finding a headband she wanted today. When I returned to Luke, he had emptied the toys from the daycare bag and strewn them around the house. I found the stuff and put it back in the bag. Then Julieanne was worried that she had forgotten to put her permission slip in the backpack, so we had to wait while she checked.

☆I'm not sure we have ever gotten out of the house on time. My son, Alexander, 9, is more interested in playing with electronics or the cat. I have to always be reminding him to keep moving or he would never finish getting ready. When I think we're ready to leave, suddenly he has to find his shoes and put them on.

Goal: Both parents want kids to get themselves completely ready before playing with anything.

Reality check: Kids often resist adult's schedule—particularly in the morning. *Development*: Although kids are able to dress with adult supervision, many of them still need reminding to dress alone. (See Household job chart, page 163). *Temperament*: Children who are natural planners (slow to adapt) will have more trouble following someone else's plan. Children who are easily distracted or have low persistence may have trouble remembering what they should be doing.

Lots of ideas

Avoid problems

1. Clarify what all is expected. Make a list (words or pictures depending on the child's abilities) and post it. When the child is goofing off, take him to the list. Ask which tasks he has done, and what he will do next. **CT**
2. Give her some control. "Finish getting dressed and breakfast will be in the kitchen when you are ready." Then walk away and tend to your own tasks. **CT**
3. Reduce stress by preparing lunch and packing bags the night before. **RS**
4. Create a five-finger check to clarify expectations. One task per finger. *E.g.,* Get dressed, brush hair and teeth, eat breakfast and put dishes in sink, collect your stuff and put it by the front door, get a hug. **CT**
5. Leave without shoes on. He can carry them to the car. **CT**
6. Make a story board. Draw a picture for each step of getting ready on a separate file card. Ask the child to plan (put the cards in order) how he will do things so he has time to play. **CT**
7. "Beat the timer." Try to get completely ready before the timer rings. **CT**
8. Make a departure goal. Record how long it takes your child to get *completely* ready: dress, morning chores (make bed), eat, collect school stuff, put on shoes, etc. Ask him how long he would like to spend getting ready (the goal.) Ask him to practice the different steps in getting ready until he can achieve his goal. **RS**
9. Start earlier. On a lazy day (perhaps a holiday), time how long it takes

your child to get completely ready by himself. Add ten or fifteen minutes. Get things started early enough to leave on time. **RS**
10. Give kids responsibility for something: Turn out the lights. Check that the pets have water, etc. Meanwhile, you collect the things you wish to take with you. **CT**
13. Say, "You can get ready quickly and have lots of free time or get ready slowly and have little free time." **2Y**
14. Say, "You can get up and get everything ready before 7:30 A.M. and I will make waffles (child's favorite breakfast) or you can prepare more slowly and eat cereal in the car." **2Y**

Acknowledge feelings

15. Reflect the child's feelings, "You feel angry when Dad (or I) keeps telling you to hurry up." **AL**
16. Say, "You are disappointed that this is not a stay-at-home day." **AL**
17. Say, "You are feeling frustrated that you can't play right now." **AL**
18. On a day with more flexibility, ask your child to share his view of what is happening and respond using non-committal comments. ("Oh," "hum-m," "I see," "really") **SL**
19. Comment, "Imagine if you had a magic wand. You could say a magic word and everything would be magically ready to go." **AL**
20. Say, "Wouldn't it be nice if we could get to school quicker? If we had a space portal and could step immediately where we wanted?" **AL**

Reward cooperation

21. Smile at him if he is working when you check on him. **AT**
22. Comment, "Marvelous! You're ready to

go super early this morning!" **PR**
23. List the things the child has completed (don't mention what is lacking). "You're dressed. You've eaten. Hair and teeth are brushed. Soon you will be ready to go." **PR**
24. Give her a star when she is ready on time. When she gets five stars, she can plan the menu for Sunday brunch. **RW**
25. Read to him while he dresses. If he slows down or stops, you slow or stop your reading. **RW**
26. Say, "I'm pleased that we all got dressed, breakfasted, and out the door *on time* today." **PR**
27. Reward with Mommy time. Set timer for departure in thirty minutes. Tell your child that as soon as he is dressed and stuff collected you will spend the rest of the time reading or playing with him. (If he dresses in ten minutes, you read for twenty.) **RW**
28. Create an incentive. Set timer for departure in 30 minutes. When he is completely dressed and ready to go, he can watch TV until the timer rings. **RW**
29. Make a points system. If she is ready to go when a ten-minute warning alarm rings, she gets ten points. If she is ready on time, she get five points. Points are accumulated for a specific item or privilege. **RW**

Set reasonable limits

30. Possible rules:
    (1) First you work (get ready to go), then you play." **CR**
    (2) Put school stuff (homework, book bag, etc.) by the front door before you go to bed at night. **CR**
    (3) Ready-set-go. *Ready* yourself (wash, dress, eat, hair & teeth brushed, etc.) first, Set all your stuff by the

front door. Go have fun (read, draw, watch TV, etc.) till it is time to leave. **CR**

(4) We leave at 8:15! In pajamas and dry cereal in the car if that is how you are. **CR**

31. Clarify consequence. If you use TV or electronics before you are completely ready to go, you will loose the privilege of using them for two days. **CN**

32. Explain, "If you can't get ready on time, you will get up ten minutes earlier the next morning (and go to bed ten minutes earlier so you have enough sleep). We will shift time until we know how much time it takes to get out without hassles. **CN**

33. Say, "If you are not ready when the timer rings, we stay home." (Be sure you can do this.) **CN**

34. Say, "My way is you are completely ready to leave before you watch TV. Your way is to watch TV while you dress and get ready. What might work for both of us?" **BW**

35. Say, "My way is that you get dressed now. Your way is that you get dressed later. What would work for both of us?" **BW**

Teach new skills

36. Make up a story about a bear who has trouble getting ready for school in the morning and what he does. (1) First,

ask the child what things he thinks slow the bear down and tell a story about that. (2) The next night tell a story where the bear has a problem. The parent and child think of three to five ideas for the bear. Leave the story open ended. (3) The next evening, pick up the story and ask the child what the bear might try and why. (4) Next evening choose a different aspect of the problem to generate ideas on. (5) Eventually, when child has a problem, ask the child what bear ideas might work. **SH**

37. Practice an "out of the house" drill with reward. When time is no issue, practice moving quickly. If everyone is in the car before the timer rings, you all go for a treat. If not, laugh, make a group hug, and return to house. **MD**

38. Model getting your stuff together the night before and comment, "It's is so much easier in the morning when I remember to put my stuff by the door at night." **MD**

39. Model getting yourself ready early. Comment, "This feels really good to be ready ahead." Bonus, you have time to help your kids. **MD**

40. When a child gets distracted, say, "Oops, you turned on the TV before you were ready to go. Let's go finish gathering your things." **MD**

School-aged ideas

- *Two alarms wake up.* If getting out of bed is a problem, set one alarm clock by bed, and another one across the room so the child must get up to turn it off.
- *Tell the child you will wait in the car.* Leave and let the child join you when his coat and shoes are on.
- *Family meeting & brainstorm.* With the whole family (not just Mom or Dad) list the problem areas. Brainstorm ideas. Create a plan that works for everyone.

Dark side tool
Nagging—keep reminding the child to put his clothes on. "How many times do I have to tell you to put your pants on?" This gives negative attention and power to the child. Try micro-encouragement instead.

Make transitions easier
Help your child visualize success.
When your child is in bed at night, help him imagine what it will be like the next morning. Discuss how he might keep himself on track and then reflect the good feeling he will have when he is dressed on time.

Triple "R" trap
Repeated Reminding Reinforces unwanted behavior. What you comment on, you get more of. Instead, catch the child being good and comment on that.

STAR Ideas Bank—Grabs Toys

Problem: Hailey, 4, won't let her baby brother play with anything. As soon as Logan, 1¼, touches anything, she takes it away. I've told her to give it back, and I've given her a time-out, but nothing seems to work. I don't know if she wants my attention or if she is jealous. Ideas, *please!*

Goal: I value cooperation. I would like Hailey to play nicely, specifically to take turns with toys and with directing the play.

Reality check: You are unlikely to get a quick fix. Most young children have difficulty adjusting to a new sibling. This may happen when the sibling is born or when he starts moving around. The older sibling may feel displaced or she may not have the skills she needs to get what she wants. *Development:* Conflict may be magnified by normal developmental stages. For example, a task of children 3 to 6 is to feel powerful. The younger sibling becomes a partner in this learning. *Temperament:* The temperament trait of slow to adapt can slow learning down.

Lots of ideas

Avoid problem

1. Tell Hailey she is special to you, that no one else can ever take her place. "You will still be my first—even if I have 100 children." **RS**
2. Look at pictures or tell stories of when she was little. **RS**
3. Tell Hailey what to do when she wants your attention. For example, she could ask for a hug, a story, dance with you, look at your picture, etc. **CT**
4. Give her special "big girl" toys that she does not have to share with Logan. Perhaps she can only play with these while he is playing with the baby toys. **CT**
5. Reduce stress (for both you and Hailey) by doing aerobics together each day. **RS**
6. Offer two yeses, say, "No grabbing. When you want something Logan has you may wait until he is done or offer him something else fun." **2Y**

Teach new skills

7. Model trading when you remove something from Logan. **MD**
8. When she grabs, say, "You forgot to trade. Try again." **RD**
9. Break the task of trading into small steps. (1) Model trading. (2) Then, give Hailey a toy to trade. (3) Next show Hailey two toys and ask her which she thinks Logan will like to trade. (4) And finally ask her to find a toy Logan might like. **SH**
10. Teach sharing. (1) Read *I Want It* to Hailey and let her choose what the character does. (2) Act out the options. (3) Pick another toy and act out how a story might be. (4) Role play three options in dealing with Logan. **SH**
11. Use puppets or stuffed animals to demonstrate and practice sharing. In the beginning ask her to identify nice sharing, then later ask her to demonstrate for the puppets. **MD**

Reward cooperation

12. Sit near the kids and watch them while they play pleasantly. **AT**
13. Describe the appropriate things Hailey does. For example, "You wanted the fire truck and offered Logan the dump truck." **AT**
14. Praise kindly behavior. "Thank you for cheering up Logan. He felt sad when Daddy left. You helped him cheer up by making silly faces." **PR**
15. When Hailey asks for attention give it to her immediately and willingly. **AT**
16. Praise effort. "I noticed you offer Logan three different toys and he didn't want any." **PR**
17. Reward effort. Each time Hailey waits for a toy give her a ticket. When she gets five tickets reward her by playing tea party with her. **RW**

18. Ignore the toy issue and let Logan learn to cope. **AT**

Acknowledge feelings

19. Listen supportively. (No questions, no criticism) **SL**
20. Reflect her feelings, "Looks like you're irritated that Logan is playing with your baby toys." **AL**
21. Say, "It must be frustrating to share me and your baby toys with Logan." **AL**
22. Give in pretend, say, "Wouldn't it be fun to be able to clap your hands and make a new toy for Logan whenever you wanted?" **GF**

Set limits

23. Clarify expectations, "Put toys you don't want to share up high." **CR**
24. State rule, "Trade for toys." **CR**
25. Explain the consequence, "If you want a toy Logan has, trade something else for it. If you grab a toy, you will need to play in a room by yourself." **CN**
26. Clarify, "Two children both want the fire truck. What can you do so you can both be happy?" **BW**

Grant in fantasy

STAR Ideas Bank—**Forgets homework**

Problem: My daughter, Freya, who's in 5th grade, is not turning in her homework assignments. She enjoys the work, but has difficulty getting it done and turned in on time. I have tried to let homework be her responsibility, but it doesn't seem to be working.

Goal: I want her to remember to get her assignment, to do her homework, and to turn it in on time.

Reality check: You are right to be concerned. Leaving kids to work this out may work *if* children have the knowledge and skills needed, otherwise you let them practice being incompetent. *Temperament*: High distractability and low persistence may make remembering more difficult.

Lots of ideas

Teach new skills

1. Teach Freya a system of monitoring herself.
   (1) With Freya, list the steps needed to get her homework to school.
   (2) Create a checklist for Freya to check off the steps when completed. For example,
   - Write down assignments.
   - Bring home assignments.
   - Look at assignments and keep them in designated location.
   - Do homework.
   - Put completed homework in the folder in her notebook.
   - Put her notebook in her backpack.
   - Put her backpack by the front door before going to bed.
   (3) Monitor Freya's follow-through with the checklist.
   (4) Establish a contract with Freya to monitor herself. **SH**
2. When she forgets, say, "Oops, you need to put your homework in your folder and check it off on your checklist." **RD**
3. Model using a checklist posted in a visible location to remember to do things. **MD**

Reward cooperation

4. Notice that her homework is in the folder, ready to go to school and give her a "high five." **AT**
5. Say, "You are doing so well learning to get your work to school." **PR**
6. Describe her effort, "You remembered to put your homework in your pack and put your pack by the front door by yourself." **PR**

7. Comment, "I noticed that you removed distractions from your study table before you started." **PR**
8. "Wow, you have remembered your assignments three times this week. **PR**
9. Freya could choose an incentive agreed upon with parent to reward herself when she turns in all her homework for a week. This will be confirmed by a list of completed homework sent home by the teacher. **RW**

Set limits

10. Clarify expectations: (a) Homework must be put in the folder of her notebook. (b) Backpack with the notebook to be left near the front door of the house at night. (c) Backpack taken to school in the morning. **CR**
11. Say, "If you forget to bring your homework assignment home, call and get the information from a friend or the teacher." **CN**
12. Freya monitors herself by checking a list posted at home. If those steps are not checked off at night, she will have to complete the checklist before she can have dinner the next day. **CN**
13. Homework done before play. **CR**
14. If she cannot get her assignment then she will work ahead or do family chores before she can play. **CN**
15. Say, "Your way is you do your homework when you feel like it. My way is you do your homework when you get home from school. What is a better way?" **CR**

Acknowledge feelings

16. Listen supportively when Freya cries frantically, "I can't find my homework that I did."

Mom: "Hmm."
Freya: "I left it on the floor."
Mom: "I see."
Freya: "But it's not here now!"
Mom: "Uh huh."
Freya: " Someone must have taken it."
Mom: "Hmm." **SL**

17. Say, "You feel disappointed that you got a C in this subject because you forgot to turn in much of your homework." **AL**
18. "Looks like you're frustrated that you forgot to bring your homework assignment again." **AL**
19. Comment, "Wouldn't it be fun if you could mentally transport your homework to your teacher's desk as soon as you're done?" **GF**

Avoid problem

20. Have a table with space on which to do homework. **CT**
21. Make location by front door for the backpack and other material Freya is taking to school. **CT**
22. Post a mini poster by the front door listing all the things she should do before she leaves in the morning. **CT**
23. Plan "activity breaks" while she does her homework to reduce Freya's overall stress level. **RS**
24. Plan twenty minutes of exercise each day to reduce stress. **RS**
25. Say, "Your homework must be completed by 8 P.M. You can chose when to start your homework or we can agree upon a time." **2Y**
26. If she forgets, say, "Uh-oh. You forgot your assignment. You can call Hailey, Sherylyn, or Mrs. Brown to get it." **2Y**

STAR Ideas Bank—**Interrupts conversations**

Problems:

☆Lily, 2¼, interrupts when I have an adult conversation (on the phone or in person, like at dinner). If I don't respond she becomes louder and more insistent: "Mom-my, talk to me!"

☆Ian, 9, has no patience whatsoever. For example, Mom and I were having a conversation and Ian barged in—like the house was on fire—and told us to come immediately and see the spaceship he had built.

Goal: Courtesy is important to me so I am willing to invest the time needed. I want my children to wait until I'm done speaking or say "Excuse me" pleasantly and wait for a response.

Reality check: *Development*: Two-year-olds play alone an average of thirty to sixty seconds. Two-and-a-half-year-olds may play an average of two minutes, but prefer their mothers with them. (See chart below.) *Temperament*: Children who are persistent, intense, and slow to adapt may need to be taught patience or self-restraint in general before learning to avoid interrupting.

Lots of ideas

Avoid problems

1. Say, "I hear you. We can talk . . . [when]. **CT**
2. Set her up with something to play with or do in another room or near you. **CT**
3. Let her play with the apps on your cell phone (colors, phonics, etc.). **CT**
4. Collect special phone toys and stuff to be used ONLY when you're on the phone or having an adult conversation. Bring out play dough only when you are on the phone. **CT**
5. Lower your expectations—be happy for any uninterrupted discussion you have. **CT**
6. Be realistic. See kids' attention span in box on right. **CT**
7. Take two minutes at the beginning of the call for her to talk on the phone with you. **CT**
8. Call/talk after she goes to bed. **CT**
9. Do some aerobic exercise with her every day to reduce stress. **RS**
10. Tell her beforehand that you can talk when done. **RS**
11. "You can sit on my lap till I'm done, or you can use the special play dough." **2Y**
12. "You can find Daddy and ask him to talk with you or make a picture for Grandma." **2Y**

Respond to cooperation

13. Let child be with you, stroking her arm so she won't feel ignored. **AT**
14. Lift her on your lap and bounce her so she will feel included. **AT**
15. Make your call very short and say, "Thank you for waiting." **PR**
16. When she waits quietly, describe what she did that helped. "You found a book to look at while you waited. Thank you for letting me finish." **PR**
17. If she is quiet a moment say, "Thank you for waiting. I could finish talking and hang up quicker." **PR**

18. Reward her for waiting for you. Each minute she is quiet, she gets a sticker or stamp on her hand. **RW**
19. Give waiting tickets. Can be used for extra story or alone time with the parent. **RW**

Set reasonable limits

20. Sit or play quietly while I'm on the phone. **CR**
21. Explain when someone wants to speak, you say, "Excuse me." [Note: Parent must be willing to stop when child says, "Excuse me."] **CR**
22. "Put your hand on mine when you wish to speak. I will cover your hand so you know I heard you." **CR**
23. When you want to be with me and I am on the phone, motion to sit on my lap. **CR**
24. When you want to talk, bring a timer set for five minutes. I will stop or take a break. **CR**
25. "If you continue to interrupt, I will go to another room and close the door." **CN**
26. "Your way is to talk now, my way is to finish my conversation. What is a way that works for both of us? (Not appropriate with toddlers) **BW**

Acknowledge feelings

27. Say, "You feel frustrated because my attention is elsewhere." **AL**
28. Say, "You feel ignored because I am not responding to you." **AL**
29. When the child is upset (or feels left out) respond with nonjudgmental comments ("Oh," "I see," "Really," etc.) (Tool not appropriate with toddlers) **SL**
30. Wouldn't it be great if you had two dads—one could talk with Mom and one could look at your space ship?" **GF**

Teach new skills

31. Practice taking turns. For example, roll a ball between you, saying "Your turn, my turn." **MD**
32. Wait for a turn to talk. Say, "I want to talk. I will wait for my turn." **MD**

33. Teach how to wait. (1) Make a picture list of three activities Lily can do while waiting. (2) Practice doing each activity until she is comfortable with it. (3) Start Lily with an activity, leave for thirty seconds and come back, so she will learn to play by herself and expect you to come back soon. (4) Gradually increase the waiting time by fifteen to twenty seconds each time. (5) Practice waiting skills in pretend. A stuffed animal needs to wait. Lily can help him wait. When she can help the bear, move to the next step. (6) When you want to talk for a few minutes, ask Lily, "What activity would you like to start with?" Praise any degree of success. **SH**
34. Teach "Excuse me." (1) Introduce the concept with puppets. Tell the puppet what behavior you want when your child is with you. (2). Practice interrupting appropriately, using stuffed animals, Thomas the Train, etc. (3) Role play "Excuse me" with three of you (you, your child, and a partner or friend). (4) Model interrupting your child with "Excuse me." Note: You must be willing to be interrupted if children say, "Excuse me." **sh**

Attention span at different ages

From *Is This a Phase?* by Helen F. Neville

18 mo.	30 seconds
2 yrs.	30–60 seconds
2½ yrs.	2 minutes, but prefer Mom
3 yrs.	3–8 minutes, if they are interested
4 yrs.	7–8 minutes if interested
5 yrs.	10–15 minutes if interested
6 yrs.	30 minutes if the activity is easy and interesting

STAR Ideas Bank—**Homework Hassles**

Problem: Schoolwork creates a is very emotional time at our house. Grace, 8, takes forty to forty-five minutes to do what should be a ten- to fifteen-minute assignment. She daydreams, agonizes over each problem, complains about how hard they are, or begs to watch TV. She thinks the homework is too hard. I don't believe that because she does better than average on the tests.

Goal: I want Madeline to begin her assignments with an efficient, can-do attitude. To read each problem and try it before asking for help. To focus pleasantly on the assignment until she is done.

Reality check: Through homework kids learn how to approach difficult (or tedious) problems, and how to motivate themselves, as well as the learn content. Temperament and experience both influence homework. *Temperament:* If a child is highly distractable, then she needs to learn how to focus. If a child is slow to adapt and believes it is hard, he needs to learn to update his expectation with reality. If a child is physically active he needs to learn to release that energy so he can concentrate. *Experience:* Children who have positive experiences learning material generally continue to find learning manageable. Children for whom it is difficult often have more trouble. Also, if the family focus is on effort it will be easier for kids to learn new things than if you emphasize the product or results.

Lots of ideas

Acknowledge feelings

1. Say, "You feel overwhelmed with all the math problems you need to do today." **AL**
2. Say, "You feel annoyed that you must finish your homework before you play." **AL**
3. When she complains about the work, give her your full attention and respond with non-committal comments like: "Uh, huh," and "I see." **SL**
4. Say, "Wouldn't it be great if you could snap your fingers and the knowledge would jump into your head?" **GF**

Avoid problems

5. Create a study area with study resources and few distractions. **CT**
6. Experiment with Madeline to find if she works better with quiet, white noise, or light music. **CT**
7. With Madeline make three schedules and see which one works best. Or, combine elements of each for a new one. **CT**
8. When she gets home from school reduce stress by letting her—
   - have a snack
   - relax a bit before homework
   - use up pent-up energy (run, dance, etc.)
   - have some social time, talk with Mom or a friend
   - read a book for a while
   - have a mutually agreed-upon schedule so there is no nagging or whining. **RS**
9. Say, "You may have fifteen minutes of free time now (before homework) or forty minutes after your homework is done." **2Y**
10. Say, "You can do your homework when you get home from school and have free time all evening, or you can start your homework right after dinner and have less time in the evening." **2Y**
11. Say, "You can have a snack before homework while we talk about your day, or have your snack after homework." **2Y**
12. Say, "You may do your homework at the big table or at the coffee table." **2Y**
13. Say, "Before starting homework you may spend a few minutes cuddling and talking about your day or have a quick story on the couch." **2Y/RS**

Teach new skills

14. Sit near her as she works and do work of your own—balance the checkbook, finish a report for work, write thank you notes, etc. **MD**
15. Divide task into small steps. Say, "First, I will do two problems for you and explain how I think them through. Then, we can work on the rest of the row together. Next, you can work on a row by yourself, or with my help if you need it." **SH**
16. Describe the steps to solve problem. (1) "Let's decide if the problem is addition or subtraction. (2) "Draw circles to match the numbers and let's count them together." (Or let's take away together.) (3) "How many are left, or how many altogether? Write that answer on the line." **SH**
17. Gradually expand her concentration. Begin with five minutes. Set a timer. Sit with Madeline as she works. When the timer rings set it for five minutes again and take a break—dance, play cards, etc. When it rings, return to the homework. Alternate work and breaks until the homework is done. After a couple of days, increase both the work and the breaks to seven minutes. Gradually increase the length of work until she can finish the assignment herself. **SH**
18. Say, "First we will read the vocabulary words out loud. Second, we will decide which are the hardest ones to remember. Third, we will go through the hardest ones first. Fourth, we will go over the ones that were easier. Last, we will review the ones you missed." **SH**
19. If she is distracted by a game across the room and begins moving toward it. I will gently turn her around, and say, "Oops, you forgot to finish your math before playing a game." **RD**

Set reasonable limits

20. Homework before playtime. **CR**
21. Try a problem before asking for help. **CR.**
22. Half an hour transition time (snack, talk, etc.), then homework before play. **CR**
23. Homework done before dinner. **CR**
24. If homework is not completed before dinner, she will not be able to watch a TV show after dinner and will have to finish homework. **CN**
25. If she starts to play before her homework is done, the "temptation" (TV or toy) will be removed until homework is done on time two days in a row. **CN**
26. Say, "Your way is to play first. My way is for you to do your homework first. What is a better way that would work for both of us?" **BW**

Respond to cooperation

27. Madeline loves to have her back rubbed, so I will rub her back while she works on the first problem or two. **AT**
28. Say, "Look, you finished that whole row by yourself!" **PR**
29. "Wow, you are becoming much more accurate with your addition problems!" **PR**
30. Sit with Madeline at the table with a small bowl of treats (beads, pennies, M&Ms®, or chocolate chips) and an empty bowl for Madeline. Each time Madeline does a problem by herself, put a treat in her bowl. **RW**
31. "If you finish these vocabulary words in ten minutes, we will have time to watch your favorite show and make popcorn to go with it!" **RW**
33. Say, "If you can finish your assignment before the big hand hits the 6, we'll have time for a special story or game together!" **RW**

STAR Ideas Bank—Teases sibling

Problem: My boys always seem to be at each other. Caden, 9, comes home from school and greets Aiden, 4, with something like, "Hi dummy." If that doesn't get a rise, he'll poke him on the back. Aiden often retaliates by hitting.

Goal: I want Caden to treat his brother with respect (not tease). I want Aiden to ignore the teasing or use his words to respond.

Reality check for child who teases: Both children have things to learn. We will start with the teaser. There are several reasons kids tease others—one, to connect with others and, second, to make themselves feel more powerful. It is possible that Caden is trying to say "Hi" to his brother. By teasing or poking he does get a reaction. It is also possible that he feels put down (powerless) at school so he is asserting himself at home. Aiden, on the other hand, needs to learn several (non-violent) ways to deal with teasing.

Lots of ideas—for the teaser

Avoid problems

1. Reduce stress by giving Caden active time outside to release his frustrations. **RS**
2. Greet him as soon as he comes in and give him a lot of attention. **RS**
3. Give him a snack as soon as he comes home. **CT**
4. Encourage the boys to play or work in separate areas. **CT**
5. Say, "When you want to be with Aiden, you can say a joke or offer to help with what he is doing." **2Y**
6. Say, "When you feel grinchy inside, you can run around the house or listen to lively music." **2Y**

Teach new skills

7. Model self-care. When you are irritable say, "I feel like yelling at the kids, but I'm going to take a break and read a book for a bit." **MD**
8. When you want to interrupt someone, say, "I want to talk with Dad now. I'm going to ask if this is a good time." **MD**
9. Model positive self-talk. "At work today, Brenda was really mean to me. I wanted to shake her, but I reminded myself that her mom has cancer and decided to let it go." **MD**
10. Decide on how Caden can approach Aiden. (1) Greet him, "Hi, Aiden" (2) Ask and listen to response. "Want to play soccer with me?" [no] (3) Collect data. "Why?" or "What would you like to play?" [Because I'm tired.] (4) Revise, "How about a board game?" [okay.] (5) Evaluate. Did it work? **SH**
11. Make a plan for how to teach approach. (1) Make a list of activities they both like. (2) Develop a strategy (See idea ten) and make a poster. (3) Decide on a way to reward Caden when he tries the process. (4) Explain the process to Caden and role play with several situations. (5) Let Caden try and reward his effort. (6) Back out. **SH**
12. Plan how to help Caden feel powerful without teasing Aiden. (1) Use simple listening to figure out if something is happening at school. (2) Talk about different positive ways to be powerful (being strong, smart, kind, funny, etc.). Ask him how he wants to be powerful. If he doesn't answer, choose "be funny." (3) Get some joke books and together make a list of ten jokes that might make Aiden laugh. (4) Ask Caden to try one or two a day and keep a record of how they work. (5) Evaluate the success and revise the joke list. **SH**
13. When Caden forgets and teases, say, "Whoops, you forgot to be respectful. Let's turn the clock back and re-do it right." **RD**

Respond to cooperation

14. Stay with the boys as long as the play is kind. **AT**
15. If teasing starts, focus on Aiden and do not speak to or look at Caden. (Remove all attention.) **AT**
16. If he tells his brother a joke, give him an okay sign. **AT**
17. When they play together without teasing, tell them you are so happy with how they played together pleasantly. **PR**
18. When no teasing happens, say, "Wow, you guys have built a tall tower together." **PR**
19. Reward Caden for trying humor or a pleasant greeting with tickets. The tickets can be turned in for agreed privileges. **RW**

Acknowledge feelings

20. When he comes home irritable, acknowledge his comments with simple statements like, "Oh?" "I see, " "Really." **SL**
21. Say, "Looks like you're feeling irritable because of something that happened at school." **AL**
22. Say, "Wouldn't it be nice if the world worked exactly as we wish? If we could get up in the morning, make a plan, and push a button and have it happen the way we planned?" **GF**

Set limits

23. "We address people respectfully—no teasing, taunting, or physical hurts." **GF**
24. "If you tease you must play/work by yourself." **CN**.
25. Say, "You want to annoy Aiden. I want you to act respectfully. What can you do that works for both of us?" **BW**

STAR Ideas Bank—Teased by sibling

Problem: My boys always seem to be at each other. Caden, 9, comes home from school and greets Aiden, 4, with something like, "Hi dummy." If that doesn't get a rise, he'll poke him on the back. Aiden often retaliates by hitting.

Goal: I want Caden to treat his brother with respect (not tease). I want Aiden to ignore the teasing or use his words to respond.

Reality check for child who is teased: Although both children have things to learn, we will now focus on the child being teased. Some kids are teased because they are different—younger, wear glasses, smaller, different color skin, etc. Others are teased because they provide a large (dramatic) reaction—crying, fighting, etc. There is nothing Aiden can do about being younger. However, he can learn to calm himself and find (non-violent) ways to deal with teasing.

A Fish Story

Dad reminded his son (who was being teased) of a fishing trip they took. They would bait a hook, toss it into the water, and wait. When a fish bit the worm, it got caught on the hook, and they'd jerk it out of the water.

Dad said, "When Butch says something mean and you cry or get angry, you are letting Butch jerk you around just like a fish." "Remember, some fish decide to swim past the worm. You can decide whether or not to bite on Butch's hook."

Lots of ideas—for the teased child

Avoid problems

1. Reduce overall stress by providing Aiden lots of physical exercise. **RS**
2. Make sure Aiden has a snack before his brother comes home. **RS**
3. Aiden could play in his room with the door closed when he expects Caden to come home. **CT**
4. Say, "When you are being teased you can walk away or tell an adult." **2Y**

Teach new skills

5. Teach him three self-calming tools. See steps on page 176 (box). **SH**
6. Teach him to evaluate the message. Say, "Aiden, are you a dummy?" If he says, "No," then say, "Then you can decide if you want to get upset or not." **SH**
7. Introduce three strategies to defuse teasing (side box). Ask which he would like to try first. Then practice it. **SH**
8. Tell him the fish story (above). Teach him to: (1) Notice the hook. (2) Decide if he wants to be jerked around. (3) Use a strategy to stay calm. **SH**
9. When a clerk is rude, say, "That was rude. I will ignore what he said." **MD**
10. If Aiden starts to cry, say, "Take a breath and respond again, stronger." **RD**

Respond to cooperation

11. When Aiden rejects teasing, give him a "high five." **AT**
12. When he uses a tool, say, "I noticed that you . . . [strategy]." **PR**
13. When he walks away or ignores the teaser, tell him, "It took courage to walk away. I'm proud of you." **PR**
14. When children play together and no teasing happens, tell them you are so happy with how they played together. **PR**
15. When he responds gently to teasing, give him a ticket. Tickets can be turned in for privileges like staying up late on the weekend, screen time, or baking with Mom. **RW**

Acknowledge feelings

16. When child tells you he was teased, respond with comments like "oh," "I see." **SL**
17. "Your feelings were hurt by the teasing." **AL**
18. Wouldn't it be fun, if every time a person said something hurtful, the words would become slime and drip on their shirt? **GF**
19. Tell the teaser, "You hurt my feelings." Note: This strategy rarely works because the teasers usually know. That is why they do it. **AL**

Set limits

20. Touch gently even when teased. **CR**
21. Act respectfully even when teased. **CR**
22. "If you hit or tease back when you are teased, you are choosing to play by yourself for a while [fifteen minutes]." **CN**
23. "Your way is to hit when teased. My way is to ignore teasing (not hurt the other child). What is something that would be okay with both of us?" **BW**

Ideas for both kids

24. Reward kindly behavior. Set up a marble jar. When the boys play together pleasantly for fifteen minutes, they can each put a marble in the jar. When the jar is full, the boys can go to a ball game with Dad. **RW**
25. Set a family goal of kindness. When the kids have demonstrated they can be kind, the family will go camping. Each afternoon and evening that both kids speak and touch pleasantly, each child will get a token. When the boys have 100 tokens they can go camping. **RW**

Strategies to reject teasing

- Misinterpret what was said. "Why would I want to buy a bunny?" Or, "My thumb's not high."
- Agree to a lesser charge. "Yes, it was dumb to leave my door open."
- Reframe the comment. "Someone needs a nap." Or, "Someone has had a hard day."
- Reject the label. "You've call me that all week. Can't you find something else? I'm going to die of boredom."
- Return the label. "Hi, dumb-er"
- Change the subject. You should have seen the . . . on TV."
- Ignore the comment. "Hi, Caden. I'm glad you're home."

Appendix C
Resources

Chapter 2: The STAR Parenting Process

Love & Limits: Guidance Tools for Creative Parenting by Elizabeth Crary. Provides a short, simple, easy-to-read introduction to the STAR Parenting process, points, and tools. Seattle: Parenting Press, 1994.

Without Spanking or Spoiling: A Practical Approach to Toddler and Preschool Guidance by Elizabeth Crary. Introduces the basic concepts of child guidance. Seattle: Parenting Press, 1979, revised 1993.

Chapter 3: Consider Your Expectations

★Development and Developmental Issues

The Child from Five to Ten by Arnold Gesell, M.D., Frances L. Ilg, M.D., and Louise Bates Ames, Ph.D. Offers a psychological portrait of each age with concrete suggestions for dealing with typical behavior. New York: Harper & Row, 1977.

Child of Mine: Feeding with Love and Good Sense, third edition, by Ellyn Satter. Boulder, Colo.: Bull Publishing Co., 2000.

The Family Nutrition Book: Everything You Need to Know About Feeding Your Children from Birth through Adolescence by Williams Sears, M.D., and Martha Sears, R.N. New York: Little, Brown and Co., 1999.

How to Get Your Kid to Eat, but Not Too Much by Ellyn Satter. Describes basic feeding principles and ways to develop and maintain normal eating patterns from birth through adolescence. Boulder, Colo.: Bull Publishing Co., 1987.

Is This a Phase? Child Development & Parent Strategies, Birth to 6 Years by Helen F. Neville, B.S., R.N. Explains what to expect at each developmental stage and provides charts and graphs that make the information quick and easy to use. Seattle: Parenting Press, 2007.

Mommy! I Have to Go Potty! by Jan Faull, M.Ed., and Helen F. Neville, B.S., R.N. Includes information showing how development and temperament affect the toileting process, when your child is ready, how to start, and how to deal with training challenges. Seattle: Parenting Press, 1996, revised 2009.

The Sleep Book for Tired Parents: Help for Solving Children's Sleep Problems by Rebecca Huntley. Provides pros, cons, and practical help for four different approaches to dealing with sleep issues and lets you decide which works best for your family. Seattle: Parenting Press, 1991.

Sleepless in America: Is Your Child Misbehaving or Missing Sleep? by Mary Sheedy Kurcinka. Distinguishes between misbehaving and missing sleep, identifies everyday activities that may disturb your child's sleep, and offers strategies to help your family get the sleep they need. New York: HarperCollins, 2006.

Understanding Temperament: Strategies for Creating Family Harmony by Lyndall Shick. Helps parents understand why family members behave as they do so that parents can change conflict into cooperation. Seattle: Parenting Press. 1998.

Your Ten- to Fourteen-Year-Old by Louise Bates Ames, Ph.D., Frances L. Ilg, M.D, and Sidney M. Baker, M.D. Illustrates the dramatic changes that take place in adolescents. New York: Dell Trade, 1989.

★Temperament

Temperament Tools: Working with Your Child's Inborn Traits by Helen F. Neville and Diane Clark Johnson. Describes eight challenging clusters of traits and how to deal with them. Seattle: Parenting Press, 1998.

Understanding Temperament: Strategies for Creating Family Harmony by Lyndall Shick, M.A. Helps parents identify children's temperament and teach skills children need to live cooperatively in the family and world outside the home. Seattle: Parenting Press, 1998.

Your Child as a Person by Stella Chess, M.D., Alexander Thomas, M.D., and Hurbert Birch, Ph.D. Based on their classic research that explains the impact of temperament on behavior. New York: Viking Press, 1965.

★Values

Using Your Values to Raise Your Child to Be an Adult You Admire by Harriet Heath. Offers three ways to identify your values, and illustrates how to convey them to your children. Seattle: Parenting Press, 2000.

Chapter 5: Respond to Cooperation

The Five Love Languages of Children by Gary Chapman and Ross Cambell, M.D. Introduces the five love languages and helps you identify which is your child's. Chicago: Northfield Publishing, 1997.

What About Me? 12 Ways to Get Your Parents' Attention (Without Hitting Your Sister) by Eileen Kennedy-

Moore, Ph.D. Helps parents recognize children's attempts to get attention constructively. Seattle: Parenting Press, 2005.

See Resources, Chapter 3: Consider Your Expections for books on eating and nutrition.

Chapter 6: Acknowledge Feelings

Dealing with Disappointment: Helping Kids Cope When Things Don't Go Their Way by Elizabeth Crary. Clarifies the skills needed for children to manage their feelings and illustrates how to teach them. Seattle: Parenting Press, 2003.

Dealing with Feelings series: *I'm Mad* (1992), *I'm Frustrated* (1992), *I'm Excited* (1994), *I'm Scared* (1994), *I'm Furious* (1994), and *I'm Proud* (1992) by Elizabeth Crary. Teaches kids to think about feelings and offers a variety of constructive ways to deal with feelings. Seattle: Parenting Press.

Feelings for Little Children series: *When You're HAPPY and You Know It, When You're MAD and You Know It, When You're SHY and You Know It,* and *When You're SILLY and You Know It* by Elizabeth Crary and Shari Steelsmith. Each board book illustrates age-appropriate self-calming tools for young children. Seattle: Parenting Press, 1996.

The Way I Feel by Janan Cain. Vivid, expressive illustrations encourage children to understand their emotions and those of others. Seattle: Parenting Press, 2000. Board book, 2005.

What Angry Kids Need: Parenting Your Angry Child Without Going Mad by Jennifer Anne Brown, M.S.W., and Pam Provonsha Hopkins, M.S.W. Helps you understand why your child might be angry and gives you effective ways to help your child. Seattle: Parenting Press, 2008.

Why Don't You Understand? Improve Family Communication with the 4 Thinking Styles by Susie Leonard Weller, M.A. Illustrates how different thinking styles can enhance or interfere with family communications. Seattle: Parenting Press, 2009.

Chapter 7: Set Reasonable Limits

Consequences for Children by Ann Corwin on YouTube. Describes when children are old enough to understand consequences.

Go to Your Room, Consequences That Teach by Shari Steelsmith. Lists consequences for more than 50 common frustrating behaviors. Seattle: Parenting Press, 2000.

Growing Up Again, Parenting Ourselves, Parenting Our Children, second edition, by Jean Illsley Clarke and Connie Dawson. Distinguishes between healthy and unhealthy forms of structure (limits) and nurture (love). Describes the "limit line." Center City, Minn.: Hazelden, 1998.

Chapter 8: Teach New Skills

Children and Chores: The Surprising Impact of Chores on Kids' Futures by Elizabeth Crary. Explains why chores are so important and shows how to start them at different ages. Seattle: Parenting Press, 2011.

Is This a Phase? Child Development & Parent Strategies, Birth to 6 Years by Helen F. Neville, B.S., R.N. Explains what to expect at each developmental stage and how to approach common issues. Seattle: Parenting Press, 2007.

Mind in the Making by Ellen Galinsky. Describes seven essential life skills kids need. New York: Harperstudio, 2010.

★Problem solving and negotiation

Children's Problem Solving series: *I Want It* (1982/1996), *I Want to Play* (1982/1996), *I Can't Wait* (1982/1996), *I'm Lost* (1986/1996), *Mommy, Don't Go* (1986/1996), and *My Name Is Not Dummy* (1983/1996) by Elizabeth Crary. Models negotiation and thinking of different ways to handle problems. Seattle: Parenting Press.

Kids Can Choose series: *Amy's Disappearing Pickle, Heidi's Irresistible Hat,* and *Willy's Noisy Sister* by Elizabeth Crary. Models kids thinking problems through themselves, anticipating how the ideas will affect others and choosing the best solution for the situation. Seattle: Parenting Press, 2001.

What About Me? 12 Ways to Get Your Parents' Attention (Without Hitting Your Sister) by Eileen Kennedy-Moore, Ph.D. Illustrates constructive ways to get attention. Seattle: Parenting Press, 2005.

★Personal safety

It's MY Body: A Book to Teach Children How to Resist Uncomfortable Touch by Lory Britain, Ph.D. Helps children learn how their feelings can help them make decisions about sharing their bodies, and how to communicate those decisions to others. Seattle: Parenting Press, 1982.

Kids to the Rescue! First Aid Techniques for Kids by Maribeth and Darwin Boelts. Provides children with the fundamentals of first aid and helps prevent accidents by making children aware of their vulnerability. Seattle: Parenting Press, 1992, revised 2003.

Telling Isn't Tattling by Kathryn Hammerseng. Helps children distinguish when to involve an adult and when to resolve the problem themselves. Seattle: Parenting Press, 1995.

Chapter 9: How to Get Started

Love & Limits: Guidance Tools for Creative Parenting by Elizabeth Crary. Provides a short, simple, easy-to-read introduction to the STAR Parenting process, points, and tools. Seattle: Parenting Press, 1994.

Closing Thoughts

Am I Doing Too Much for My Child? Getting Your Child on the Road to Responsibility and Independence by Elizabeth Crary. Introduces four levels of support (or parenting) and shows how to use them for different situations and at different ages. Seattle: Parenting Press, 2011.

Growing Up Again, Parenting Ourselves, Parenting Our Children, second edition, by Jean Illsley Clarke and Connie Dawson. Provides insight and parenting skills many parents did not receive when they were growing up. See chapter 7. Center City, Minn.: Hazelden, 1998.

Help! The Kids Are at It Again: Using Kids' Quarrels to Teach "People" Skills by Elizabeth Crary. Introduces four people skills children need and uses the STAR Parenting tools and processes to encourage them. Seattle: Parenting Press, 1997.

How Much Is Enough?: Everything You Need to Know to Steer Clear of Overindulgence and Raise Likeable, Responsible and Respectful Children from Toddlers to Teens by Jean Illsley Clarke, Ph.D., Connie Dawson, Ph.D., David Bredehoft, Ph.D. Clarifies the line between enough, abundance, and overindulgence. New York: Marlowe & Company, 2004.

Internet Safety and Your Family by Linda Carlson. Designed to prepare you to make choices regarding your family's Internet use: from cyber bullies and pornography to identity theft and sexual predators. Downloadable book. Seattle: Parenting Press, 2005.

Pick Up Your Socks . . . and Other Skills Growing Children Need! by Elizabeth Crary. Presents information helpful in raising a capable, responsible child. Includes a household job chart explaining when kids do selected tasks. Seattle: Parenting Press, 1990.

Self-Esteem: A Family Affair by Jean Illsley Clarke. Presents how to build positive self-esteem in your family and how to take care of yourself. Center City, Minn.: Hazelden, 1998.

Why Don't You Understand? Improve Family Communication with the 4 Thinking Styles by Susie Leonard Weller, M.A. Illustrates how different thinking styles can enhance or interfere with family communications. Seattle: Parenting Press, 2009.

Index

Good Books for Children and about Children from Parenting Press

Feelings for Little Children series:
When You're Mad and You Know It . . .
When You're Happy and You Know It . . .
When You're Shy and You Know It . . .
When You're Silly and You Know It . . .
These charming, colorful board books are designed to offer very young children alternatives for dealing with their feelings. Written by Elizabeth Crary and Shari Steelsmith, illustrated by Mits Katayama. For ages 18 months to 3 years, $7.95 each, or 4 for $31.80

The Way I Feel by Janan Cain and *The Way I Act* by Janan Cain and Steve Metzger. These books provide both concepts and vocabulary: to help children express their emotions, and to invite them to think about their actions and the affects of those actions. Expressive, colorful illustrations by Janan Cain with short rhyming verses. For ages 2 to 9 years. Hardback, $16.95; board book of *The Way I Feel,* $7.95

What About Me? 12 Ways to Get Your Parents' Attention (Without Hitting Your Sister) by Eileen Kennedy-Moore, illustrated by Mits Katayama. Twelve positive, practical, and possible ways for a child to get attention from a grown-up when feeling left out or ignored. Especially helpful to children with new siblings. For ages 4 to 8 years. Hardback, $14.95

Self-Calming Cards by Elizabeth Crary, illustrated by Mits Katayama. Thirty-six activity cards in English and Spanish, with directions in both languages. The 24 self-calming tools and 12 activity cards help children (and adults) learn self-calming strategies while having lots of fun. For ages 2 to 12 years. Boxed card deck, $12.95

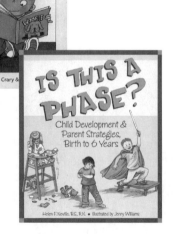

Children's Problem Solving series:
I Want It, I Can't Wait, I Want to Play, My Name Is Not Dummy, I'm Lost, and *Mommy, Don't Go* by Elizabeth Crary, illustrated by Marina Megale. These six, 32-page books teach children to think about their problems. The reader gets to choose among a variety of solutions and observe the results. If she or he doesn't like the ending, another one can be chosen. For ages 3 to 8. Paperback, $7.95 each or 6 for the price of 5 ($39.75)

Is This a Phase? Child Development & Parent Strategies, Birth to 6 Years by Helen F. Neville, B.S., R.N., illustrated by Jenny Williams. An authoritative reference on children's development as it affects their day-to-day behavior: what to expect and when to get help, or relax because the phase will pass. Filled with interesting and useful charts and tables. For adults. Paperback, $23.95

Contact your bookseller, library, or www.ParentingPress.com for these materials.
Prices subject to change without notice